JOE
The Autobiography of
A TRENCHARD BRAT

Boom Trenchard loves us!
Boom Trenchard loves us!
Boom Trenchard loves us!
And so he bloody well should!!
(Halton Apprentices' Song)

The Author

JOE
The Autobiography of
A TRENCHARD BRAT

W/Cdr Joe Northrop,
DSO, DSC, AFC, PFF

A Square One Publication

First published in 1993 by
Square One Publications
Saga House, Sansome Place, Worcester, WR1 1UA

© Mrs Pamela Northrop 1993
ISBN: 1 872017 69 X

British Library Cataloguing in Publication Data.
A catalogue record for this book is available from the
British Library.

Typeset by Avon Dataset, Bidford on Avon, in Times 10 on 13pt and
Printed in Great Britain by
Antony Rowe Ltd, Chippenham, Wiltshire

For Filly

Without the encouragement and assistance of Jim Spencer, who edited my late husband's autobiography, the Trenchard Brat might never have found a publisher, and I gratefully acknowledge his contributions to Joe's book . . .

Pamela Northrop

Contents

Editor's Introduction

Joe Northrop was the archetype 'Trenchard Brat'. He joined the RAF, as a 'Halton' apprentice in 1929, at the age of 16. For three years Joe endured the harsh Halton regime during which he was given a thorough grounding in aircraft maintenance. On successfully completing his apprenticeship he became an aircraftsman and plied his trade at the newly completed Cranwell Staff College, firstly in the engineering workshops and then servicing the aircraft of the Cadet Training flights. During the later part of his service at Cranwell, Joe had his first experience of flying, albeit as a passenger on air tests of 'his' aircraft. Some of the instructors allowed him to handle the controls on these flights, awakening within him the ambition to become a pilot himself 'one day'.

A routine foreign posting followed Cranwell, to Abu Sueir in Egypt. While Joe was in Egypt Mussolini embarked on his adventure in Abyssinia, ringing alarm bells in Britain and leading to plans to expand the airforce. This gave Joe the chance to achieve his ambition. Volunteers were called for from suitably qualified aircraftsmen to train as pilots. He applied and, thanks to an exemplary service record, was accepted and returned to England to be trained.

★　　★　　★

By the time World War Two started Joe was a fully qualified pilot flying Fairey Battle day bombers. Initially it was as a sergeant pilot but in 1940 he was promoted to pilot officer. As was the normal practice for those promoted in wartime his was a 'Hostilities Only' commission, something which was to have unfortunate repercussions at the end of the war.

For the first two years of the war Joe was employed on secret work, flying to detect and plot the position of the radio beams the enemy was using to direct its aircraft in the night attacks that followed the Battle of Britain. He was chosen for this work because his navigational training had been more thorough than was normal and initially he flew as a navigator in the aircraft searching for the beams. It is a fascinating story told by someone on the inside. This work was followed up by flying to test the British beam systems then under development, now as a pilot. Joe's skills as a beam flyer resulted in him being 'blooded' on operations. He flew as an additional pilot in several raids by the newly introduced Stirling aircraft on the German Battle cruisers Scharnhorst and Gneisenau at Brest, taking over from the normal pilot in the final beam controlled stages of the bombing run. For his work on the beams Joe was awarded the Air Force Cross.

★   ★   ★

With his navigational skills and his experience of beam flying it was inevitable that Joe should eventually find himself in the Path Finder Force. In 1943 he joined No 83 Squadron flying Lancasters. The rest of the story is, as the saying goes, history. Joe will always be remembered as a Lancaster pilot, taking part in, and sometimes acting as controller of some of the heaviest and most dangerous raids of the war. In No 83 Squadron he attacked the most strongly defended target of all, Berlin, no less than eight times. On these raids aircraft losses averaged 5% of those taking part and on 'Black Thursday', and including those lost in accidents, reached a horrifying 11%. In recognition of his service in Lancasters Joe was awarded the Distinguished Flying Cross.

'Tour Expired' on heavy bombers Joe was offered and accepted the command of 692 Squadron by Air Vice Marshall Bennet on the condition that he limited the number of operational flights he made himself. 692 Squadron, flying Mosquito aircraft, was part of the Light Night Striking Force of the Pathfinder Group which attacked the enemy on every possible occasion, often in conditions in which the heavy bombers could not operate. Despite the limitation Joe seized every opportunity to fly and completed a further 12 operations, including yet another attack on Berlin. The command of 692 Squadron was the zenith of Joe's career. Early in 1945 he was once again 'Tour Expired' and was taken off operations to become the Chief Flying Instructor of a Path Finder Training Unit. At the same time his long and successful operational flying career and his devotion to duty and enthusiasm was recognised by the award of the Distinguished Service Order.

★   ★   ★

With the end of the war the qualities for which Joe had been decorated were seemingly of lesser importance in the RAF. By now a Wing Commander, Joe applied for, but was at first denied, a permanent commission. Instead he was offered and had to accept a medium service commission in the newly formed Air Traffic Control Branch. He served the RAF loyally in this new field in a number of traffic control, signals and administrative posts. Eventually he was given that which he so desperately wanted, and had surely earned, a permanent commission. After a course at the RAF Staff College he returned to general duties and was able to resume a flying career, taking a refresher course followed by a jet conversion course. In the 14 years following the end of the war he filled a number of administrative posts, mainly in Germany, and in an ironical twist of fortune found himself heavily involved in the Berlin Air Lift. His last post was President Permanent Courts Martial in North West Europe. However, unlike other 'Brats' who missed the 'hostilities only' trap, he received no further promotion.

After retiring from the RAF in 1959 Joe held a number of civilian jobs but his heart remained with his old service. This is reflected in the story of his life, which he then started to commit to paper. The result is this book. Unfortunately he died before it was complete, hence the need for an editor to bring it all together.

★   ★   ★

Joe tells a many-faceted story, differing in many ways from the stories of his contempories. First of all it is the story of an intensely family man. He married his wife Pamela just before the start of the war and his daughter was born in 1940. He frequently tells of the struggle to maintain a 'normal' life with Pamela as she followed him from one posting to another across the country to set up 'homes' outside station *gates. Could any fighting men in history have lived such a life, switching in hours from life at home with one's family to desperate battles over an enemy land, then back to a few precious days, or hours, of domesticity?*

Another side to the story is the sheer dedication and professionalism Joe brought to his 'trade' of airman. How many pilots, noticing a loss of oil pressure in one engine of a twin engine plane, were capable of landing at an airfield on route, identifying the split oil pipe, taking it to the workshops, welding it, refitting it and resuming the flight? And the list of aircraft which Joe flew would gladden the heart of an aviation museum curator. It is virtually an inventory of the RAF's equipment in the inter-war and war years. Avro 504s, Bristol Bulldogs, Hawker Harts, Fairey Battles, Vickers Wellesleys, just to name a few. To these after the war he was able to add jet aircraft.

★   ★   ★

A serious side to Joe's pre-war experience is the revelation of how ill equipped and poorly trained the peace time air force was. For example, the Wellesley, the last word in bombers being brought into service in 1938, just in time for the war, was found to have a 'minor' problem. It could not release its bombs in typical European weather conditions. And the Fairey Battle bomber with which the RAF started the war was found to be virtually unflyable at night because the flames from the engine exhausts blinded the pilot. Dead reckoning navigation as practiced by the RAF at the start of the war Joe describes as a farce, despite him having come top of his specialised navigation course. But what about Astro navigation, which it was believed would overcome the problems of dead reckoning, and for which aircraft were being equipped with astro hatches and bubble sextants? After a course on this Joe came to the conclusion that while in favourable weather conditions it might have its use for maritime reconnaissance, it was hopeless as an aid to a bomber force. He sums up navigation at the start of the war as being 'by guess and by God'. When trying to plot the position of the German beams, for example, he found it an impossible task out of sight of the ground.

★   ★   ★

For the rest of the story the words are largely Joe's own. There are, however, discontinuities in the manuscript which he left covering, unfortunately, the most glorious part of his flying career, his service as a Pathfinder in No 83 Lancaster Squadron. It is interesting to speculate the reason for this. Was the experience so emotionally draining that he could not bring himself to write about it? Or was it so physically exhausting that he did not have the energy left to write the notes on which to base a full story? Fortunately continuity is supplied by his flying log book which had to be completed after each flight. Some pages of this have been reproduced together with descriptions, by Joe, of the most notable raids. These are of great historical interest in that some of them reveal the stresses which existed within Bomber Command.

Growing Up

Yorkshire is a county famed for its broad acres and the white rose emblem. It was my good fortune to be born there in the small town of Knottingley, little more than a year before the start of the Great War of 1914 – 18 so that my earliest recollections of childhood days are of junior school during the war that was meant to end all wars.

I played a minute part in that struggle against German might, my contribution being a once-weekly purchase of a war savings stamp in the classroom – I remember those savings stamps quite clearly, as they depicted battle scenes of trench warfare and bursting shells in colour.

My father was a pre-war regular naval officer who had served his apprenticeship as a shipwright and then joined the small band of commissioned shipwrights, a rank retained by the Royal Navy from the late 18th century. He was thus brought up in the best Naval traditions, serving on all kinds of ships from before the turn of the century, through the Boxer uprising of 1900 and the Great War until he was finally retired from the service in 1928. A tall man of erect bearing, he made an imposing figure in full dress Naval uniform of cocked hat, frocked coat with the sleeves and shoulders heavily laced with gold rings and epaulettes, complete with belt and naval sword, and wearing his medals. He was a man of strong principles, and as straight as a die in all his dealings. He was also a strict tee-totaller all his life. When I was older I realised that his loathing of alcohol stemmed from his own unhappy experiences with his father, who had been a heavy drinker, and that he had left home to join the Navy to get away from it all. He became a life member of the Rechabite anti-drink order. Even at my wedding reception when every other guest was drinking champagne, he stuck to his principles and asked for a glass of water with which to join the toasts.

★   ★   ★

During the first years of my early childhood we lived in a small two-storey terraced house near the outskirts of the town. The town itself was on the fringe of the industrialised West Riding of Yorkshire and pit head gear and the tall chimneys of woollen mills were in evidence to the west. It seemed, however, that the industrial encroachment on the green country to the east had halted there. The town's prosperity was based on the three large glass works and a chemical works that were the biggest employers of labour. But one could walk out of the town in any direction other than north and within minutes be in country lanes skirting the rich farm lands and the long worked limestone quarries so abundant in the area that had for centuries provided Yorkshire farmers with the agricultural lime they needed. To the north was the River Aire, a wide river but un-navigable on this stretch and for this reason by-passed by the Aire and Calder canal that snaked its way eastwards throughout the town, crossed and recrossed by many bridges that turned the place into a northern Venice. Throughout the day fussy little steam tugs dragging long strings of wooden barges or square steel coal containers passed to and fro on their way between the West Riding industries and Goole docks. Occasionally a single barge drawn by a horse ambling along the tow path could be sighted and periodically a dredger would operate clearing out the silt deposit to keep the canal at the right depth. To a child it was all fascinating and I never tired of watching.

As I grew older the problem of overcrowding in the already cramped accommodation of our small house became more and more acute. The building boom was, however, still in the future and it wasn't until well after the end of the war that the sort of house that we wanted became available nearby and we were able to move into a spacious three storey building.

Looking back over the years I can only remember being with my father once during the war and that occasion only sticks in my memory because it is associated with other events. During the second or third summer of the war he was shore-based at a training establishment at Shotley, near Harwich, for a while and mother snatched this opportunity to join him for a short stay and took me along. That weekend I was taken to tea in the wardroom at Shotley and was made a great fuss of by some of the other naval officers who kept feeding me with huge black cherries then being picked locally. I made such a pig of myself that I ended up by being violently sick, a disgrace that I shall never forget. Also, during that visit I can clearly recall being carried out into the open fields one night and being sufficiently awake to watch the huge cigar-like shape of one of the Kaiser's Zeppelins passing overhead the searchlights lighting it up as they caught it in their beams. On another night a Zeppelin was shot down in flames nearby and father brought some pieces of aluminium girder from the wreckage for me to give to the small museum we kept at my first school. The souvenir pieces are probably still in the same place gathering dust some sixty years and yet another war against the same enemy later.

With the signing of the Armistice and the end of hostilities there were spontaneous celebrations and thanksgiving services all over the country. At my school we had a magnificent party and every one there received a souvenir mug and a medal with a red, white and blue ribbon to commemorate the occasion. The souvenirs are long since gone, broken or lost, but each year we still celebrate the day, November 11th for the simple reason that it happens to be my birthday.

The following summer father came home on an extended leave before leaving for abroad on another long commission and mother decided that it would be a good opportunity to renew family ties by paying visits to some of the closer relatives who lived within a reasonable distance of us in the West Riding. Some of them lived quite close by but were not served very well by the L.M.S. or L.N.E.R. railways so for those visits we hired a coach and the family travelled the seven or eight miles each way in style. One of the less formal visits I enjoyed was when we visited some cousin of my mothers who had a farm on Sharleston Common; we messed about with the animals and played ducks and drakes on the many ponds around and had a thoroughly good time. Before leaving we were called in to take Yorkshire high tea with all the grown-ups and as a special treat a monster of a goose egg was put in front of me; it proved too rich for my stomach and once again I disgraced myself by being sick. It gave me an aversion to eggs that stayed with me for the next decade.

When visiting further afield in the Leeds and Doncaster areas we travelled by train and completed the journey on the electric trams. Near the Pennines riding on the trams was as good as going on a switchback at the fair with the additional fun of being able to collect a bunch of the multi-coloured tram tickets on the route.

Just as we were getting used to having father around his leave ended and he had to return to Chatham to join his next ship on a commission that included Canada and Australia in its itinerary. As a treat I went to Doncaster with my mother to see him off from the main line station. After that the only way we could keep track of his movements for the next two years was from his letters and the post cards sent to each one of us from every port of call; over the years we each built up a world-wide collection of postcards in our own albums.

When he came home at the end of that commission, sometime in 1923, it was to move the family into a larger three storey house a short distance from our old one. It was spacious, with tall glass-panelled double doors at the front that faced south and caught the sun all day. The doors opened into a wood-panelled hall and on each panel father had mounted a crest of a ship in which he had served, each on a polished mahogany base. They really looked something special. The top two spare attic rooms he rigged up with benches and used for carpentry, and I spent many rainy days there doing fretwork and amateur carpentry, usually ruining my father's tools in the process.

From where we lived it took only a matter of minutes to reach open country. As most of my school friends came from farming stock we could always be certain of a grass field in which to play our innumerable games of cricket and football athough the field might often be liberally decorated with cow pats or piles of horse manure. My friends were usually co-opted as part of the farms labour force when away from the school and in turn I would also be pressed into service for whatever work was in hand. We would bring the milk cows in from the pastures nearby, cling precariously to the broad backs of the plough horses returning from a day in the fields and take part in the haymaking, harvesting and picking the pea and potato crops. In the autumn we had great fun stacking the dried haulms in great piles and burning them. We roasted left over potatoes in the embers eating the burnt offerings when we felt hungry. The big event of the year for most of us was the annual farmers shoot held on Boxing Day. We were always co-opted for the day as beaters, being ferried from one farm to the next in the farmers' cars and covering many heavy miles.

There was always a glorious cold lunch with huge pork pies and cold meats brought out and hot drinks or something stronger served halfway round. We always finished the day dog-tired but well rewarded financially and usually with the added bonus of a brace of birds or a hare if the shoot had done well.

Looking back they seemed halcyon days indeed when the only disaster capable of casting a shadow was if the county cricket team failed to win at Headingley. During father's long absences at sea my Aunt Hannah, mother's elder sister and a spinster, lived with us to keep my mother company and help run the house and keep us under control. She was a superb cook and performed culinary wizardry on the large coal-fired kitchen range we used. Bread and cakes were home-baked and the massive pork pies, cooked hams and iced Christmas cakes that appeared not only at Christmas but on other high days and holidays were out of this world. Throughout the summer she made jams, 20 lbs at a time in a large brass preserving pan; starting with strawberry, my favourite, and followed up with raspberry, Victoria plum and damson, ending up with blackberry or bramble jelly. In readiness for the winter she prepared huge demi-johns of pickled red cabbage, shallots and salted down runner beans; and she made many gallons of elderberry wine that we had regularly as a mulled bedtime drink throughout the winter months. She also attended to our other needs and was always ready to dose us with syrup of figs or brimstone and treacle, having utter faith in these two remedies for all childhood ills.

★   ★   ★

So the months and years slipped by quietly and smoothly for me until the Spring of 1924, by which time I was in my 11th year and had reached the top form of the local school. My teacher then was the Deputy Head of the school, a burly middle aged Yorkshire man. He was a friend of the family and devoted much of his time to farming activities in the area. Some two years earlier he had entered my brother for the competitive examination for the Kings School, Pontfract, the nearest grammar school. He passed with flying colours. Now I was old enough to sit and that summer I was entered for the examination and passed without any difficulty. My school broke up for the summer holidays shortly afterwards and I was faced with the glorious prospect of having nothing to do except enjoy myself until the Autumn term started at my new school in late September.

King's School was situated in extensive grounds on top of the hill near to the ruins of Pontefract Castle. It consisted of a motley collection of buildings, many with historical connections, completely enclosed by a high wall. Entering the main gate one passed between huge twin bastions and under a grille, the only thing required to complete the illusion of entering a mediaeval castle was a drawbridge. In the past the building had at some time been used as a barracks, and it was still connected to the Castle by an underground passage. Another legacy from those days was the excellent covered-in rifle range used by the school Rifle Club each day in the lunch period. In the days of the Civil War, Cromwell and his Roundheads had laid siege to the nearby castle and used his artillery to such effect that it and the church lower down the hill lay in ruins, never to be occupied again.

At this time I experienced my first real set-back. Each year the school held its Speech Day and Prizegiving in the Town Hall, and in December 1925 the whole family attended for the first time, as my father was home. We returned home late in the evening and whilst making a hot drink before going to bed, I spilled a kettle of boiling water over my feet. It took nearly five months before the raw flesh healed enough for me to walk again, and when I could resume schooling I had missed a term and a half, and was naturally a long way behind the rest. It was also a long time before I was able to play games — I remember that in the autumn of that year I was watching some of my friends kicking a football around, and as it rolled near me I took a kick at it without thinking. The impact pushed my toes back about an inch into my soft foot and scared me silly. It was a year or two before they were really strong again, and even today I still have the great scars on my ankles to remind me that I was lucky to get away without more serious injuries that would had put paid to any thoughts of a flying career later on...

That year my brother sat for and obtained his Cambridge Matriculation certificate, and moved into the sixth form to prepare for the Northern Universities' examination. He was Captain of the School and Head Prefect, and also captained the school Elevens at football and cricket. He had decided to take up a career in teaching and would soon be leaving for college.

I hadn't thought very much about my own future up to then, apart from deciding that the last thing I wanted to do was to enter the teaching profession or join a bank as so many others wanted to do. Until my father finally retired from the Royal Navy in the summer of 1928; the family had been able to live fairly comfortably on his pay but when he retired on half pension his income was so reduced that it was clear that he would not be able to keep both my brother and me on full time education at school and college for the next three or four years. As I had not yet matriculated it was up to me to do something.

I discussed the matter with my Housemaster and he suggested that I might be interested in entering my name for the next competitive examination for an engineering apprenticeship in the Royal Air Force, a step taken by two or three old pupils over the past two years. Without knowing very much about it I agreed subject to my father's approval; he raised no objections being secretly pleased at the turn of events. When the time came to sit the examination I turned out to be the only candidate from the school and I worked through the papers without too much effort. When the results came through in November I had achieved a reasonable placing in the first hundred from around eight hundred passes from all over the country. Soon afterwards I received detailed instructions and a single rail warrant to Wendover for a day in the first week of January, 1929.

I remained at school until the end of term then made my

farewells and severed my connections with the school. After the Christmas festivities we had a cold spell of weather and father and I went skating together for the first time on some flooded fields nearby that had now been frozen solid. This was followed by some fairly heavy snow and I spent my last day at home tobogganing on the local slopes.

Next morning I was up bright and early with the few personal necessities that I would need packed into a small suitcase; father insisted on accompanying me as far as Doncaster and waved me off in the Kings Cross train as I had done to him some years earlier when he returned to Chatham from leave. As the train pulled slowly out of the station and gathered speed I closed the window and sat down feeling very much alone for the first time in my life.

Trenchard Brat

Boom Trenchard loves us!
Boom Trenchard loves us!
Boom Trenchard loves us!
And so he bloody well should.

(Halton Apprentices' Song)

As it turned out I wasn't alone in the compartment for more than a few minutes of that January day in 1929 before the sliding door to the corridor was opened and another boy of my own age joined me. We were soon in conversation and it turned out that he came from Wakefield, was also another would-be apprentice and like me had never been as far south as London before. By the time the train pulled into Kings Cross station we were like old friends and sorting out the underground for the next stage of the journey to Baker Street together became an enjoyable adventure.

On reaching Baker Street station I had my first glimpse of a Royal Air Force uniform, an uncommon sight in the North. It was worn by one of the number of sergeants who had been sent from Halton to meet the new entry of apprentices as they arrived from all directions and to shepherd them on to the special train laid on to take them to Wendover, the nearest rail station to Halton Camp. At the time I thought what an unenviable task the sergeants had as there were already around 300 of us milling about the platform with more arriving each time a train pulled into Baker Street. However, with infinite patience and much checking and rechecking of lists of names we were at last herded onto the waiting train.

The short winter's day was already drawing to a close as we

detrained, travel weary and hungry, and climbed into waiting blue-grey painted lorries. At that moment all we craved for was hot food and drink and bodily warmth. The powers that be must have divined our needs for after the snort and bumpy ride from the station and through Wendover village the lorries turned through the guardroom gates of what turned out to be No 4 Wing and disgorged us on a vast expanse of asphalt in front of some brightly lit barrack blocks. Here we were split up into parties of twenty or so and led to a nearby dining hall where we were served with big plates of sausage and mash and mugs of hot strong tea. We were then led off to a long barrack block dormitory, allocated a bed and left to our own devices. The long day had taken its toll and I was now feeling very tired so despite the strangers around me and the unfamiliar surroundings I was in bed and fast asleep by nine o'clock, dead to the world.

Next morning we were awakened by a trumpeter sounding reveille, a sound that was to herald each dawn for me for the next three years. Our ablutions were soon over as few of the 16-year-old-chins needed a razor, and once again we were herded into a shambling and un-military looking group and taken to the dining hall for breakfast. Once that was over the serious business of the day began with a very strict medical and dental examination that weeded out the unfit applicants, who were sent back home without further ado. This was followed by the documentation of our particulars. We then signed on officially as Aircraft Apprentices in the Royal Air Force. Now that the die was cast there was no going back. I was whisked away to the clothing stores where I was issued or rather had thrown at me a full RAF kit, the service tailor in attendance taking note of the alterations needed to my new uniforms. Items of kit were stamped with my personal number (563257) using black marking ink or metal stamps that indented the number on wooden backed brushes, aluminium mess tin and leather boots. To end the day we were led like lambs to the slaughter to the Barber's shop, where the hard-pressed staff who having to get through shearing 7 – 800 of us within the next few days, treated us all with a fine disdain.

The next day the blitz started, the aim being to indoctrinate us into the Royal Air Force routine the hard way with two full weeks of drill, discipline and Physical Training designed to crush individuality. During this time we were at the mercy of the many sadistic senior N.C.O.s who had started their careers as drill instructors in the Army or the Royal Marines. Their sole object in life seemed to be to drill us into the ground.

On the acres of barrack square we paraded to start the day with the hoisting of the RAF ensign, and followed that by being drilled in every movement in the RAF manual by squads, then Flights and then forming into Squadrons. The last hour of the afternoon was reserved for Wing drill with a drummer sounding the movements under "Sammy" Marshall the Wing Sergeant Major, a most terrifying character. In between the drilling to make sure we were fully occupied we changed into P.T. kit and did exercises, had lectures on every aspect of the Service, or had sections of the Air Force Act read to us.

The intensely cold weather of that January made matters worse for me, I had never worn boots until then and although those issues were of a light pattern they chafed my feet so that I developed blisters and I hobbled around for some days. My head ached from the weight of the service cap and the tightness of the hard leather sweat band and my neck was raw from the continued chafing of the service great coat worn fully buttoned up in the biting wind. All in all I was pretty miserable and had it not been for a streak of Yorkshire obstinacy that made me determined to stick it out I would have brought to an end my Air Force career within the first 48 hours; indeed a number of people did just that, having decided that there was too much hardship involved in reaching the stars. Time proved to be a great healer in my case for after the sheer misery of the first week my feet toughened up and I found to my great surprise that I was actually enjoying all the unaccustomed exercise in the open air.

No. I School of Technical Training (Apprentices), Royal Air Force Halton, had been established shortly after the end of the Great War when the Royal Air Force was still in its infancy in pursuance of the policy laid down by the first Chief of the Air Staff Lord Trenchard. The objective was to create technical and flying corps élite to meet the future requirements of the new service. The camp was spread along the ridges and steeply wooded slopes of the

Chiltern Hills lying between Wendover and Tring amid some of the most beautiful beech woods and countryside in Buckinghamshire. For many years the land had formed part of the Rothschild estates and had then been presented to the nation by the family. Halton House the original mansion became the Officers Mess and the three Apprentice Wings were built in red brick and laid out in neat geometrical patterns around asphalted drill squares on sites on the chalky hillsides. They overlooked the many acres of workshops, school buildings and playing fields that stretched down to the Grand Union Canal and to the sports stadium and Halton village, with a small grass aerodrome just beyond.

Apprentice Training for the aircraft engineering trades took a full three years; similar training for the wireless trades was given at Cranwell and a two year training was given at Ruislip for the clerical trades. Numbers 1, 2 and 4 Wings were at Halton and there were two new intakes annually allocated to the Wings in numerical sequence as an entry passed out on completion of its three years training. Thus each wing comprised a Senior Entry and a Junior Entry with 18 months between them. As the Seniors completed their three years and moved out the Juniors then automatically became the Seniors and the new intake the Juniors. In No. 4 Wing, of which we were now part, the 13th Entry had left just before Christmas. The Junior Entry, the 16th, were now the Senior Entry and we, the new intake and the 19th Entry, now became the Junior Entry and the lowest of the low.

By the end of our two weeks of concentrated square-bashing, we could march and drill with the best, and basic technical training and schoolwork started to a set weekly programme, which in my case was one of the top Engine Fitters' classes. If your particular class appeared on the programme for morning workshop training you attended morning parade at 8am in overalls, and marched down the hill to the skirl of the bagpipes or to the music trumpeters or fifes and drums before dispersing to one of the various bays in the workshops for tuition. The first test job given us was to use various cold chisels and files to chip and shape a hexagon out of a length of four inch mild steel bar and for weeks afterwards it was possible to recognise the fitter trainees from their damaged knuckles and gashed hands.

17

Wednesday afternoons were set aside for organised sports. If you weren't good enough to be selected for one of the many team sports arranged you were detailed to take part in a five mile cross-country run, or if an important rugger match was being played, turn up to give vociferous support from the touch line. There was no known method of opting out of the cross-country run as the route was manned at intervals by staff NCOs wielding rubber office stamps which were used to mark some part of the anatomy of each runner as he staggered by. Any one returning to base without the full number of stamps on his person had to go round again.

Saturday mornings were always reserved for kit and barrack room inspections preceded by long sessions of cleaning and polishing everything possible including broom handles. Windows were polished with metal polish, kits in the tin lockers squared up, and the brown lino floor covering liberally dressed with Ronuk and then shone by using floor pads made from old blankets until it resembled a mirror. After the inspection there was the inevitable Squadron and Wing parade lasting until mid-day, but then we were free for the rest of the day.

Sundays meant Church parade, wearing puttees. The RAF still had this unwanted legacy from the Army as part of "best Blue" for all ranks up to Flight Lieutenant, above which the puttees gave way to field boots. Winding long swathes of horse bandage around the legs, varying the starting point and degree of tautness to line up the seam when finished, making sure that the 'rings' round the legs were equidistant, was something not to be recommended even to one's worst enemy. They were designed for maximum discomfort. No matter how painstakingly I adjusted the puttees, coming back from church up the steep hill, they tightened up on my calves and gave me cramp. No doubt the Royal Horse Artillery liked them as they rode astride the horses on the gun carriages, but they were certainly not designed for marching up hills!

I now lived in Room 3 Block 2 of "C" Squadron No. 4 Wing together with 17 others of roughly my own age we were generally supervised by a "Leading Aircraft Apprentice" from our senior entry who lived in a small room or bunk just inside the barrack room door. We were a hetrogeneous bunch of ruffians as I recall; Bill Redding was a fellow Yorkshireman from Scarborough,

18

Nicholls from Durham a little further north and my great friend Johnny Stroud also came from that area near Bishop Auckland. Scotty Robertson was a Glaswegian, Nicholson a Liverpudlan and Paddy Stanley was from the Emerald Isle. Coming further south Al Stone was a Cardiff man, Happy Steele from Nottingham and Radford from Leicester. Rowe was a Plymouth man, Roberts from Dover, Sharman lived in Sheerness and Rapley and Peters were Londoners; all in all they represented a good cross section of the United Kingdom.

As members of No. 4 Wing we wore a red cap band instead of the normal black mohair band on our service caps and behind the RAF cap badge a yellow disc denoting our squadron; Nos I and 2 Wings wore green and light blue bands respectively and A Squadron had black discs and "B" Squadron white ones. All Apprentices wore the brass wheel, a four bladed propeller in a ring on the left arm of the tunic.

During our first two years of training we were paid at a whole shilling a day going up by sixpence during our last year; every Friday afternoon the pay parade was held, another drill routine, at the end of which we collected three shillings in cash the other four shillings being credited to us and paid out before each leave period to ensure that we had sufficient funds for the rail fare. It was rather like being at school again with three terms and three holiday periods at Easter, Summer and Christmas when we were paid our credits and lived like lords for as long as the money lasted.

Smoking was one of the more serious crimes in the book and was forbidden anywhere in the Wing. At the age of 18 one became eligible for a smoking permit but then only permitted to light up outside the Wing gates. Lack of money was a more effective means of deterring would-be nicotine addicts as seldom as we have the price of a packet of ten between us.

Our little world revolved around the Station cinema located roughly equidistant from the three wings; it was small, holding 4 – 500 people and the seats were uncomfortable. As there were some 3,000 apprentices in the wings to say nothing of the staff and the Princess Mary's RAF Hospital personnel the manager had to provide three changes of programme weekly with two houses every evening. The seats ranged from fourpence to a shilling and there was always a long queue for the cheaper ones. A few of us were lucky enough to be "remittance" men whose doting parents sent them a small weekly postal order usually on a set day of the week. By the time the post came in there would quite often be half a dozen of us literally "willing" the letter to arrive so that we could all see a particular film mid-week. "Talkies" were something we had read about but had not yet arrived in our neck of the woods; it wasn't until the autumn of that year that they were shown in Aylesbury and a party of us squandered a weeks pay going by bus on Saturday afternoon to see our first one. I can still recall the first song: "If I had a talking picture of you" sung by Janet Gaynor and Charles Farrell not quite synchronised with the lips but sheer magic in those days.

That first term in the long cold winter of early 1929 dragged on with the temperature seldom above freezing and there was ice on the aerodrome lake right through to the end of March; then suddenly Spring arrived and we went on our first Easter leave the day before Good Friday in really hot weather perspiring freely in our thick serge uniforms. The previous day our credits had been paid to us and I had bought my rail ticket home at the temporary booking office set up in the workshops.

At the station that morning I joined up with the three other ex Kings School scholars who were also at Halton; Tom Colley was in the 16th entry, the senior entry of my No 4 Wing, Fred Robinson in the 17th entry in No 1 wing and Len Wood and Eric Gardiner in the 18th entry in No 2 Wing. Until now our paths had not crossed but today we all travelled together in one party, changing stations at Sheffield and leaving the connection at Pontefract where we split up, Len and I then catching the bus for Knottingley.

After the welcome home the rest of the leave turned rather sour for there was little for me to do and I now found that I had nothing in common with the few old school friends I met. I seemed to spend most of my time going for long walks with the dog or sitting alone at a matinee performance in one of the local cinemas and sometimes joining my father in the evenings at his club for a game of snooker or billiards. To tell the truth I was bored and missed the routine and companionship of the new life I had begun; I was secretly glad when it was time to return to Halton for the second term.

★   ★   ★

I enjoyed the long hot days of the summer term and the time passed pleasantly, divided between school, workshops practice and sporting activities. Just before our long leave started in August the station sports were held in the Stadium; I enjoyed watching the events, particularly the high hurdles won by Don Finlay in superb style, and there and then decided to participate in the next ones.

It was pleasant to start off home again on three weeks leave and have the benefit of drawing our biggest credits of the year to spend while away; this time there seemed much more to do and the days went by pleasantly cycling, fishing and playing snooker and billiards when it was wet. I even played cricket a couple of times for the town second eleven.

The leave was soon over and once again the five of us met on the station platform at Pontefract for our return to Halton. The autumn was a delightful season in the Chilterns with the beech woods changing colour and the scent of wood fires around. From now to the end of the year we would finish off our workshop practice during which time we would have completed a wide range of test pieces designed to exercise our skills with hand tools and measuring instruments. We would be regrouped on our year's results ready to start in the new year in the aero-engine workshops.

With but a few days to go to the end of term and Christmas leave one of my room mates fell ill and was quickly moved into the isolation wing of the hospital suffering from diptheria. That started a bit of a panic and the remaining occupants of the room were immediately placed in isolation and subjected to a daily round of throat "swabs" the results of which would show whether any of us were carriers without actually having caught the disease. For more than a week we stayed in splendid isolation with time hanging heavily on our hands in the confined space and we watched miserably from our prison windows as the remainder of the Wing left in high spirits for Christmas leave. Luckily we received a clean bill of health the next morning and leaving the room and contents to be sealed up and fumigated we were hurriedly sent off that same afternoon. Although it was Christmas Eve I managed to connect with the last train from Sheffield and walked the last three miles from Pontefract, arriving home in the early hours of Christmas Day.

★   ★   ★

At the start of 1930 our small party assembled once more on the platform of the railway station at Pontefract in time to catch the Sheffield train for the first leg of the journey back to Wendover and the start of the new term. With the memory of the previous years Arctic conditions still fresh in my mind I had reconciled myself to expect similar "brass monkey" weather for the next three months but my fears were groundless; the first weeks of 1930 proved to be nothing like as cold.

As a result of the re-grouping exercise based on our first year's results I was now in 19 FI, the top class of the Aero Engine Fitter fraternity. Half my new classmates were total strangers to me but this soon changed as we were introduced to the mysteries of the Bristol Jupiter 9-cylinder engine. Using the special tools and jigs we stripped and re-assembled the engine and major components, quickly breaking the ice as we worked together.

As the summer approached the "C" Squadron Commander, Johnny Walker was posted. The new CO, who was younger and possibly had private money, tried to stimulate greater interest in athletics by initiating a novices competition and providing prizes for the winners paid for out of his own pocket. I had intended to try my hand at athletics anyway so I promptly put my name down for a few track and field events and started to practice in the evenings. I discovered that I had a natural aptitude for both the long and high jumps and also the hurdles. In the ensuing competition I also tried my hand at putting the shot and ended up either winner or runner-up in all four events being awarded the Victor Ludorum medal. From there I went on to more victories in the Wing sports and Londonderry Cup competition and was selected for the Wing team competing for the Barrington-Kennet trophy.

As the year wore on, our Senior Entry, the 16th., were approaching the end of their three years apprenticeship and the final written examinations, test jobs and viva voces to decide their classifications on passing out into the mens service as fully qualified aircraftsmen, were in full swing. Once the 16th., had left my Entry automatically became the Wing Senior Entry and new boys due to arrive in September, the 22nd Entry, would then become our Junior Entry. In readiness for that a number of apprentices from the 19th would have to be made up to Leading Aircraft Apprentices (Leading Boys). They would take charge and maintain discipline in the barrack rooms of both entries and thereby take much of the load away from the regular staff senior NCOs during off-duty hours. My name must have been sent in by someone for this doubtful honour. I was detailed to attend the next special drill course designed to fit me for such duties being run by "Sammy" Marshall, the Wing Sergeant Major. He was a tough disciplinarian, the very mention of whose name was sufficient to strike panic into parade ground slackers. Somehow I managed to survive the week under that formidable figure and was then authorised to report to the main stores and tailors shop to have the visible symbols of my new authority, three inch strips of chevron tape, sewn on both sleeves of my tunics just below the brass Apprentices' wheel. My new status brought me no increase in pay and little in the way of privileges. I was now responsible for every action of the twenty or so new Entry boys in my room. On drill parade I was likely to be called upon to act as a marker. Off-duty I took my turn on the duty L/AA roster for evening duties in the NAAFI restaurant and games room. An occasional duty was to serve as ADC and general dogsbody to Air Commodore Bonham-Carter, the Air Officer Commanding Royal Air Force Halton. He was an ex-Royal Flying Corps officer, utterly dedicated to the service. Although he had lost a leg in the Great war he did not allow that to affect his career and made a point of taking major parades or inspections mounted on his own white horse. On one occasion when watching a PT class he decided that not enough effort was being put into the exercise and dismounted on the spot and demonstrated on his one leg just how it should be carried out. He absolutely refused to admit to his disability as I found out for

23

myself when the day came for my turn to be his ADC; I reported bright and early to the official residence in Halton village to find that the great man was still at breakfast and waited in the hall with some trepidation for him to emerge. His own old Renault car and personal driver were waiting outside and when at last he came out he completely ignored me, stomping past to get in the back seat of the car. I chalked up my first gaffe of the day by darting forward and attempting to assist him only to be blasted by him for being so presumptious, to the great amusement of his driver who must have seen it happen every morning. For the rest of the day I managed to restrain myself from providing any assistance and we got along well; I was subjected to a continual barrage of questions on every subject under the sun, however, and by the end of the day when he dismissed me, my stumbling answers must have convinced him that he was dealing with the village idiot.

The RAF uniform for Corporals and below was a thick blue serge tunic with a hooked up collar, in which it was difficult to look smart and which most of the time looked like a sack tied in the middle. Faced with having to wear this many Apprentices turned a blind eye to that part of Kings Regulations and Air Council Instructions threatening death and such like punishment for any unauthorised alteration of service uniform. With imagination and the judicious use of needles and thread pantaloons could be taken in at the knee to give a tighter fitting and allow the breeches to curve away in a drooping wing effect. Uniform caps, hard and flat looking when issued, also provided a challenge to individual taste, the ultimate goal for most being the German style high up in front and drooping at the rear; this effect was achieved by inserting a metal strip to strengthen the normal spring and hanging the hat on one of the metal uprights of the bed with some weighty object tied to the back of the crown to stretch it to the required shape. I had the bad luck to be caught out by the service police with a "stiffener" in my hat and was promptly hauled up on a charge before the Squadron Commander and awarded three days C.B. for such a heinous offence.

That was my only experience of C.B. in my three years at Halton and I resolved never to get caught again. The routine of early morning reporting, mid-day reporting, missing out on the evening meal to change into best blue and attend defaulters parade at 6 p.m. followed by an hours drill in fast time and up to a further two hours of fatigues in the Wing Guardroom made me decide against a life of crime.

When that summer term ended and I went home for the three weeks leave I found that my mother had received the third and last report on me from the Officer Commanding No. 4 Wing. (Wing Commander Bill Hicks who was an ex Airship pilot of the First World War). On my first report he neatly summarised my achievements all round with the comment "Has the makings of a good airman"; on my second one "Has the makings of a very good airman" and on my third and last "He has the makings of an excellent airman". Praise indeed, but today I wonder if the reports on all the apprentices were couched in exactly the same terms, regardless.

Before I came home my father had obtained permission for the two of us to fish a large private lake on a big estate near Darrington a few miles away and on the first fine day we cycled over with our rods and a luncheon basket to try out luck. It was unfortunate that the only boat available had been sunk and we were thus confined to the shores but we spent many enjoyable hours trying out new swims without catching anything. What infuriated us was the sight of a large shoal of monster fish basking near the surface of the lake about a hundred yards out and beyond our reach all the time we were there, visible evidence that the lake was well stocked.

Once again I filled in for a couple of cricket matches for the town club, spent some time on the snooker table and generally lazed around the district but it was soon time to don uniform again and head back south.

That autumn we had an Indian summer and it was good to be alive and watch the beechwoods around us changing to gold and smell the fragrant blue wood smoke from cottage and garden fires curling up into the still air as we meandered along the cart tracks in the surrounding hills. On the rare occasions we had a few pence in our pockets we would call in at one of the many small inns and refresh ourselves with a half of Benskins bitter. We climbed up to the monument on Coombe Hill and gazed down at Chequers the country residence of the Prime Minister. From the monument it was possible to see parts of Berks, Bucks, Oxon and Herts.

The fine weather soon changed to cold and damp as we settled down to our second year of training an another type of engine. In November I reached the ripe old age of 18 an event that brought me a postal order and a parcel from home. I remember that it was a Wednesday and the post was late so I had to make a mad dash to the Camp Post Office to cash the order a minute before closing time. Six of us went to the cinema that evening, living it up with a couple of bars of Sharpes toffee each and a small packet of cigarettes between us, returning to devour the parcel of goodies to the last crumb; such was happiness in those far-off days.

That term we drew rifles and started drill that was to go on until the end of our training by which time the rifle had become an integral part of each of us. There was more variety for us in the workshops, too, and we spent three weeks in the Metallurgy Laboratory being instructed in the properties of metals and the recognition and testing of different types and of their alloys. This was followed by a week on the types of ancillary equipment such as the fuel and air equipment and the generators in current use on aircraft. By the time Christmas leave came around Tom Colley and Fred Robinson had left us and our train party had been reduced to three.

★   ★   ★

I think that Christmas leave was the most boring of any. The weather was cold, wet and miserable and I spent most of the time either reading at home or at cinema matinees. I was glad to be back with my cronies when I returned to Halton in the New Year. This was to be our final year and we were soon at work sorting out the mysteries of the Napier Lion engine. The rear cover on that engine was a work of art in itself as it housed practically everything except the cylinder blocks and pistons and the special tools for working on it occupied half an engine bay.

Other courses were now coming at us thick and fast. We had a week of fault finding and tracing in the static engines shed followed soon afterwards by installing an engine in a wingless fuselage and running it at night to check the colour of the fuel mixture. After the short Easter leave we fired our first .303 musketry course and accustomed ourselves to the "kick" of the Lee Enfield rifles. And we spent more time than ever on the wing parade ground practising the "Advance in Review Order" and marching past by Squadrons and as a Wing presumably so that we wouldn't disgrace ourselves at the end of the year on our passing out parade.

At Whitsun Johnnie Stroud and I were invited to stay at Joe Martin's home near the Peak district of Derbyshire; Joe's father was a retired Captain in the Inniskilling Fusiliers. On our return after an enjoyable time rambling around the district I had a letter from home to say that I had been invited to spend a weekend in London at the home of one of my mother's relatives who lived in Paddington Green in a cottage in a quiet backwater; I could also bring one of my friends if I wanted.

I had never met the family before but had several times seen the eldest daughter Louise Fawcett pictured in the newspaper when training in Battersea Park for the AAA championships. A year earlier she had been selected for the British team and had gone to Scandinavia with them. Her speciality was the javelin and the discus. As Joe Martin and I intended to go to the RAF Pageant at Hendon that year it seemed a good idea to combine the weekend with the Pageant and to take Joe with me.

Louise and her sister met us on the Tube station by the simple expedient of waiting until everyone else had hurried off leaving just the four of us eyeing each other dubiously, then introducing ourselves and soon breaking the ice. The cottage was in a little green oasis of a garden tucked away out of sight behind the church, and the head of the family was like something out of the past, smoking a long clay churchwarden's pipe continuously. The weather was hot and after a meal we played croquet on the lawn and sat out in the garden catching up on family history and getting to know each other better. Next day the weather was again hot and perfect for the display, and Joe and I set off by Tube in good time for Colindale, the Hendon station. We enjoyed our first Hendon Display very much but the crowds were such that it took us most of the evening to travel back and we perspired freely in our thick serge uniforms.

I think it was at the Hendon Air Display that I determined to become a flier. Until that moment my thoughts hadn't gone any further than the end of my Halton training and there had been no opportunity to get into the air to date. Soon after our return from summer leave, however, we were sent on the aircraft handling course held on the small grass airfield on the far side of Halton village. The aircraft in the Flight served a dual purpose by providing ground handling and propeller swinging experience for the apprentices, and practice flying for the General Duties officers on the staff. At the time I was there the aircraft were mostly of First World War vintage such as the Bristol Fighter, D.H.9A, Avro 504 N and a slightly more up to date Fairey IIIF. After a familiarisation flight in the Bristol I could hardly wait to get up in the rest. The IIIF was unserviceable most of the week but late on the Friday afternoon it was made serviceable and the new C.O. of the Wing, Wing Commander Herring came along to give it an air test and took me up. It was a beautiful afternoon and he flew the aircraft towards Oxford and then followed the river back to Marlow at a lowish altitude, landing back on the long grass of the aerodrome with scarcely a bump, an experience never to be forgotten.

From then on the tempo of life seemed to quicken as we started revision in all subjects in readiness for our passing out examinations. All too soon they started with the inevitable bench test piece followed by the major written paper of the trade. I did well on both, scoring well over the 80% of marks required for the top classification. These were followed by a series of viva voce tests by different examiners on the three types of aero-engines on which we had been trained and a more general test covering metallurgy, properties of metals, hand tools, screw threads and such like things. With the exception of the Siddeley Jaguar test I took these in my stride and was on top of the world. On the Jaguar test, however, the examiner was a weedy Flight Lieutenant already in a bad mood before we started. As he examined me on the master rod assembly of the engine he asked a silly question on why the big end bolts were waisted and I replied that it was obvious, to reduce weight. At this he exploded and took umbrage saying that I was there to answer his questions and not to tell him that anything was obvious. Looking back I can see that he had a point but it was too late then to retrieve the bad impression I had given and I was penalised for it by being given an average mark only. When the overall final results were listed I found that my unfortunate remark had cost me dear, for it had pulled my final percentage down to 79.86, thus missing the top classification by a whisker.

It also destroyed any small chance that I might have had of being considered for one of the two or three cadetships given to each entry and selected from the top thirty or so in the order of merit. It would take me another 18 months before I could get another attempt at reclassification at the start of my struggle to become a pilot.

A few days before Christmas 1931 the ceremonial passing out parade of the 19th Entry took place on the Wing parade ground. We marched past the visiting top Brass by Squadrons, then as Wing, and finally in review order. Back in the barrack rooms after the parade the yellow cap discs and red Wing bands were taken off our caps and the apprentice wheels removed from our arms; we were now men and part of the Royal Air Force proper.

Lists were now being pinned up on the notice boards detailing the individual postings. Scanning the pages rapidly I found that I was being posted to the staff of the Cadet College at Cranwell next day. I spent the evening packing and saying farewell to the many friends I had made during the past three years and early next morning set off for Wendover station for the last time, carrying all my worldly possessions in the pack and kit bag on my shoulders en route for my new life.

★ ★ ★

On the journey to Cranwell I watched the flat and mainly uninteresting countryside flash by without much enthusiasm. After the beech woods and the Chiltern Hills of Buckinghamshire the grass and ploughed fields of Lincolnshire seemed deadly dull.

Few people appeared to be around when we arrived at the West camp, as most of the Flights and Workshops staff had left earlier that day on either long leave or the four-day Christmas break. Much to our delight as soon as we had completed the required booking in formalities we too were able to fill in leave passes and were then free to go. I caught the green Lincolnshire bus that passed by the West Camp Guardroom an hour later en route for Newark and from here the mainline train to Doncaster. An hour after leaving the train at Doncaster a South Yorkshire bus dropped me at Knottingley, where I took my parents completely by surprise.

I spent a quiet Christmas at home with my family and returned to Cranwell to take up my new life and duties on the College staff the day after New Year's Day, 1932.

Joe and fellow apprentices at Halton, 1930
(Joe second from right, back row)

Aircraftsman Northrop

Royal Air Force Cranwell, like Halton, sprawled over several square miles of flat Lincolnshire land. It was located to one side of the main Sleaford to Newark road approximately four miles from Sleaford before the length of dead straight Roman road known as the "Leadenham Straight" started. The road split the station into two parts known as East and West Camps. East Camp housed the Signals Apprentice School training the Wireless Operator mechanics for the service. West Camp was made up of the Cadet College and its associated flying training flights and technical training school, together with the back-up workshops facilities required to maintain the training aircraft.

A start had been made on the construction of the new permanent Cadet College with an imposing facade on a site across the road from the old black wooden huts then accommodating the cadets, but it was still a long way from completion. All other personnal on the staff of the training flights and workshops were housed in the single storey buildings that lay between the cadet quarters and the hangars of the West Camp aerodrome. These had been built during the First World War t house the Women's Services of that era.

Probably arising from the luck of the draw in these matters I had been placed in the main Engine Repair Section of Station workshops where major overhauls and repairs were carried out on the Armstrong-Siddeley 14-cylinder Jaguar and 7-cylinder Lynx engines used in the Avro 504N's, dual Atlas and Siskin aircraft of the Cadet Training Flights. On my first working day I paraded on the road at the back of the Sergeants' Mess with the rest of the workshop staff where roll call was held by the Warrant Officer "Fonso" Ellison. Fonso sported the Observers' half brevet over his medal ribbons and was well known throughout the service as a character, having achieved fame in the Royal Flying Corps as McCudden's observer.

Fonso would wander around the engine bays in his supervisory role and regale the staff with the most outrageous anecdotes about his personal and wartime experiences. Much of it must have been authentic for when he left the service both the "Flight" and "Aeroplane", the well known aviation weeklies published several articles about him, a signal honour for a Warrant Officer in those days.

After roll call we marched off to the Engine Repair Shop (ERS) and on arrival I reported to Fonso in the office. He sent me off to find a Corporal Somerville with whom I was to work.

"Slim" Somerville lived up to his name, a tall thin individual with a serious expression. An ex-apprentice himself from one of the earliest entries he had seen quite a bit of overseas service. He had been involved in peacekeeping operations against the warring tribes on the North-West Frontier and formed part of the air-craft crew in the old Vickers Vernons and Victoria troop carriers during the evacuation of Kabul. Right from the start Slim and I got on well together and I learned a lot from him as we worked side by side in the engine bay stripping down engines which were due for overhaul or which had been damaged in a crash. The component parts were cleaned and checked minutely for wear or damage and if necessary replaced. Lastly, the engine was re-assembled on its stand and run on the test bench with a graded propellor to check the power output and fuel consumption. The cylinders were then inhibited against rust and the engine was placed in storage until required for installation.

The E.R.S. staff was a fairly small group of skilled personnel who were engrossed in their specialist tasks for most of the year with little in the way of variation from their daily routine.

Every Saturday morning during the College term, unless one had a long weekend pass, we paraded alongside the cadets for the weekly colour hoisting ceremony marching off afterwards to the sound of the Cranwell band playing the College march, "The Lincolnshire Poacher". Once off the parade, unless one happened to be caught for some special fatigue, we were free to change out of uniform and pursue our weekend activities. Throughout the time that I served in the ranks fatigues formed a bone of contention in the Royal Air Force and was probably the worst of the legacies passed to us by the other two services, who saw nothing wrong in making use of highly skilled technicians in a labouring capacity at any time.

After a few weeks had gone by and I had settled down to my new way of life I went home on a long weekend pass. Up to then the general remoteness of Cranwell had not bothered me at all but that journey convinced me that it was really necessary to have some form of transport of one's own to travel from door to door. The ordinary bus and train services were too few and far between and too overcrowded quite apart from the cost. To run a car on the sort of pittance I was then earning out of the question and it looked as though I would have to settle for power on two wheels.

A few days later I bumped into Fred Robinson who had been posted to Cranwell a year earlier and who was now well established in "E" Flight as a member of a dual Siskin ground crew. Fred was running his own motor-cycle and offered me a lift home on the pillion seat on my next weekend to see what I thought of it. We set off just after two o'clock the following Friday afternoon and covered the seventy odd miles mostly along the Great North road in roughly two hours arriving in time for tea. Had I gone by bus and train I would have still been on the station platform at Newark and wouldn't have reached home for another four hours or so. Petrol in those days was only a shilling a gallon so that the pair of us would do the return journey of a hundred and fifty miles in a third of the time taken by public transport for a shilling each, a 20th of the rail and bus fares.

This was the sort of economic reasoning that made sense and I started to look around for a reasonably priced machine. Some weeks later I went to Lincoln to look at a 500 cc New Hudson that was advertised and after a little haggling over the price with the owner bought it for twenty pounds and drove it back to Cranwell in triumph, my first trip as a driver. Now that I owned a machine I was accepted into the circle of riders who kept their machines in a small section of hangar partitioned off from the part used for storing the Panther motor cycles issued for use by the cadets as

33

required. Our section of the hangar was marked out in bays and numbered and I was allocated one of these for my use. I promptly acquired a very large wooden box fitted with a hefty lock in which to keep my rubber waders and other bad weather kit handy and to keep my tools safe from prowlers. From then on I was home and dry so to speak.

Any time from then on if I was at a loose end I could wander along to the dry and well lit garage "club-room" to work on the New Hudson or to chat with some of the other members who would be there. Much loving care was lavished on the machines. I can recall George Kennedy's stately Sunbeam, that took his owner to York every other weekend, and the latest camshaft Norton bought by Mac who had come with me from Halton. Later that summer he lost a leg, and nearly his life, when late at night he was hit from the side by a drunken car driver and left for dead in the road. There were a number of B.S.A.'s from 250 cc upwards, an Ivory Calthorpe, a New Imperial, a Rudge "Ulster" and a Scott "Flying Squirrel" seldom mobile. The one that really was kept in superb condition was a Triumph 500 cc O.H.V. whose bespectacled owner stripped it down completely after each weekend run home to Sheffield and then spent the next week assembling it in time for his next run out.

During the light evenings the "Club" made use of the nearby Leadenham Straight as a testing ground and speed track; in addition to being dead straight for four or five miles and with little traffic, there was a small filling station and garage boasting a small café at the Cranwell end known locally as Bayards Leap where we could sit and have a cup of tea in between forays along the "Straight".

Easter came and I took my machine home for the first time; six weeks later I again rode it to Yorkshire for the short Whitsun break. Because of the crowds and travel difficulties normally experienced on Bank Holidays, College staff had the concession of reporting back by 10 a.m. on Tuesday morning. I set off bright and early on a lovely summer morning looking forward to a pleasant ride back when about six miles from Newark the engine overheated and the bike slowed down and stopped the engine seizing up solid. Nothing could be done there and then so I pushed

34

the now useless piece of machinery back along the road to a small garage I had passed earlier and arranged for it to be left there for a few days. As I left the garage Fred Robinson came haring along on his bike and stopped to pick me up thereby solving my immediate problems of getting back to Cranwell on time. The following day being a normal Wednesday and half day Fred took me back to the garage and we towed my bike back to Cranwell in a quite illegal manner.

That evening we stripped down the engine and found that the oil pump had failed and caused the seizure; some scoring of the cylinder bore had resulted but the worst damage was to the cylinder head which had cracked near one of the valve ports. I had the cylinder bore skimmed and a new piston and rings fitted and sent the head away to Barimars for specialist welding, cast iron being tricky stuff. It came back a few days later not very well done. Up to that moment I had intended to keep the machine but knowing now that I would never be assured in my mind that it would hold up in use I decided to change it.

Pride & Clarke, the big London firm of motor cycle dealers had a big sales drive on at the time and were offering very attractive terms in part exchanges for the new Rudge radial valves that had just come on the market. I wrote to the firm and asked for a price for my machine and when I was offered more than I had paid for it originally I decided it was an offer I couldn't refuse and went ahead with the deal. I forwarded the now assembled New Hudson by passenger train from Sleaford and two weeks later while home on leave in Yorkshire collected a brand new chromium and black Rudge 350 cc O.H.V. from the Knottingley railway station.

It was a dream of a machine, quiet and powerful, that seemed to run largely on fresh air by comparison with the larger 500 cc engine of the New Hudson. That holiday my father developed a taste for travelling on the pillion and together we visited relatives I had heard of but never met. Two lived near Leeds and Bradford and one in Doncaster. One had started up the huge motor firm of Appleyard of Leeds and lived in the Manor House at Linton on Wharfe. He was now in the millionaire class and had two boys Geoffrey and Ian, who had visited us a few years earlier while at Bootham School prior to going to University.

35

Joe (standing) and friends in front of Avro Tutor at Cranwell

On my return to Cranwell I decided to do something useful during the coming winter and entered my name for classes leading to Part I of the RAF Higher Educational Test. To obtain the three parts took three years. Apart from improving ones general and specialist knowledge and any personal satisfaction one obtained from the classes, the fact that one had obtained one or more parts of the Test was noted in one's records and counted in ones favour when being considered for promotions, courses or other benefits. With reclassification in mind and, after that, selection for a flying course it would be enough to tip the scales in my favour in some future interview.

One highlight of the Autumn evenings before winter came was the annual six-a-side football competition in which teams from each of the thirty or so barrack huts competed against each other. Over a period of two weeks hard fought battles took place to a chorus of cheers, groans and cat-calls from the supporters. By the time the final was took place the dark nights were drawing in and the damp and cold of the Lincolnshire winter in this exposed site was making itself felt. I was glad then that I was working in a well-heated workshop.

I continued working with Slim for the first two months of 1933. During that time a number of overseas postings linked to the current trooping season took place creating gaps that had to be filled and a general reshuffle resulted. I was caught up in this and was moved into "C" Flight at the beginning of April.

"C" Flight was one of the two *ab initio* training flights on which the cadets carried out their first year training on the Avro 504 N's. These were of First World War vintage made of wood and fabric and only differed from the earlier models in that the old rotary Rhone Gnome engine had been replaced by the radial Lynx and the ungainly wooden nose-skid had been removed. The hickory "U" shaped wing tip skids and the tail skid were retained. During their second year on advanced training the cadets moved on to the Armstrong-Whitworth Atlases of B and D Flights and the dual Siskins of E Flight.

On my first day I paraded with my new Flight for roll call on the road outside the billet and we were then marched as a body to the hangar and dismissed to change into working overalls and start the day's work. The early detail of half a dozen men and a junior NCO had gone straight to work after breakfast to open the hangar doors and roll out the aircraft on the flying programme and these were already parked in two neat lines on the grass and the wheels checked ready for the ground crew to start up the engines. The fitter and rigger of each aircraft, now in overalls, checked and signed for daily inspections on the aircraft Form 700, the counter signature of the Flight Sergeant was then obtained and the aircraft was ready officially to be taken into the air.

The ground crew then went out to start up the engine. The only way to start the engines, other than sending out an SOS for the one old model "T" Ford Hucks starter kept for use in emergency, was by turning the laminated wooden propellor by hand. Whoever was in the cockpit then operated the engine switches and primed the induction manifold from the Ki-Gas pump mounted there. The mixture was sucked into the cylinders as the propellor was turned.

With the engine set on a good compression the operator stood clear, the man in the cockpit operated a hand starter magneto that supplied a fat spark to the plug in the cylinder under compression and, hopefully, the engine fired as the main switches were put on.

Round about 8.30 a.m., the first Flying Instructors would be emerging to carry out short test flights on their aircraft in readiness for the first of their instructional periods with the cadets. Usually the fitter or the rigger on the aircraft would opt to go up on this flight and for that purpose a few old flying helmets with home made Gosport tubes fitted were available in the Flight store.

After a few weeks on the aircraft I had been allocated the NCO pilot/instructor who usually flew it became quite friendly. He had served with fighter squadrons for five years before qualifying at the Central Flying School as an Instructor and was never happier than when he was doing aerobatics. Every time I went up with him I knew what to expect. His favourite gimmick was to line up the Avro into wind over the gasometer at Lincoln, turn the aircraft on its back and throttle back the engine. In a fair wind the aircraft would drift away downwind giving the impression to someone on the ground below that it was flying backwards. On these occasions the engine would cut out through fuel starvation as the gravity float mechanism of the carburettor ceased to function in the inverted position and he would then roll the aircraft back and dive it to restart the engine with the windmilling propellor. I could never get the cockpit straps tight enough to keep me in my seat and would dangle upside down in the slip stream hanging perilously loose and praying that they would hold. Sometimes I would be allowed to fly the aircraft for most of the flight and would be given elementary instruction. Before long I became quite proficient in the air and this served to whet my appetite for flying, making me more determined than ever to become a pilot.

By the time the test flight was over and we landed back at Cranwell the first detail of cadets on the flying programme would be kitted up and ready so the engine would be kept running. Part of the ground crews job was to see that the cadets were properly strapped in. They would then hang over the tailplane to make sure the aircraft didn't tip up on its nose as the engine was run up and checked for RPM drop on each magneto. After this the chocks were removed from the wheels and the pilot assisted in turning by dragging on a wingtip or strut until finally waved away.

All this man-handling on the ground was very necessary for the 504's had no brakes and relied solely on a combination of engine, rudder, elevator and ailerons for control when taxiing. In a fresh wind or on sloping ground they became unmanageable without additional assistance. Whenever our aircraft was flying either my rigger or I would be constantly on the look-out for it coming in and we would sprint from the hanger to hold on to the wing tips and guide it safely into a vacant space in the parking area and chock the wheels before the pilot switched off.

My rigger and I thought that we had this surveillance off to a fine art until one blustery day a notoriously dim cadet lost himself on the last detail of the day and landed in a panic at Wittering some 30 miles away. As it was getting dark he was kept there overnight and we were told that he would be coming back the next morning. However, there was a very strong wind blowing then and his take-off was delayed until it moderated. We were still waiting for news when he arrived and came in to land at the eastern end of the aerodrome over a mile away. Trying to taxi in with no one on the wing tips in the gusty wind he ended up on his nose, damaging the propellor and putting the aircraft out of action for an engine change. By the time we could get there on foot it was all over.

"Daddy" Holmes, the Sussex county cricketer, commanded "C" Flight and when he heard of the incident he was absolutely furious and told the Flight Sergeant to place the ground crew on a charge for not being available as soon as the aircraft touched down. My rigger and I were brought before him the next morning. Our protestations that we had not been informed of the aircraft's return, and that we could not possibly have reached it in time to prevent the accident as it landed a mile away, were brushed aside by Daddy who obviously wanted a scapegoat. The punishment of three days C.B. was completely unjustified and rankled for some time.

The five aircraft Flights took it in turn to be Duty Flight for a week at a time and during that week there was usually some variation in the normal routine when we had to deal with all types of visiting aircraft, mostly service but sometimes civil types. Also during that week the instructors had the daily chore of going out to the forced landing practice fields in the area before the programme started and hoisting the circuit flags on the signals masts and at the end of the day taking them down again. I usually went on this job as we tried to do it in a minimum of time by hedge-hopping from take-off and side-slipping in to the field to shorten the landing run.

Many visiting aircraft were flown by ex-cadets trying to impress their juniors. The Bristol Bulldogs and Hawker Furies always put up a good show taking off or landing in Fight formation, the distinctive roar and crackle of the stub exhausts of the Furies being unmistakable.

In 1933 almost all Royal Air Force aircraft were bi-planes with fixed landing gear. All aircraft were fabric-covered apart from vulnerable areas to the rear of the engines, which were fitted with detachable cowlings, and the points where inspection covers were used. Day bombers and fighters were finished in silver dope, usually embellished with the Squadron marking, and night bombers wore their dark and sombre camouflage. Among the visitors were aircraft such as Hawker, Harts, Demons and Army Co-op Audax's, Fairey IIIFs and 'Shiny Twelves' Foxes, Westland Wapitis and Wallaces, and Vickers Vildebeasts. And there were the occasional Fleet Air Arm Blackburn Darts or Ripons. Sometimes an old Vickers Virginia or trundling Hyderabad would appear, or a later Boulton and Paul Sidestrand. On rarer occasions some of the smaller civil and private aircraft of that era paid landing fees, and we managed to get close ups of the Parnell Pipit, Comper Mouse, Avro Avian, Westland Widgeon and Blackburn Bison, and other rare species.

The limited speeds and low ceilings of many of the Service aircraft taking part in the annual Air Defence of Great Britain Exercises that were held in the Autumn led to some laughable incidents, such as the occasion when Cranwell was used by the "Blue Force" of Sidestrands taking off to bomb London. Approaching the Capital a squadron of Bulldogs came up to intercept them whereupon the Bombers simply pushed open their throttles and left the pursuing fighters "stranded".

However, some progress was being made. Attached to 'E' Flight at Cranwell was the Fairey Monoplane K1991, being prepared for an attack on the world long distance record, to be flown by Sq.Ldr Gayford and Fl.Lt. Nicholetts. The monoplane was, to all intents and purposes, a huge flying petrol tank powered (or under-powered) by a specially tuned Napier Lion 12-cylinder engine, that gave a fantastically low fuel consumption under cruising conditions. The problem was getting the overloaded aircraft into the air and in the absence of a more powerful engine, that meant a longer take-off path. That was why Cranwell had been chosen as the starting point. A very long runway could be improvised using both the East and West Camp aerodromes and providing an additional length of hardstanding in an adjacent turnip field. Even then the aircraft became bogged down on several occasions.

Fortunately a hard frost in the late autumn came to the rescue and enabled the overladen aircraft to waddle along the full length of the runways to become airborne and set a new world distance recorded by flying to Walvis Bay non-stop. The aircraft was written off at the end of the flight by landing in a mangrove swamp.

Maintenance schedules on the aircraft in the flight were based on flying times of 20 and 40 hours between inspections, give or take an hour or two either way. At the end of that time the machine was placed unserviceable by an entry on the From 700 and pushed into a convenient space in the hangar where the crew could start their inspection. The schedule of work done and checks by supervisory NCOs before the aircraft was signed for as serviceable to fly again appeared to be fool proof until the day a dreamy fitter of long experience proved otherwise. Mac, the culprit, had removed the huge laminated mahogany propellor and hub from the splined engine shaft to check for cracks and damage and inspect the phosphor bronze centralising cones for wear and chatter. Having done this he re-assembled everything correctly finger-tight. He then went off to the crew room for his cup of tea and a cigarette intending to finish the job and tighten up and lock the hub to the engine shaft with the special tool provided in the engine kit. On returning he forgot all about it with the result that the aircraft was signed up as serviceable and rolled out of the hangar on to the grass to be given an engine run-up. The Corporal Fitter climbed into the cockpit and the Hucks starter connected in readiness to turn the engine over. The moment the engine fired the heavy propellor was cast off the shaft and whistled through the air like a boomerang until it splintered on the tarmac and finally came to rest without doing any other damage. I shall never forget the look of horror that came across Mac's face at that moment as he realised what had happened.

Towards the end of that summer the hangar and aircraft were prepared for the A.O.C's inspection; each machine was washed using hot water and soft soap then pushed out of the hangar to dry. The big wooden drip trays used under the engines were given a new coat of paint and a line of men abreast using the big platform brooms went up and down in swathes until all the loose dirt and dust had been swept up and collected. The hard work then started, we changed into rubber wellies and using bass brooms attacked the well established oil, grease and paint spots by sloshing buckets of hot caustic soda solution on them and scrubbing away. As we moved along the men behind sluiced away the caustic with clean water; by the time we finished the floor was spotless.

Next day we finished off the job, lining everything up from drip trays to propellors and polishing everything on the aircraft from brass switches to external copper pipes that was capable of taking a shine. Daddy Holmes carried out a preliminary check in the afternoon and approved everything, and we then repaired to the billets to prepare out kits and carry out the necessary spit and polish for the parade.

That took place in the morning, with the cadets and the Cranwell band in attendance. In the afternoon the Flights were inspected, each fitter and rigger standing by his aircraft. Afterwards the whole Flight, officers, NCOs and airmen assembled in front of the central aircraft for a Flight photograph and the College closed down for summer leave.

During the summer months I had been playing quite a lot of tennis with a chap from Doncaster whom everyone called "Hopkins" for no apparent reason. He had recently become a member of the motor cycle club when he had purchased his first steed, a Triumph 350 cc and was keen to do some touring on it. Shortly before summer leave we had agreed to spend a week touring the lake district and calling in to see some relative of his on the way who lived near Whitehaven. So, a week or so after I had arrived home Hopkins turned up one fine morning and we set off northwards.

We pottered through part of the Dales then headed for the west coast and spent the first night in Morecambe. Next day we started along the coastal road and stopped to have a picnic lunch on the pebbly beach in the shadow of Black Combe. Here we met up within two Scots lads who had been touring Britain in a little Morris Minor and were now returning home; we spent the afternoon on the beach and set off northwards in a convoy attending to call in at Whitehaven that evening. As we ran along the coastal road, one minute in view of the sea and the next climbing or descending wooded hills or valleys as the road snaked inland, the affair developed into a race between us and as mine was the newest and fastest machine I quickly piled up a big lead. Unfortunately, flashing downhill towards a U bend I made the mistake of looking back for the others and hit the high bank bordering the road at well over sixty. The impact jerked me backwards off the saddle on to the rear mud-guard and I clung to it as machine careered along, losing speed unti the engine stalled and I was able to control it and bring it to a stop. Needless to say for the rest of my motor cycling days I never looked backwards again!

The rest of the holiday was both enjoyable and uneventful and when I returned to Cranwell come days later there were two items of good news for me. I had passed the first part of the Higher Education Test. I could now go ahead with the next part during the coming winter months. Also the Flight Sergeant had put my name forward for the next Board to be held for re-classification to Leading Aircraftsman and I would be going to West Drayton for trade testing on the following Monday.

This was good news because I had to be reclassified as a Leading Aircraftsmen before I could go any further towards achieving my ambition to become a pilot. For the rest of the week I spent every spare moment I had swotting up my engineering basics and aero-engine manuals determined to make sure of passing. My efforts proved worthwhile for the following week I sailed through the written and the inevitable test job with marks in the nineties and didn't give a wrong answer in the viva voces. I returned to

43

Cranwell on the Friday evening to receive the congratulations of the rest of the Flight and to buy drinks all round. My "props" were recorded by an entry on P.O.R.s. giving me a back-dated pay increase that brought me to 38s. 6d. week.

With the future still in mind I went ahead and entered my name for the second part of the Higher Education Test and also volunteered for a series of new technical classes that were starting that winter with the object of broadening the scope of Aero-Engine Fitters to include Motor Transport work so that they could be used in either role. I little realised at the time just how big a part these voluntary classes were to play in realising my ambition for pilot training. At the time I simply found them interesting and useful in passing the long winter evenings.

In November I celebrated my 21st birthday, now a seasoned veteran with almost five years RAF service behind me. In December I went home for a few days Christmas leave returning to Cranwell to see the New Year in and settle down to meet whatever it held in store for me.

The spring of 1934 saw a number of changes taking place at Cranwell; the magnificent new College buildings were at last completed and handed over by the contractors and the Cadet Entries moved in, leaving the tarred black wooden huts on the opposite side of the road that had served so many cadets so well for so long a time.

As if to mark the occasion A. V. Roe and Company brought out their new trainer aircraft the "Tutor", a much smaller and more compact biplane than the old 504 N and of all metal welded tubular construction although still fabric covered. The engine was basically the same well-proven Siddeley Lynx 7-cylinder radial modified to produce slightly more power. The Townsend ring now enclosing it gave more effective cooling to the cylinder heads and improved the appearance of the aircraft. The best innovation of all was the independently sprung legs of the split landing gear with doughnut tyred alloy wheels fitted with differential brakes. This made the Tutor easy to manoevre when taxying and capable of stopping without ground crew assistance at the wing tips.

"A" and "C" Flights were re-equipped with the new trainers as they came off the factory production line and were brought into service. Shortly afterwards the ancient Atlas and Siskin aircraft of the other three Flights were replaced by the more modern Hawker Hart and similar types.

For the next few months we had teething troubles with the new aircraft but then a serious defect caused all aircraft to be grounded until an immediate modification had been done. It came to light one afternoon when my aircraft was flying on an aerobatic exercise. In the middle of a loop there was a heavy thump on the bulkhead just in front of the cockpit causing the pilot to abandon the exercise and land as quickly as possible. On removing the side panels we found that the single big fuel tank that rested in a transverse cradle mounting between the engine and the cockpit bulkheads had come adrift. It was clamped in position by two flexible metal straps and had moved backwards under the gravity forces created during flight. Fortunately the main fuel feed pipe hadn't fractured otherwise fire would almost certainly have occurred. All aircraft were grounded for several days by which time A. V. Roe's were able to design and produce new fastenings that cured the trouble for all time.

Throughout that summer I took every opportunity I could to fly on the short early morning air tests and I also managed to get in a few long weekend trips away by air. On one occasion I flew with Cocky Spencer to Weston Zoyland in glorious weather and spent the weekend under canvas near Blue Anchor Bay where the Army Ack Ack on the cliffs at nearby Watchet loosed off round after round at the pilotless drone aircraft sent up as targets. "Cocky" left me to do much of the flying on the way back, possibly because he had a hangover or he might still have been suffering from the multiple injuries he received in a crash some months before. He had been giving a display of aerobatics in a small private aircraft at Skegnesss and the aircraft spun into the ground; after some near miracles by RAF surgeons and many months in a hospital bed "Cocky" turned up at the Flight on crutches and insisted on taking up his old Avro 504 N to get in some practice flying. As he side-slipped to lose height in the final stages of a practice forced landing in a field near Rauceby he found out too late that he was unable to apply enough rudder with his damaged leg to check the descent and the aircraft just carried on until it hit the ground. The crash was reported by a local farm labourer and the Flight Commander took me along with him in my aircraft to find out what had happened. We landed in the same field and taxied to the heap of wreckage to find "Cocky" sitting on his parachute pack nearby nursing the small hand fire extinguisher that he had grabbed in case of fire. It was lucky for him that no fire started, for without his crutches he could barely have crawled away in time to save himself.

That year I took part in the Station Sports for the first time at Cranwell and won the High Jump, coming second in both the Long Jump and the Hurdles. On the strength of these showings I was selected for the Cranwell team entered in the RAF Championships at Uxbridge a week or two later. During the week of the meeting RAF Uxbridge was literally bursting at the seams in trying to accommodate teams from all over the United Kingdom; many had to sleep under canvas and I finished up on the floor of the Station Gymnasium. Despite this discomfort I had an enjoyable time and met up with many old friends. I was disappointed that our team didn't even manage to be placed, as the year before it had won the High Jump and my hopes of an RAF Championship medal had been high. However, I did have three Cranwell medals to show for my efforts.

I arrived back at Cranwell and for the first time was able to put in a formal application for flying training and appear before the Chief Flying Instructor for interview. Much to my chagrin I was passed over as being the most junior of the large number of applicants. The competition was fierce with only two applicants being chosen despite of the size of the field. To succeed at the first attempt one had to be outstanding at something as in the case of Don Finlay the Olympic hurdler who was selected first time. I was only a good "all-rounder".

I had now been at the RAF College for over two and a half years, about the usual length of stay for a posting in the United Kingdom, but there was no indication that I would be moving so far. Life was very pleasant anyway, so I carried on enjoying it without a thought for the morrow. My interests had turned to cars since Mac, who had been the culprit in the propellor incident the year before, had exchanged his Rudge "Ulster" bike for a brand new B.S.A. three wheeler that had come on the market. It was much more comfortable going out in the car than getting kitted out to take my bike out in wet weather. Some of my other friends were going in for four wheels. Smithy came back one weekend in an old bull-nosed Morris Cowley and Cooper, lately promoted to Corporal, sported a massive old Talbot Darraq two seater with a huge "dickey" seat that could carry six at a pinch. The best of the lot was an old red British Salmson racer picked up for a song by half a dozen of us clubbing together. It was a superb looking machine with three cockpits that had to be stepped in as it had no doors. The rear cockpit was a single, way out in the tail behind the rear axle. We ran it up and down the Leadenham Straight and there was great competition to be in that seat for the thrill of going round bends in the road when all the sensations of a tail gunner in a turret could be experienced.

Unfortunately, during one of these outings a connecting rod broke and came through the side of the crankcase causing irrepairable damage to the engine. After trying unsuccessfully to obtain another engine we were on the point of scrapping the car when by a miracle one fell into our lap. In the hot weather several of us went open air swimming in a lake on a nearby estate that had been thrown open to the public. During the afternoon there was a heavy thunderstorm and we took shelter in an old barn near by until it passed over. In one corner half covered over with rubbish was an identical model. We could hardly believe our ears when the farmer who owned the barn gave us his blessing to take it away. We returned the next day with tools, tow rope and the wheels and tyres from our car. We soon had it in the garage at Cranwell and the engine removed, and it wasn't long before our red bomb was on the road again.

Egyptian Interlude

Early in 1935 with Spring just around the corner an overseas posting came through for me. Up until then I had started to think that Records had lost my service documents and that I might well finish my career at the RAF College. I suppose that the Italian Dictator, Mussolini was largely responsible for my move. Pursuing expansionary aims in North Africa he prepared to invade Haile Salassi's Abyssinia while the League of Nations met and dithered ... My name had been added to an extra list of postings for the reinforcement of stations in the Middle East.

It was a relief to be leaving Cranwell after over three years. There I seemed to be getting nowhere fast with my applications for pilot training, being up against a large number of other applicants for the few nominations available. Cranwell was a very large command under it's own Air Officer. I had the feeling that I would stand a better chance in a smaller pool and I wanted to put it to the test.

I was sent on leave until the day before embarkation and left for Yorkshire on my motor bike to spend the leave at home and say my farewells to the family.

I had been wondering what arrangements to make about disposing of my trusty Rudge. That problem was solved for me when I stopped for petrol at a small garage on the North Road, just outside Newark. The proprietor admired the machine so much that on hearing I would be disposing of it in the next fortnight, he promptly offered to buy it. After a bit of haggling we agreed a price and arranged the deal. True to his word, when I returned a week later he had the cash waiting.

Less than 48 hours later, in company with other service personnel from all quarters of Britain, we arrived on the quayside at Southampton and boarded SS *Lancashire*, one of the oldest of the Bibby Line troopships, as equally famous as her sister ship, SS *Yorkshire* which featured in barrack room ballads throughout the Services. The Bibby Line had been operating these troopships for many years. They were small and cramped, and unstable in any but the calmest of seas. Like the French "voitures" of the First World War they barely came up to the standards normally required for transporting four-legged animals.

For the next three days the ship ploughed along the English Channel in the teeth of wintry gales. When it headed into the notoriously rough Bay of Biscay it was tossed about until nearly everyone was seasick below decks and conditions became simply nauseating. Our party occupied a mess deck at the first level down and thus had easy access to the main deck and the fresh sea air. The Army personnel were not so fortunate in the lower mess decks and suffered accordingly. The smell of sick humanity that permeated the atmosphere below decks was too much for me and I spent every moment I could braving the elements on deck and subsisting largely on tea or coffee and packets of dry biscuits from the ships canteen. I went below only to respond to calls of nature, take a shower or crawl into my hammock to sleep.

It says much for the endurance and resilience of the men in the Forces that under these miserable and nauseating conditions below decks in the rolling and pitching ship they could still manage a laugh. I remember going to the "heads" one morning when the ship was pitching heavily fore and aft and staggering away helpless with laughter at the sight that met my eyes. The toilets consisted of troughs continuously flushed by sea water to take away the by-products. To accommodate the needs of the large complement of troops on board the maximum number of loo seats had been installed over the troughs at the expense of privacy, only token partitions separating users with nothing restricting the frontal view. Under reasonably stable conditions the system worked well but with the ship pitching heavily anyone using the 'heads' who wanted to keep his nether regions dry had to attune his movements to those of the ship. As the bows went down a sort of miniature "Severn" bore rushed madly along the troughs slapping at any posteriors still occupying the seats. As the bows rose again the direction of the wave reversed. The sight of the two rows of half-

49

naked men standing up and sitting down as if by numbers or to the strains of music in a ballet was hilarious.

As the old *Lancashire* steamed steadily southwards the weather gradually became warmer the sea grew calmer and the grey skies turned to blue, morale improved all round. By the time the ship dropped anchor off Gibraltar to allow Army replacements for the Rock garrison to be ferried ashore the sun was shining and it was as warm as a summer's day in Britain. Feeling the welcome warmth on our backs we hung over the ships rail and bargained with the occupants of the many "bum" boats hovering round the ship selling fresh fruit and souvenirs; occasionally someone tossed coins into the sea to be retrieved by grinning boy divers.

After a stop of two hours the anchor was raised and the *Lancashire* headed eastwards into the Mediterranean between the "Pillars of Hercules" escorted by a school of dolphins racing alongside, the first ones we had seen on the voyage. It now became more of a pleasure cruise with each passing day as we lounged on the warm deck, sun bathing and chatting as the ship's Tannoy broadcast the popular tunes of the day. At intervals during the day there were "Housey Housey" sessions run by old Army sweats on the make and in odd corners below decks we were invited to gamble and "find the lady" by con-men in the crew who made a regular income out of troops on passage.

Some days later the ship dropped anchor just outside the harbour of Valetta and we were able to see some of the ancient forts and buildings of the Knights of Malta. The troops for the garrison and Luqua aerodrome were shipped ashore by tender and then it was up anchor and away on the last lap of the voyage.

We arrived in Alexandria and berthed along the quayside in the early hours of the morning. Most people were still asleep. Breakfast was earlier than usual after which those of us due to disembark collected our heavy kit from the bowels of the ship and paraded on deck to be checked off as we passed down the gangway. An Egyptian Railways train was waiting with steam up to deliver people to their various destinations between Alexandria and Port Said. In my own case it would be No. 4 Flying Training School, Abu Sueir, close to the Suez Canal and about six miles from the town of Ismailia.

Half an hour later the train pulled away and we settled down for the long journey overland. The sun was well up in a dazzling blue sky by now and the temperature in the carriage started to climb. We were still in the thick blue service dress we were wearing in the British winters just 10 days ago. We took off our tunics and yet still felt hot and sticky, despite the open windows of the carriage. Every time the train stopped at a station we were besieged by hordes of platform vendors of fruit and coloured drinks clamouring at the open windows. We soon learned to almost close them each time the train started to slow down for a stop. Each platform also had its own "gilly gilly" man, the Egyptian equivalent of "find the lady" using little wooden cups and live yellow chicks as he demonstrated his skills at sleight of hand. However we had been well briefed and took no chances, either on buying contaminated soft fruits or drinks, or gambling on the chick. We sat tight in the hot dusty carriage until the train started off again.

Late in the heat of the afternoon, by which time we were visibly wilting, the train juddered to a halt at Abu Sueir. The only indication that it was a railway station was the name in both Arabic and English at the side of the track and a collection of flat topped "mutti" buildings and hovels. A familiar blue RAF lorry was waiting to take us the last mile of our journey to the aerodrome. Once there we washed away all traces of the journey and headed for the dining hall where a first class meal was served by Arab waiters dressed in long white gowns and red tarbooshes.

Replete, I returned to the cool bungalow where "Nebby", the general factotum of that particular building had prepared a bed and tucked in the huge mosquito net to reduce the chances of one getting inside before I did. I pottered over the few yards to the showers and luxuriated under the cool spray before changing into a long sleeved white shirt and drill slacks, the dress worn by most people in the evenings when the mosquitoes were at their most active.

I spent much of the evening chatting to the other occupants of the bungalow and picking up as much useful information as I could on the routine at Abu Sueir. I found that I was the odd man out as a Group I tradesman as the others were all M.T. drivers and comprised the entire staff of the M.T. Section. Assuming that I was merely being housed for the night it didn't seem odd at the time. However, on booking in at the Station Orderly Room bright and early next morning it was a bit of a shock to find that I was to be with them permanently. The only reason I could think of was that the voluntary M.T. training classes I had undertaken at Cranwell the year before had been duly entered on my service documents and on the strength of this entry someone had earmarked me for Fitter duties in the M.T. Section Workshops. Having only just left Cranwell where the most up to date training aircraft in the RAF had been in use for some time it was like going backwards in time to find the airspace above Abu Sueir filled with old Avro 504s and Atlas's; this accorded with the normal Air Ministry practice of leaving the Overseas Commands until the very last for any form of re-equipment in the air or on the ground.

However, in many other respects and certainly from the sports aspect, the facilities at 4FTS and generally within the Canal Zone were very good indeed. This was largely the result of enterprise on the part of successive generations of airmen stationed there. In the thirties the length of a normal overseas tour of duty in the Middle East was five years. With lots of time on their hands and few places to go on their meagre pay the bored residents turned their various skills to building sports complexes providing club and bar facilities that could be enjoyed by members at low cost. Most buildings were ingenious conversions of old wooden packing crates in which aircraft were delivered overseas in those days. The clubs were well organised and quite opulent in appearance; the tennis club boasted three hard courts overlooked by shady verandah and was extremely popular. The Golf Club, with a nine hole course and sand greens designed to develop a raging thirst in the player, tended to attract a small hard core of drinking types quite content with their single long table around which they could pursue their hobby and hold rumbustious smoking concerts.

The Sand Yacht Club was the oldest and most élite with the 30 or more yachts each of distinctive design lined up on each side of the club-house. Most of them had been salvaged from old aircraft fuselages. Some dated back to the First World War, and after ending an honourable career in the air through old age or accident, had been seized upon by a potential club member for conversion purposes. The wheels, tyres, axles and steering fitments all came from the same source leaving the owner to purchase the mast rigging and sails made to measure at the chandler's shop in Ismaila. There were other clubs for keen photographers and marksmen. In addition the Station provided an excellent swimming pool, a modern cinema, football and cricket pitches beautifully level but lacking the green, green grass of home. A station bus with smart Egyptian driver in red fez was available most days to deliver sports teams to their local fixtures or take anyone over to Lake Timpsan a few miles away for an afternoon of salt water swimming, canoeing in Kayaks or water polo in the lake. For sports fixtures over longer distances it was usual to enlist the aid of a Valencia troop carrier, from 216 Squadron at Heliopolis, to ferry the team on a "training" flight.

Having arrived in the late Spring of the year the weather was rapidly starting to hot up. Within days the temperature began to soar and the heavy blue serge uniforms in which we had arrived were stored away and khaki drill became the order of the day. For every day work this meant modified Air Force blue shirts with Khaki Drill shorts, stockings and black shoes and a large pith helmet. In the evenings the usual dress was K.D. slacks or grey flannels, leather sandals and white shirts with long sleeves.

Each night before turning in it was a wise precaution to make a thorough search of the inside of the mosquito net enveloping the bed for the smallest tear in the net was sufficient to let in a marauder; any missed were easily seen next day for they would be hanging in the netting bloated to obscene proportions and bright red from their feast of blood.

The Army and RAF medical staffs carried out numerous experiments in vain attempts to kill off the mosquito larvae in the breeding swamps. Most of the waste engine oil drained from aircraft engines and M.T. vehicles during maintenance inspections was poured on the surfaces of stagnant pools without visible effect. One keen RAF Medical Officer even went so far as to obtain authority to purchase fish from South America for his experimental work; they were reputed to thrive on the larvae of mosquitos. The fish eventually arrived in large tanks and these were taken to the shallows of the heaviest breeding areas and the fish released watched by an excited local population. Within the next few days they had netted and eaten the lot!

I quickly slipped into the overseas routine making new friends daily and really enjoying the sunshine and the warmth after the British winter. My day began when "Nebby" the hut bearer and general factotum woke me around 5.30 a.m. with a large and steaming mug of tea, returning a few minutes later with my shoes polished to a high gloss and to lay out clean drill shorts and take away any items for laundry. After carrying out my ablutions I dressed and walked the short distance to the Mess to be served breakfast by one of the native waiters in white gown and red fez. By the time I returned to the bungalow to collect my pith helmet Nebby had already made up the bed and closed all the louvred shutters so that the interior would stay cool and dark throughout the heat of the day.

One "perk" that came my way as a matter of course was that I never had to go on any parades because most of the drivers in the Section went off bright and early on fixed driving details around the Camp, or ferrying Flight personnel out to the forced landing grounds in the desert. I was left to make my own way to the M.T. Workshops each morning, where I joined the two Corporals, Bill and Bud, as they arrived from the Married Quarter area at the other side of the Camp.

After nearly six years of training and workshop experience on an assortment of aero engines the antiquated list of vehicles brought in for major overhaul presented few problems other than the difficulty of obtaining spares which led to much of the work being treated as a challenge in expendiency and "making do". The first vehicle to come into the workshop for my attention was the old Ford Model "T" Hucks Starter that had been in use there since the mid-twenties. It says much for Henry Ford's products that despite the heat and dusty conditions, when I stripped the engine down after around ten years of desert running it was just as good as new.

Next in line for overhaul came an old solid-tyre Leyland, almost a museum piece, to which I fitted four new big-ends. It was rather like working on a railway locomotive. This was quickly followed by one of the two "Brooke Bond" Trojan vans on the strength

54

The Trojan van.

which needed new main bearings. However, almost as soon as I started to remove the engine from the van the Trojans were made obsolete and the RAF Depot at Aboukir signalled for them both to be returned there at once. At that time I was waiting for new main bearings to be delivered before I could make it roadworthy so I volunteered to accompany Wally, the driver detailed to return the other Trojan to Aboukir, and act as armed guard on the trip.

The Armoury issued me with a .303 rifle but without ammunition clips, the theory being that the mere sight of the rifle would keep any would be attackers at bay. In the meantime, Wally, a driver with lots of experience in Iraq and Egypt, had collected together enough food rations and equipment to keep us going for a week and had fuelled and loaded up the van in readiness.

We set off next morning at the crack of dawn aiming to reach Heliopolis on the outskirts of Cairo by mid-day after which it would be too hot for driving. For some two hours we passed along dusty roads through small villages where street markets jammed the road, reducing our speed to a crawl and enabling the local urchins to hang on to the tail-board while trying to remove anything not securely lashed down inside the van. I spent much of the time rapping any hands that appeared over the knuckles with a cane I had brought along for the purpose.

Then, at a suitable spot well away from any signs of habitation and near a cultivated area flanked by date palms, we stopped for breakfast. While Wally set up his cooking equipment I collected

55

some luscious tomatoes from a nearby field and within a very short space of time we were tucking into a veritable feast of bacon, eggs and fried tomatoes washed down with a mug of strong sweet tea. Sustained by this we hardly noticed the next two hours driving. We booked into the RAF Station at Heliopolis, on the outskirts of Cairo, in time for the mid-day meal.

After a siesta in the transit block we prepared the Trojan for an early start next morning, refuelling and checking the vehicle thoroughly. A quick shower and change and we were ready for a trip to the local open air cinema, my first experience of one. It was delightful sitting in the cool of the evening beneath the stars drinking iced lager and nibbling prawns and nuts while watching an up to date film on a massive screen that appeared almost as big as one of the nearby pyramids. After the show we returned to the transit block to spend a hot, sticky and scratchy night trying to sleep on straw-filled palliasses. It was a relief when the time came to get up and start the last stage of the journey to Aboukir.

The journey proved uneventful and we made good time reaching the Depot and being able to hand over the Trojan complete with documents before having our midday meal. We were then free to do as we pleased until we returned to Abu Sueir by train on the Monday.

All new equipment for the RAF in the Canal Zone came through the Depot at Aboukir having first been delivered via the main seaport at Alexandria a few miles along the coast. Likewise, all aircraft, engines, vehicles and other items requiring major overhaul and full workshops facilities were returned to Aboukir. Over the years a large permanent work force from the locality had been built up to deal with the work involved and the Depot was run on factory lines with as few changes in the RAF supervisory staff as possible. To keep them happy there were plenty of off-duty facilities available on the Camp and two magnificent beaches from which to swim, sail and carry out under-water exploration. As at Abu-Sueir many large wooden aircraft crates had found their way to the sand dunes of "Brighton" beach where they had been skilfully converted into seaside chalets that could be lived in quite comfortably for weeks at a time at little or no cost. Airmen came from as far afield as Iraq and Aden to spend local leave under these conditions and we managed to get a chalet allocated to us for the weekend.

We spent a delightfully lazy weekend swimming near the ruins of what was purported to have been Cleopatra's Palace, soaking up the sun and chasing the thousands of multi-coloured lizards that inhabited the rocks and dunes. Food was no problem as there were several small bar cafés a short distance away where we went for cold drinks. With each round came plates of local prawns, salted nuts and crisps, free with the drinks. All too soon the weekend was over and for the second time I boarded the Egyptian Railways train at Alexandria for the return to Abu Sueir.

Back in the Section once again I began to get involved in more and more activities. Having been roped in for the water polo team I soon found myself in the swimming team for the relay and backstroke events, the athletic team for the high and long jumps and the Station cricket team. In between fixtures I played golf, started to take an interest in photography and walked for miles around the area looking for subjects to take.

The drivers were a mixed bunch but as nice a crowd as one could hope to meet and even now nearly 45 years later I can recall most of them quite clearly. There was Charlie Hans, then into his fifth year of service overseas, a short and wily character and the regular driver of the solid-tyred Leyland that went round the Station daily collecting the refuse with a gang of native labourers. Charlie was always the first with any news. Sam Tykeiff, well over six feet in height and always impeccaby turned out, was the Station Commander's driver of the official Morris open tourer. Bill Beardsworth was short and dapper with wavy hair and short moustache who played the saxophone in the station dance band and was never happier than when he was dressed for the part in his white Tuxedo and bow tie. "Haggis", a dour Scot from Aberdeen, played golf with me whenever I could manage it and the rest of his off-duty time was taken up practicing sending Morse signals on a buzzer hand key or trying to decipher Morse that he picked up on an old radio set; his consuming ambition was to remuster to Wireless Operator. "Wally" had served two years in Iraq before being posted to Abu Sueir and kept very much to himself, lavishing all his affection on a little black mongrel dog named

Joe's Sand 'Yacht'.

"Pooch" that he kept on the verandah outside and took with him on his driving details. "Mac" McKenzie was a small bandy-legged Scot with a ready sense of humour who always looked scruffy. Later I pooled finances with him and we teamed up to buy the skeleton of an ancient sand yacht that had started life as a DH9A

Joe at the wheel of the 'Yacht'.

fuselage. We spent many afternoons working on it with temperatures well over the hundred mark before we christened it the "N.I." and ventured on our first test run in it.

Percy Parrish, Dinger Bell, King and half a dozen others whose faces I can bring to mind without being able to put a name to them made up the full complement of driver. In addition "Bombshell" Mills from Hull an ex-Ruislip Clerk-Apprentice kept the Section Records and "Nobby" Clark a raw Aircraft Hand from Battersea kept a general eye on the running of the bungalow and domestic requirements through Nebby, our native bearer.

By now, Mussolini's invasion of Abyssinia was imminent, and Italian ships loaded with supplies and troops, displaying huge posters of Il Duce, passed daily along the Suez Canal en route for the Red Sea.

The mid-summer weather was really hot and it seemed a good idea to hold a Section outing to the banks of the Canal where we could bathe and picnic. We watched the Italian activity at first hand, and expressed our disapproval with catcalls and rude gestures as the ships steamed slowly by.

Everyone in the section had cooperated and there was no shortage of food and drink, with two large dustbins filled with cracked ice, spirit stoves, and our two bearers, Nebby and Mustapha to look after our needs for the day. Wally's little black dog had joined the party, barking furiously at everyone who passed by as if to join in the fun. We had found a suitably shady olive grove and enjoyed splashing around in the warm salt water of the Canal. I picked up one of the inflated inner tubes, we had brought with us and with an old trilby hat on I floated off in the hot sun, closing my eyes and dozing gently, at peace with the world. How long I slept I don't know, but I was rudely awakened by a huge bulk flopping on top of me knocking all the breath out of me, and forcing me below the surface of the cool water. I rose to the surface gasping for breath to see a shoal of porpoises moving away along the waterway snaking in and out of the water in line astern. During my nap I had drifted away from the shallow water near the bank and was now in the middle of the canal. The thought struck me that I was indeed lucky that it had been only a big fish — it could well have been a passing ship.

The Sweetwater canal that passed nearby Abu Sueir on its path parallel to the Suez Canal and Ismailia supplied all the water, heavily chlorinated, used by the Camp. It hardly lived up to its description for the canal was teeming with a great variety of organisms, in particular tapeworms, to which the locals had become immune but which were deadly to newcomers. The decomposed carcasses of dead camels, donkeys and other small animals not to mention the occasional human remains were often caught up in the filters of the main supply pipes. It was an object lesson to pass along the main road to Ismailia by the side of the waterway where it was quite normal to see a number of villagers standing or squatting in the shallows to perform natural functions while a few yards away on the bank veiled and black robed women from the same village would be filling chatties with water for drinking and other household needs. The water was considered to be so contaminated and dangerous that we had strict orders to report sick if at any time we accidentally came into contact with it even though it might only be a splash. One Sunday morning, however, when I was with the Station cricket team in the Camp bus nearing the outskirts of Ismailia we were horrified by the spectable in front of us. On the other side of the water from us a large Army tent encampment had been set up and splashing around in the water enjoying a morning swim in total ignorance of the danger were a large number of Army personnel. This puzzled me until I remembered that some days earlier on the Pathé Gazette news and on the radio there had been a lot of fuss about British Army units who were returning to U.K. on completion of their tour of duty in British Guiana being diverted to the Middle East. On arrival at Southampton the troops were sent on almost immediately to the Canal Zone after a few hours spent with their dear ones at a reunion held in the Customs sheds on the quayside. The soldiers we were watching must be those troops who were normally accustomed to bathing in the clean river waters around the Caribbean. We stopped the bus at the first Army post in the town and reported what we had seen to the N.C.O. on Guard duty and left him to start the ball rolling. A few heads must have rolled over the huge sick lists that would have resulted from that episode.

As the hot summer wore on I became more and more established in the Transport Section taking my turn with the drivers on duty in the office after normal duty and often joining them on the early morning runs ferrying personnel and equipment over the desert to the practice forced landing grounds a few miles away. These trips gave me the opportunity to drive the old Leyland solid tyred three tonners being used and I could always squeeze into one of the dual Atlas aircraft for a short trip along the Suez Canal. These flights served to renew my determination to become a pilot. When, however, the opportunity did arise it came right out of the blue and I had nothing to do with it. It so happened that the Flight Sergeant had been passed the Engineering file asking for suitable applicants who could be recommended for pilot training on the grounds of age, service experience and keenness. He was about to send in a nil return when he suddenly remembered that he had me on his strength. Sticking his head out of the office window nearest the workhouse he yelled for me and I went over still holding the con-rod I was fitting in my hand. "Would you be at all interested in applying for a flying course?" he asked, to which I replied, "Yes please Flight", and my name was added on the spot. I could hardly believe that what I had dreamed of and worked towards for so long had been achieved so easily now. Ten days later I appeared for an interview with the Chief Flying Instructor, Squadron Leader Gardner who dismissed me with what sounded like a grunt of disapproval after making a few caustic comments about the state of my best K. D. uniform that, donned at short notice, was a mass of creases. I remember thinking disconsolately afterwards "Well, that's my lot as I'll probably never get another chance," only to find a few days later that I would appear for a final selection interview with Air Vice Marshal MacClean, the Air Officer Commanding Middle East Headquarters at Heliopolis. I made sure this time that my uniform was uncreased and sailed through the interview and the pilot's medical examination that followed at the Middle East Central Medical Board I returned to Abu Sueir clutching the precious certificate that pronounced me "fit for full flying duties".

For the next few days I walked on air and could hardly settle down to my mundane duties in the Section. I liked the life at Abu Sueir and I was hoping that I would be earmarked for the next training course there, scheduled to begin at the end of the year. I was already on the spot and raring to go. But I should have known from previous experience that a simple solution as such would not suit the plans of the Air Ministry and as the weeks went by and nothing happened I began to despair and threw myself wholeheartedly into more Camp activities.

Although the Camp was only a few miles into the desert wastes from Ismailia it was isolated to a large degree by the lack of adequate road and rail communication and the population was predominantly male. There were a few married quarters well away from the main area of the aerodrome and quarters but the inhabitants were seldom seen other than when they attended the cinema or used the small swimming pool during normal hours of work. Thus, apart from the usual sports activities, the male population was provided with entertainment by the Station cinema through a change of programme three times a week. There were long intervals so that everyone could purchase ice-cream and cold drinks and to allow all doors to be flung open and a cooling stream of night air let into the building. Other entertainment depended on the talent available to put on a good show at the open air smoking concerts held periodically in conjunction with the Station Band on the patio outside the NAAFI building. Impromptu concert evenings were a feature of the makeshift club-houses of the tennis, golf and sand yacht clubs and some uproarious evenings were held fuelled by the large quantities of McEwens and Youngers bottled export ales consumed by the audience. There was no shortage of talent. I recall in particular one of the leading lights of the Golf Club who brought the house down regularly with his Stanley Holloway rendrings of "Sam and the Duke of Wellington" and "Albert and the Lion".

During August, the hottest month I had experienced so far, the annual swimming sports were held in the Camp pool. I took part in the water-polo and relay race and the individual two lengths back stroke which I won. On the strength of that performance I was selected for the team to represent Abu Sueir in the Middle East Championships at Heliopolis at the beginning of September. These were held in the magnificent pool and surroundings of the Sporting Club on the outskirts of Cairo over three days starting on the 5th. September. I was beaten in my heat on the first day by the eventual winner but there was some consolation in being out of the action. Next day several of us who were no longer involved in the swimming decided to have a days sightseeing and take in the Sphinx and Pyramids at Gizeh.

As the evening would be our last at Heliopolis and we were washed out by the day's sight-seeing we decided to relax in comfort at the open air cinema nearby. Sitting in comfortable seats in the warm night air watching a good film on a giant screen and being able to order refreshment throughout the programme is the most enjoyable way I know of going to a show! Next day we watched the finals of the Championships and the presentation of prizes by the AOC in C and then returned to the aerodrome at Heliopolis from where we were to be flown back to Abu Sueir in the evening. No. 216 Squadron was based at RAF Heliopolis and was equipped with twin engined Vickers Valentia troop carrier aircraft. As part of the normal training programme the members of our team were to be taken back to Abu Sueir in a Valentia, taking off at dusk and landing by wing tip flares. Partly because of the bulbous shape of the nose of the aircraft and the unpleasant manner in which it wallowed through the air during hot weather, hitting every air pocket en route, the Valentia was aptly named the "Flying Pig" by the Services. Few passengers ever completed a journey of any length without throwing up. A silent testimony to its reputation was the stack of paper bags always carried in the back. Fortunately for us our flight over the star-lit desert in the cool of the evening was as steady as a rock and the experience of landing at night amongst the camel-thorn by the light of magnesium flares was one I wouldn't have missed for all the world.

On the 3rd October 1935 some three weeks later war was officially declared between Italy and Abyssinia and precautionary measures were brought into force by Middle East Head Quarters. Slit trenches with sand-bagged parapets appeared overnight in the sandy areas between the bungalows and everyone was issued with First World War type "tin hats", gas masks and rifles or revolvers. Parades wearing this equipment became the order of the day and very hot and sticky they were too; however the panic soon died down and we breathed sighs of relief and returned to normal routine.

Work on a new aircraft hangar that had been in progress for some time took on a new urgency when two Hawker Hart trainers were delivered, signalling the start of the re-equipment of No 4 FTS. Regrettably they never came to be used. In the autumn during early morning flying a low lying sheet of mist or low cloud sometimes formed, being quickly dissipated as the sun rose higher. One morning soon after the arrival of the Harts the two aircraft, resplendent in silver dope, were lined abreast near the new hangar when the mist formed. A number of Atlas's were flying around above the mist unable to land but making futile attempts. The Duty Pilot stepped out of the Watch Hut and began to fire off red verey light to warn these aircraft off. Unfortunately the trajectory of the first verey light was such that it fell, still burning, on the centre-section of the nearest Hart. The resultant fire reached the other Hart before it could be moved and in a matter of minutes all that remained were the charred skeletons and the promise of a

Court of Enquiry and eventual Court Martial for the careless Duty Pilot.

I was still waiting for news of my next move to a Flying Training School and as each day passed by I became more and more frustrated, yearning for some action. With the cooler weather at this time of the year the change over from khaki drill to blue serge uniform became effective and that was the signal for the inter-bungalow six a side annual football competition to start. Our bungalow fielded a strong side and for the next two or three weeks we struggled hard to reach the final, only to be beaten by the odd goal in the semi-final. I was selected to play for the Station eleven against the Scots Fusiliers and shortly afterwards for an RAF Canal Zone team to meet an Egyptian eleven in the stadium at Port Said. I was a bit shattered when we scored our first goal and the team was assailed by the crowd and had to retreat to the centre of the pitch under police guard to get out of range of the hail of coca cola bottles and other objects thrown by the spectators. We never finished that match!

Half-way through December with local dust storms making life a bit of a misery and plans for Christmas in the air, my posting back to U.K. came through. Back home an RAF Expansion Scheme hurriedly approved by the Government was rapidly being implemented and airmen from the Overseas Commands were to be returned to U.K. for flying training.

At the time of the Italian invasion of Abyssinia the S.S. *Cameronia* a 20,000 ton liner normally sailing on the Atlantic run had been hurriedly requisitioned and fitted out for trooping purposes. Her first job had been to take reinforcements to the Far East and Hong Kong and now she was on her way back to U.K. with time expired Naval and Army personnel. She was scheduled to pass along the Suez Canal the day after Boxing Day. The plan was to squeeze on board as many airmen trainee pilots as could be gathered together from the Middle East Stations. The Cameronia would lose way on her passage through the Bitter Lakes and let down her companion ladder so that the airmen could come alongside by tender and scramble up the ship's side to board her. I would be one of that party of scramblers.

Knowing that I had less than a fortnight to go, and with the

Christmas celebrations intervening, the time began to flash by. The day before Christmas Eve I cleared from the Section and Station and it only remained for me to pack up my kit and be picked up by transport and taken to Abu Sueir railway station on the day after Boxing Day. The time was most appropriate for saying my farewells as in readiness for the annual competition for the best decorated bungalow, every Section had a bar of sorts over Christmas. One had even gone so far as to convert the exterior into some thing resembling a troopship complete with funnels, admittance being given when coming on board by ringing a large ship's bell commandeered from heavens knows where.

On Christmas morning I managed to get round half the Camp having a farewell drink in each bar before having the official Christmas dinner served in the Mess by a bevy of officers acting as waiters true to the tradition of the Forces at Christmas. After a short siesta most of Camp then started paying visits to each others' bars and the celebrations carried on non stop into the early hours. I got up next morning with a shocking hangover to play in the comic football match and take part in the donkey polo. Later I again said my farewells in the bars of the three clubs.

Next morning, feeling the need for some fresh air, MacPherson and I rigged up our sand yacht and went for a spin in the desert; the breeze died away near the sand hills marking the line of the Sweetwater canal and we had to leave the N.I. and walk back some distance to the clubhouse where I handed over all rights of ownership to Mac.

Early that evening I had my last meal at Abu Sueir checked over my kit and boarded the transport that was to take me to the station to catch the train for Port Said. Many of my friends in the M.T. came along for the ride to see me off and the air was thick with ribald remarks. The banter was tinged a little with envy for I was on my way back to the U.K. after less than a year in Egypt, while many of them had already served three or four years and would not return until they completed the full four or five years.

The weather passing through the Bay of Biscay in mid-winter was atrocious. However, SS *Cameronia* had been built to stand up to worse conditions on the North Atlantic run and took everything the Bay threw at her in its stride. Not so the occupants of the troop-decks below who appeared to be permanently sea-sick. The Naval ratings on the other hand, seemed to enjoy the voyage so much that a couple of them slung their hammocks from stanchions on the after-deck and snoozed happily away with the deck awash and spray breaking over them.

Eventually the ship turned along the English Channel in the teeth of what must have been a Force seven gale. The Captain was unable to heave-to off Plymouth to disembark the Navy ratings at their home port in these conditions and steamed on for the shelter of the Solent, berthing at Southampton in the early morning. The tannoy was soon blaring out instructions for leaving the ship and after identifying our sea kitbags and suitcases, we filed down the gangway in turn to clear Customs and board the London train.

Our relatively small RAF party was soon en route for Victoria and from there we took the Underground to the RAF Depot at Uxbridge. On arrival we were informed that our allocations to Reserve Flying Schools had not yet been worked out and we were sent on leave for a week. We were assured that on our return all would have been organised.

I arrived home the following day taking my parents completely by surprise but I have to admit that all I remember of that week was huddling by the fire to keep warm against the continuous rain and cold.

The Greatest Moment of My Life

After a week at home my conspicuous Egyptian tan was beginning to fade. I was eager to get back to Uxbridge to join my companions and to discover my next move. As a change, the threat here at home was not Mussolini, as it had been in the Middle East, but Adolph Hitler, who was seen as a major threat to world peace. Belated efforts were being made to expand and re-equip the fighting services. For the RAF the first step had been to set up Elementary and Reserve Flying Training Schools (FTSs) at small civil aerodromes. At these, a new influx of pilots would be trained by civilian instructors, who were ex-RAF pilots now in the RAF Reserve.

We found that we were to undergo our training at one of these F.T.S.s as all the Service course were already filled to capacity. We would move on later to RAF Training Schools for our advanced training. While at these civilian schools we would wear civilian clothes and be billetted in lodgings provided locally. I was being sent, with half a dozen others, to Woodley, the Phillips and Powis aerodrome on the outskirts of Reading, the others being sent as far afield as Perth. Before leaving, we were issued with flying kit, Sidcot suits with teddy-bear linings, flying boots, goggles, gloves and Gosport earpieces. Then it was off to the FTS, by train and bus for the last part of the journey.

On arrival we were directed to a newly-built two-storey instructional block where the School staff were waiting to book us in and allocate billets. Mine was bout half a mile distant, in a fairly modern bungalow shared with another trainee, named Woodcraft.

Next morning the pair of us walked along to the aerodrome where the whole course of 30 to 40 students were milling about in the instructional block waiting for something to happen.

Eventually the formalities of enrolment and documentation started and we were issued with manuals and air publications and weekly programmes covering classes and tuition on the ground and in the air. In the afternoon I met my flying Instructor Bill Skinner who I immediately recognised from Cranwell days when he had instructed Flight Cadets in the dual Siskin aircraft of "E" Flight. His Service engagement had ended and for the better, as he was now an Officer in the RAF Reserve and a civilian instructor with the Flying School with occasional free-lancing as test pilot on production aircraft of Phillips and Powis.

Training at Woodley was carried out in both Tiger Moth bi-planes and Miles Hawk monoplanes and I was to receive mine in the Miles Hawk. Bill Skinner took me over to one of the Hawks and showed me round the aircraft; we carried out pre-flight checks together then donned flight helmets and parachutes and were soon in the air for a first familiarisation flight. During my time in the College Flight at Cranwell I had managed to put in quite a bit of passenger flying in the 504 Ns and the Tutors that replaced them, both types of aircraft were fitted with dual controls and many of the pilots I had flown with had either let me handle the controls in the air or had given me elementary flying instruction. Bill Skinner was well aware of this and soon had me through all the standard instructional manoevres of stalls, spins and recovery and steep turns that I took in my stride. Thinking that he would get me off solo in record time he then concentrated on Take-offs and landings in readiness for a solo check by the Chief Flying Instructor. With this in the offing I suppose I developed some sort of reaction for I would start the day's instruction with Bill doing superly straight take-offs then mess up the landings completely; Bill would curse me and spend the rest of the period concentrating on landings until I appeared to have them sewn up. On the next period I would snake all over the place taking off but my landings would be as smooth as rose petals touching down.

This stupidity went on for some time until I had clocked up nearly ten hours of dual instruction and was almost sending Bill up the wall; something had to be done and it had to be fairly drastic, as what confidence I had started with was fast ebbing away. Bill, seasoned instructor as he was, realised my problem and on my next

Joe's group at the start of Flying Training at Woodley
(Joe 4th from right, back row)

Joe and a Tiger Moth

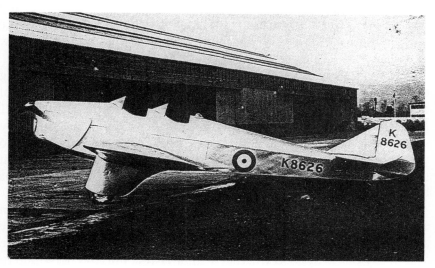

The Miles Hawk in which Joe trained

trip with him as we took off and climbed away from Woodley I was startled to see him waving the control stick that he had removed from his cockpit round his head and singing merrily. Next moment his voice came over the Gosports "She's all yours now, you really have her, show me that you can fly because I can't do anything about it".

After the initial shock I turned into the circuit with a newly-found confidence and executed a text book landing with Bill still waving the stick at me but saying nothing. As we stopped at the end of the landing run he heaved himself out of the cockpit, fastened the seat harness straps in position, stopped by me long enough to say, "Right, do that again without me and God help you if it's not as good." With that he was gone still carrying the control stick in one hand, the other holding his parachute straps across one shoulder.

I took a deep breath then taxied into position for take-off and did a repeat performance concentrating on flying the machine so much that I was hardly aware that I was alone in the air for the first time. As I taxied back from the landing run and parked the aircraft and switched off the engine Bill arrived back from his long walk and gave me a "thumbs up" sign and a grin. It was just two o'clock in the afternoon on 25th February, 1936, the greatest moment of my life, when, after eleven hours of dual instruction, I entered the magical figure of five minutes flying in the solo column of my new and shiny pilot's log book.

The weather was very kind to we novice pilots in the early spring of that year for in the course of the next four weeks remaining of our *ab initio* training I managed to pile up a creditable total of 51 hours flying time, enjoying every minute. Perhaps I should qualify that a little and say almost every minute. There were at least two occasions during that time when, still wet behind the ears and in the over-confident stage that all new pilots pass through, I was brought to realise my own inexperience in the air.

The first occasion was when I came off second best in an encounter with a huge thunder cloud to the south of Reading one afternoon. Up to that moment all my flying had been done by the seat of my pants in good weather with a visible horizon on which to keep the aircraft straight and level or to refer to in a climb or glide.

I had no experience at this stage of cloud flying or of using the limited instruments in the cockpit without an horizon. Thus when I became adventurous that afternoon and decided to investigate the black interior of the huge cumulo-nimbus towering upwards I got more than I bargained for. I entered the base of the turbulent grey mass with my altimeter reading just under 4,000 feet. After being tossed about with everything misted up I began to feel very uncomfortable in my straps and could hear a strange whining noise. No wonder, for at that moment the aircraft came out of the cloud heading almost vertically for the ground and spinning furiously. I barely had time and height to gather my wits together and apply corrective action to stop the spin and ease the aircraft out of the resultant dive. Afterwards, I flew back to Woodley still feeling very wobbly at the knees and landed the aircraft carefully, a shaken and much wiser young aviator.

The second occasion was almost at the end of the course when someone at the Air Ministry sent a Qualified Flying Instructor (Q.F.I.) to check the standard of flying of some trainees. He was Flight Lieutenant Sinclair (later Air Marshal Sir Lawrence Sinclair KCB, GC, CBE, DSO). I happened to be picked out as one of the Hawk trained pilots to be checked. It was a clear cold day with not much wind as we took off and I forgot to check the heading by setting the compass verge ring. Sinclair told me to carry out a number of manoeuvres and I completed all these seemingly to his satisfaction. I was then told to head back to Woodley. Assuming quite wrongly that the test was as good as over I was lolling back in the cockpit feeling pleased with myself when the throttle lever was suddenly yanked shut and Sinclair's voice came over the Gosports: "Engine failure – carry out a forced landing please". I trimmed the aircraft into a glide looking frantically about for a large field with a grass surface and a tell-tale plume of smoke to give me wind direction, but couldn't see anything. Making a wild guess at the wind direction I picked out a longish but narrow field to port and carried out gliding turns across the heading, back and forth, losing height and trying to keep the field in view for the final turn in. This proved difficult, and little wonder, for as I came to line up for the landing much too high and too fast I realised that I had committed the cardinal sin of attempting to land down-wind.

Sinclair, of course, had watched my efforts with great patience and now took over the controls, slating me all the way back to Woodley. Never again after that episode did I ever fly without the wind speed and direction at take-off indelibly printed in my mind.

Towards the end of my stay at Woodley one of the first "Flying Fleas" built in France as the "Poux de Ciel" arrived to give a demonstration from the aerodrome. In zero wind the strange looking craft, obviously underpowered to the n'th degree, took the full length of the aerodrome in trying to take off. It progressed in a series of hops rising a few feet then sinking back on to the grass. As it ran out of aerodrome the French pilot panicked and yanked the control stick hard back in a last attempt to clear the hedge on the boundary. The Flea jumped the hedge then stalled into the ploughed field the other side in a cloud of dust and tangled wood and wires. The pilot walked away unhurt, impressing us more than his plane's performance.

The course ended on the 26th March 1936 and it was quite a wrench to get back into RAF uniform and return to Uxbridge for a taste of service discipline after the free and easy weeks of civilian life at Reading. At the Depot the same old faces who had been on the *Cameronia* turned up again at the end of their *ab initio* training. We found that most of us, including Nick Carter, Roger Reece, Cooke, Woodcraft and Smithy were being sent to the RAF's 6 FTS at Netheravon for our service training on Hawker Harts and Audax's. As we weren't due there until the third week of March it would be a good opportunity to take some of the leave due to us so next day once again I boarded the train at Kings Cross Station and headed north to spend two weeks in Yorkshire.

The fortnight at home simply dragged by as by now I had lost all contact with my old school friends. Occasional frames of snooker at my father's club with his cronies or lone visits to the cinema were a poor substitute for the companionship I had left. It was with a sigh of relief that I headed south again at the end of the leave and rejoined the rest at Uxbridge.

I left there the following day in uniform loaded like a pack mule. My full kit and all my flying gear were crammed into two large kit bags and a huge leather suit-case I had purchased in Ismailia. I arrived at Netheravon in time to settle in and have a meal; the date was 20th April.

★　　　★　　　★

Netheravon, situated on Salisbury Plain, was one of the first aerodromes to be used by the Royal Flying Corps before the First World War. As at Cranwell, many of the original single-storey buildings were still in daily use.

The Camp was scattered along a ridge of chalk Wiltshire Down. It straddled the principal road that ran along the ridge starting at the main Guardroom and ending at the relatively modern aircraft hangars over a mile away.

The main grass area of the aerodrome was to the right of the road, on the sloping flank of the ridge. A secondary landing area beyond the hangars created an 'L' shaped aerodrome, large enough to be used as two separate take-off and landing areas on different circuits under certain weather/wind conditions.

A few miles to the north along a similar parallel ridge and clearly visible most days was Upavon, another old RFC aerodrome with a history. A year earlier, the Central Flying School (CFS) of the RAF had moved to Upavon from Wittering. All potential Service Flying Instructors passed through the CFS to qualify for their QFI rating. When they had acquired instructional experience they returned for short periods either for refresher courses or to be re-categorised, thereby keeping fully up-to-date in the latest aspects of flying training. In the past, RAF Flying Training Schools had provided both *ab initio* and further flying training on a service-type aircraft to 'wings' standard. Pilots were then posted to squadrons to undergo a further long period of advanced training in gunnery and bombing as well as a conversion on squadron-type aircraft so that it could be a further six months before they became proficient squadron pilots.

The needs of the current expansion scheme had caused this policy to change. As some of the first trainees to complete our *ab initio* training at Reserve Flying Schools, we would fly service type aircraft from Netheravon and would, on completion, be awarded our 'wings'. We were to spend a further four months with the newly formed Advanced Training Squadron and receive training in gunnery and bombing and other squadron activities culminating in live firing practice and bombing on the ranges at an Armament Practice Camp. Hopefully we would then be fit to join one of the new squadrons being formed, requiring only a few hours conversion to type to become front line pilots.

To those who had returned to U.K. with me on board the *Cameronia*, "Nick" Carter, Roger Reece, Ginger Barwick and Tich Baugh, were now added Ken Cooke, Morfill and Smithy plus half a dozen more from U.K. locations. Timetables covering the Ground and Flying syllabusses were pinned on the notice boards in the huts and from them I found that my Flying Instructor was a Sergeant Berry and that I could be reporting to him at "B" Flight hangar first thing next day for first dual on the Hawker Hart.

Razz Berry, as he was known to all and sundry, turned out to be a small man with a florid complexion and eyes that seemed to pop out of their sockets when he was worked up, which was quite frequently. This had earned him the reputation of being a bit of a fire-eater in some circles and it was with some trepidation that I started to make his better acquaintance. I need not have worried. We got on well together in the air and he was absolutely first class as an instructor.

On that first day he showed me round the Hart trainer and ran through the pre-flight checks and cockpit drill before taking me up on a short familiarisation trip. During the course of the next few days I received four more short periods of instruction. Then on the 28th April he passed me over to the Officer Commanding "B" Flight, Flight Lieutenant Jacques for solo check; on landing I was sent off for the first time by myself.

I really enjoyed flying in the Hart trainer and the Audax variant that we used for solo practices for they were beautiful aircraft with no vices whatsoever. All the Hawker aircraft were powered by the Rolls Royce Kestrel liquid cooled engine with an output of between five and six hundred B.H.P., the forerunner of the much more powerful Merlin series then being developed. The Kestrel was an utterly reliable normally aspirated power plant. The altitude control to ensure the correct petrol/air mixture at height was controlled manually by the pilot from the cockpit. The aircraft itself was built of light alloy tubular construction covered with fabric and was strong enough to stand up to almost any punishment that could be meted out to it by ham-fisted pupils practicing take-offs and landings all day.

After our first two weeks at Netheravon everything was running smoothly for us. Making our way around the Camp to attend lectures and flying we were expected to march in step as a body with one of us in charge. The question of who that should be was answered almost immediately. Nick Carter, who had been the AOC's personal clerk in Iraq and was older than any of us, was called to the Station Orderly Room one morning to be informed that his promotion to Corporal had come through so from then on he automatically filled the role of senior airman pupil.

We were a happy go lucky crowd who got on well with each other and we quickly adapted to the free and easy routine. "B" Flight hangar was the furthest point we had to reach when we were on the flying programme. If weather prohibited flying or we were attending lectures on ground subjects such as Armament, Signals etc. they all took place in buildings en route and fitted in well with our daily itinerary. Each day as we swung along the mile long road one of us would start up with some old tune to lighten our steps and soon the whole party would be harmonising "Chinese Laundry Blues" and "In the Moonlight by the River" for all we were worth, to the great amusement of passers by. In between lectures we competed in pairs to be the first to complete the Daily Telegraph crossword puzzle and some of our times would have earned a mention in the Guinness Book of Records.

On top of our normal first class tradesman pay we were all receiving flying pay that almost doubled our basic, and as such were considered members of the affluent society. But we were all regulars and highly skilled tradesmen and it had taken each one of us seven or eight years of intense competition before being selected for pilot training. Even so the increase in pay wasn't the incentive for I am sure that any one of us faced with the option of carrying on flying but having to forego pay would cheerfully have done so. I certainly would have.

In the classroom we worked hard to achieve the standards demanded. At that time all communication between aircraft in the air and ground to air was done in the good old fashioned way involving visual signalling by Aldis lamp and flag using the Morse code or hand and other special signs made for the purpose and Verey pistol coloured cartridges. We practiced the morse code on "buzzer" keys and earphones and flashed by Aldis lamp to each other until it became second nature to read the dots and dahs. We stripped and re-assembled the Vickers gun lock visually and by touch blindfolded until we reached a stage of confidence that should the occasion arise in the air we would be able to deal with almost any stoppage of the gun.

Map reading and air navigation using the old brass Course and Distance Calculator, Engineering, Meteorology and Air Force and International Law were also included in the syllabus. Finally, for good measure a few sessions on the drill square taking it in turn to bellow out the orders to the squad on the move.

Notwithstanding all this frenzied activity those summer months of 1936 were some of the most enjoyable I ever spent during my service. This was despite the fact that Netheravon, in common with most other Army and RAF Establishments dotted about Salisbury Plain, was an isolated community and not well served by public transport. The nearest cinema was at Amesbury a good six miles distant and a long haul on foot if one had to walk it even one way. The only answer to give some freedom of action and a change of scene now and then was to buy a small car so I scraped together the fifty pounds or so I had saved and watched the For Sale columns in the local paper for something that I could afford. Nothing turned up, however, until Morfill, whose parents ran a public house in Salisbury, mentioned that there was a used car market in Devizes where I might be lucky. So with Roger Reece in support, we took the bus there one Saturday afternoon for a look around. There in a small garage and filling station we came upon 'Amy', a small and shapely Austin Arrow tourer in pale green, fitted with bucket seats in the front and with a narrow bench seat at the rear that enabled it to be described as an occasional four-seater. A short test drive helped me to decide and within minutes of first seeing her I had bought Amy for the princely sum of £45. Covering insurance was effected on the spot and Roger and I returned carefully back to Netheravon, well pleased with our purchase, and parked her alongside our quarters on the grass where I could see her from the window by my bed.

From that day onwards Amy provided a free taxi service for as many of the course as could be squeezed into her and and there were numerous occasions on which her springs bottomed under the excess loading imposed when in use as an occasional five or even six seater.

The Sunday evening cinema show in Amesbury was the most popular run out and we greatly appreciated the ham and eggs and coffee on the way back from a small café that never seemed to close. Once or twice in hot weather we ran down to the coast at Highcliffe, conveniently parking Amy on the low cliffs above the beach while we had a swim or just sun bathed and larked around. There was always something going on. That Whitsun Smithy invited a bunch of us to his home in Weymouth where his family ran a small guest house. We went by train, the one occasion when we couldn't all squeeze into the car with our luggage, and we thoroughly enjoyed the change. Unfortunately the shingle beach was heavily contaminated with fuel oil probably washed ashore from the Naval base at nearby Portland and it took some time to remove the filthy stuff from our swimming trunks and bodies.

During June and July under the able tuition of "Razz" Berry I became more and more proficient in the air and began to develop that extra sense of good airmanship that comes with experience. After nearly fifty hours of flying the Hart I had mastered most of the manoevres that could be carried out including some aerobatics, and had made four long cross-country flights. The end of service training on type was in sight.

Towards the end of July we prepared for the A.O.C's annual inspection. This consisted of a parade and inspection in the morning and ending with a march past on the small parade ground. In the afternoon the A.O.C. inspected the main areas of the Camp and watched a short flying demonstration laid on for his benefit. Frank Foster from the senior course had been selected to demonstrate air to ground camera gun attacks on a target set up in the centre of the aerodrome. Flying one of the few Hawker Fury single seater aircraft on the strength of the newly formed advanced training Squadron he took off and commenced the attacks pulling up in a half loop after his first shot, then half rolling off the top before turning into his next attack so that he wasted no time. Unfortunately half-way through his act Foster failed to pull out of a dive and the Fury hit the solid Wiltshire chalk at a fair lick. There was no fire but the pilot should have been killed by the impact. By a strange freak of chance, however, the structural weakness of the fuselage at the cockpit saved Foster for it snapped in two as the nose hit ejecting him a short distance forward of the wreckage still strapped to his seat. Apart from a few bruises and minor concussion Foster was virtually unhurt and he returned to flying within a week. We all considered that he bore a charmed life after such a miracle escape and it came as a bit of a shock some time later when we heard that he had lost a leg in a motorcycle accident which ended his flying career.

With but a few days more before qualifying for my "wings" Razz started to cram in lots of instrument flying practice for me under the hood. Almost all of the dual control Harts in "B" Flight were fitted with a green canvas hood that could be pulled up and over the rear cockpit, thus denying any visual external references to the occupant and limiting him to the sparse instruments available on his panel. When not being used it folded back rather like the fabric hood of an early touring car. Under the hood the pilot has no visible horizon to fly by. He had to control the aircraft by reading the air speed indicator, an altimeter that only read to the nearest 200 feet, a compass subject to turning and acceleration errors, and a turn-and-bank indicator. The latter was the only gyro-driven instrument actuated in flight by a venturi mounted externally on the fuselage and pointing in the direction of flight. If the aircraft was banked at an angle of 55 degrees or more, however, the gyros in the turn-and-bank indicator toppled and it became useless until they could be re-erected.

To fly on a steady compass course and keep the aircraft straight and level while under the hood needed tremendous concentration and could only be kept up for short periods. Banked turns were considered highly dangerous as they invariably ended up as steep diving turns due to the outer wing travelling faster in a turn and giving more lifting, causing the aircraft to overbank and slip in to a nose-down attitude. For that reason flat turns without bank using rudder to skid the aircraft round a change of direction were practiced. Razz made me sweat blood carrying out triangular cross-country flights with changes of altitude en route, some lasting a full 40 minutes and even went so far as to make me try take-offs under the hood. At last he expressed himself as being satisfied and the hood took a back seat.

On the afternoon of 13th August without giving me a hint of what was to follow Razz took me on a 30 minute refresher flight and made me go through every practice manoeuvre in the Manual of Flying Training. Landing back at Netheravon and taxing to the tarmac apron I assumed that I had finished flying for the day. However, over the Gosports he told me to keep the engine going. He then climbed out of his cockpit and his place was taken by Squadron Leader Toogood the Chief Flying Instructor, who had been lurking in the background waiting for me. As soon as he was strapped in safely I was instructed to take off and go through the whole show once again including a simulated forced landing. At the end of the flight he made no comment but my performance must have satisfied him. It was the final test in the air for me and qualified me for my wings. During the next week the examinations in ground subjects were held and to my intense satisfaction I finished up with the top marks of the course overall. Finally came 28th August 1936, when the Station tailor sewed onto my tunic the RAF wings for which I had striven for so long, and so hard. There were no formalities, not even a presentation parade – just the signing of an ordinary Demand Voucher from the stores. And it would be another four or five months before promotion to SNCO would take effect. We had no failures on our course and this delighted me, for a keener and more dedicated bunch of airmen would have been difficult to find anywhere.

We were rewarded for our efforts by three weeks leave, with instructions to join the Advanced Training Squadron commanded by Squadron Leader Ivelaw-Chapman on our return. I spent my leave fishing, walking on fine days and playing snooker when it rained, returning to Netheravon refreshed and ready to complete the final phase of my training in 'D' flight. Most of the aircraft were Audax, apart from a couple of single-seater Furies and the inevitable Tutor with instrument flying hood on which we could pair up, taking it in turn to fly under the hood, or act as safety pilot.

To date all our training had been directed towards turning each one of us into a competent pilot to whom control of the aircraft both in the air, and in take-offs and landings, would be an automatic function.

From now on everything we did in the air would be aimed at using flying skill and the machine and the weapons it could carry, in the most efficient manner should we be called upon to do so against an enemy in a future war. In simple language we knew how to fly an aircraft but not how to apply it to gunnery, bombing, photo-recce and other war-time activities.

To start with we crewed up in pairs, taking it in turn to act as pilot or as bomb-aimer/navigator during practice wind finding and bombing exercises. This was followed by air to ground and air to air gunnery practices on ground targets, and flags or sleeves towed by other aircraft using camera gun films to assess the accuracy. In between came practice formation and simulated attacks on pin-point targets at the end of long cross-country flights taking oblique photographs. On a clear night that autumn Bill Jenner gave me my first taste of night flying and demonstrated a couple of take offs and landings on a goose neck flare path. I quickly got the knack and after his second landing he got out of the aircraft and I carried on solo for an hour or so. I enjoyed flying in the dark immensely and looked forward to more but unfortunately that was the sum total allowed during the course. Over the next two months and despite the generally poor weather over Salisbury Plain at that time of the year, I managed to amass another 40 hours of flying in my log book.

Squadron Leader Ivelaw-Chapman, O.C. Advanced Training Squadron, now considered that we were ready for Armament Practice Camp (APC) where more tangible results could be achieved on the ranges using live ammunition and standard 11½ lbs. practice bombs. The A.P.Cs were mainly on the coast well away from populated areas and were clearly defined as danger areas on air maps for obvious reasons. We were to go to North Coates on the flat Lincolnshire coast south of the Humber. Clearly we were going then because it was the worst time of the whole year for fog in that locality and no regular squadron would take the chance of getting weather-bound at North Coates over Christmas.

As the movement order covering the proposed move of aircraft and personnel to North Coates took shape it became clear that only a minimum number of machines would go, and that they would be flown by experienced Staff pilots each taking one passenger in the rear cockpit; thus the majority of the course pilots would have to face the long and tedious journey by train via London.

As the odds against my being detailed as one of the air passengers seemed pretty big, I decided to ask for permission to drive up to North Coates under my own arrangements and take Roger Reece as passenger. My application was approved with the result that after the main body had left by lorry and train, Roger and I were left to drive leisurely north to Yorkshire on the last Saturday of November; there I had arranged for us to break the journey and stay overnight at my parents' home intending to complete the journey next day.

As always the unexpected happened for after a pleasant drive and a good night's rest we got up for breakfast to find freezing fog blanketing the area and almost nil visibility. Not very pleasant in a little open top tourer and something we hadn't bargained for during the previous day's run in fairly good weather. We hung around all morning in the vain hope that conditions might improve but the fog hardly lifted and it looked as though it would clamp down completely as soon as it got dark. There was nothing for it but to get going while it was still light. Having made the decision we put on our warmest items of flying gear and wrapped up well, removing the car side screens so that we had direct vision of the road verges, and set off about two o'clock on the cold and hazardous drive along unfamiliar roads to the coast. We made steady but slow progress until darkness fell when the windscreen iced up and the wipers ceased to function. To see ahead we folded back the hood and laid the windscreen flat along the car bonnet and crawled along, completely exposed to the elements. By the time we arrived at North Coates we were both covered in white rime and ice and chilled to the bone, looking for all the world like abominable snowmen. It had taken us six hours to cover fifty miles!

83

Once settled in our warm billet and thawed out in hot baths we soon felt better although our effort proved in vain; the fog persisted for a further two days leaving us to pass away the time reading or playing cards. Then the fog cleared as suddenly as it had formed. The aircraft arrived from Netheravon and we went into a flurry of activity, being briefed on range procedures and making out programmes for the next day. Next morning, the last day of November, I fired my first live rounds from the air on the ranges and saw the spurts of sand raised behind the targets as the bullets hit the ground. After that first day the weather closed down again and played havoc with our daily programmes. In the three weeks before the A.P.C. closed down for Christmas I managed to fly only eight times and that was better than most of the others were able to manage. I drove back to Yorkshire for the holiday dropping Roger off at a railway station en route to catch a train for his home. I returned to Netheravon the day after Boxing Day in time to fly twice more before the year ended to give me a grand total of 160 hours in the air, a good average for a year in the thirties.

The morning of New Year's Day 1937 I spent flying in an Audax around the Plain. The weather was pretty grim and it stayed like that for most of the next week. As a result I only managed to fly once again from Netheravon and that was in a Tutor skating over the Downs at tree top height. In the end it was the weather that ensured our passing out. Squadron Leader Ivelaw-Chapman had given up all hope of us getting in more flying before his next batch of trainees turned up, so he checked through our flying records and on the sparse results we had achieved at North Coates expressed himself satisfied as to our advanced flying capabilities to get rid of us!

On 10th January we were promoted to Sergeant/Pilots and the Station tailor's shop worked overtime sewing the chevrons on to our uniform jackets. The big moment for me came that evening when as a full-blown member I was welcomed into the Sergeants Mess by Razz Berry, my former explosive little Flying Instructor, and Bill Jenner who had taken me on my first night flying trip. Six months ago they had been tin gods as far as I was concerned, now I was accepted into their midst as one of them and the drinks were coming at me from all directions. Strangely enough I never ran into them again after that evening and in later years I was never destined to become a Q.F.I. by passing through the Central Flying School. Had I done so I am sure in my own mind that I would never have become half as good at instructing or had anything like the patience and skills of those two characters.

Next morning I woke up with a prize hangover to remind me of the previous night's junketing but after breakfast, my first meal in the Sergeant's Mess, I made my way back across the square to the billet where I had lived for the past nine months, packed up all my kit and belongings and stowed them in Amy. I was on my way to join the 35(B) day bomber squadron at Worthy Down, only a short distance by road from Netheravon. Worthy Down was also the home of No 207(B) Squadron and No 49(B) Squadron. Nos 35 and 207 Squadrons had formed the Mobile Wing sent out to the Sudan under the command of Group Captain Collishaw, a well known Canadian veteran of the First World War, to show a British presence on the Sudanese/Abyssinian border as Mussolini's troops invaded Haile Selassie's kingdom. The Wing had only recently returned to the United Kingdom and had been moved straight to Worthy Down instead of returning to its old home at Bircham Newton in Norfolk. Both Squadrons were still using the same old Fairey Gordon bi-planes they had brought back from the Sudan. By then their performance by modern standards was unacceptable. The aircraft were basically the old Fairey IIIF designed for the Fleet Air Arm and naval use using the Napier Lion broad arrow liquid-cooled engine. This had been replaced by the more powerful Armstrong Siddeley Panther 14 cylinder radial engine to improve its performance, albeit by a small amount.

As might be expected the aircraft were in poor shape after their long period of exposure to desert conditions and the numerous operations of dismantling, crating and re-assembling that had to be undertaken to get the machines to the Sudan and back.

The Journey to Worthy Down only took an hour and a half via Andover; at the last moment Woodcraft asked for a lift there as he was being posted to the other unit, No 49(B) Squadron then

85

equipped with Hawker Hinds. We arrived in time for lunch and reported to our respective squadrons in the afternoon. Arriving at Worthy Down I was interviewed by the Squadron Commander, Squadron Leader A. G. Thackray. My first meeting with him didn't go down too well as he seemed to take an instant dislike to me. At last when I felt that I couldn't do a thing right he informed me that I would be joining "B" Flight and told me to report to the Flight Commander Flying Officer R. N. Wardell. "Rusty" Wardell, so called on account of his red hair, welcomed me to his Flight and passed me over to Paddy Flynn, one of the sergeant pilots who had been at Halton with me. Next morning he showed me round the cockpit of one of the Gordons then took me up as a passenger to demonstrate a couple of take-offs and landings before I took it up to practice later by myself. There were no dual aircraft on the squadrons then and it was a case of trial and error when flying a new type for the first time. However, everything about the old Gordon was pretty basic and after a few hours practice in the air I soon became proficient in the general handling of the aircraft and ready to take part in the squadron training programme.

There was still lots of fine desert dust and sand that had accumulated in the more inaccessible areas of the fuselage and main planes and to skid or slip in during a steep turn usually filled the cockpit with a cloud of fine powder. The engines lacked power and threw out engine oil mist through the crankcase breathers that streamed back in the slipstream and covered the windscreen and pilot's goggles in true World War I fashion. Quite apart from such troubles with the aircraft it was mid-winter and extremely cold on the Hampshire Downs at that time of the year. As the Squadron training programme progressed it concentrated more and more on medium and high level bombing practice on the nearby Porton range. Weather permitting, the exercise usually involved climbing the aircraft to around 15,000 feet, a long process with no oxygen and exposed to the elements in an open cockpit, and to combat the intense cold at that height one had to dress accordingly. The issue flying clothing was bulky to say the least, a waterproof Sidcot suit that zipped over a brown fur inner lining on top of ordinary uniform with fleece-lined flying boots. The hands were encased in silk liners covered by woollen gloves under huge leather gauntlets that became mittens when a flap held on the back of the gloves by a press stud was pulled over the fingers; the ensemble was completed by a leather flying helmet and goggles with dangling Gosport tubes and a suitably warm scarf of the pilot's choice wound several times around the neck.

Having dressed and stuffed maps and pencils and message pads into the various openings on the Sidcot, it became quite a feat to waddle out to where the aircraft was standing carrying one's parachute. And climbing into the cockpit trying to find the toe holds in the side of the fuselage was quite a challenge. Once in the pilot's seat with parachute straps tightly buckled and safety straps further restraining any movement it was difficult to operate much more than the control column, rudder pedals and actuating gear flaps. It was just as well that the Gordon had few other knobs or switches to select during flight as the huge gauntletted hands and frozen fingers of the pilot would have had difficulty in operating them.

Crews also presented a problem, for up to this time no Air Observers as such had been trained by the Royal Air Force since the end of the 14 – 18 War. The general policy was to have two pilots per aircraft on heavy bombers, leaving the second pilot to do the navigation and bomb aiming. On day bombers, however, pilots were expected to navigate themselves, mainly by map reading. Sometimes we were accompanied by air gunners, usually ground crew volunteers who were locally trained and qualified in the Lewis gun and the operation of the bomb sight. They wore a brass winged bullet badge on the arm and were paid flying pay at the princely rate of a shilling and sixpence a day when flying regularly with the squadron. Wireless Operator presented no problem in those days as only one of the squadron aircraft had a radio. That was only used about twice a year when the full squadron was airborne and going some distance. In "B" Flight we had four qualified Air Gunners and two others undergoing training by Sergeant Stewart the Engine Fitter SNCO, who was also a very experienced Air Gunner but had stopped flying regularly on his promotion. He liked flying with me whenever his technical duties allowed and we made a good team in my early days with the squadron and achieved some very accurate high level practice bombing results.

The training programme came to an abrupt halt half-way through April when the squadron was sent off at short notice to Aldergrove in Northern Ireland to fill a two week gap in the programme of the Armament Practice Camp located there. Our aircraft carried no flotation or survival gear that would have enabled us to fly a direct route there in one hop. Instead we were routed via Sealand, refuelled while the crews had lunch, and then had to follow the coastline round to Stranraer to make the short sea crossing to Larne.

On landing at Sealand one of the pilots from "A" Flight complained of engine vibration and a quick check by the duty crew revealed several loose sparking plugs hurriedly tightened up finger tight and forgotten or missed later. Surprisingly the loss of power on two or three cylinders out of the fourteen hadn't been noticed on take off.

Approaching Aldergrove for the first time there were so many white crosses visible on the ground that it looked more like a churchyard than an aerodrome. It was situated close to Lough Neagh, the largest fresh water lake in the British Isles, and the saucer-shaped grass field was like a bog after the winter's rain. The crosses indicated parts of the field unfit for landings. At first sight it seemed impossible to find a suitable landing run in any direction. Undaunted, "Rusty" Wardell our leader signalled us to form echelon to starboard and land independently, and started his approach to land near the middle of the field. We saw him touch down and run for a few yards then his landing wheels bogged down in a soft patch and the aircraft slowly turned over on its nose and came to a standstill upside down in a muddy pool. The mainplane centre-section and rudder took the brunt of the impact leaving Rusty hanging upside down in his seat straps. Sergeant Stewart who was in the rear cockpit was, however, only held by a longish "monkey" wire attached to the floor to give him some freedom of movement in the air. He was not so lucky and finished dangling like a pendulum with his face in the muddy water unable to reach up and operate the quick release mechanism on his harness. Fortunately for him, rescue was soon at hand from the standby fire engine crew. The fate of the leading aircraft served as a warning to the rest of us not to take chances and in turn each of the other pilots landed gingerly in the tracks of the previous one, picking his way around the crosses as if in a minefield.

For the next two weeks we had lovely Spring weather and despite the shocking state of the aerodrome we managed to get through a full air firing and practice bombing programme each day on the Lough Neagh ranges. Practice Camp was always enjoyable as it was the only time of the year that the Squadron personnel worked together as an entity without the distractions of married life and other problems to divert them from their tasks. There was tremendous competition between individuals and Flights to achieve the best scores in the front and rear gun exercises with live ammunition on the drogues and ground targets and many ruses were employed to boost the results.

As if it were an afterthought, the Gordon was armed with a single Vickers .303 machine gun mounted on the port side of the fuselage where the pilot could just about reach it with his left hand. The gun fired forward through the Fairey Reed metal propellor being activated by a device known as the C.C. gear (after its inventor Count Constantinesco), developed during World War I. This ensured that the gun fired single shots triggered to fire each round when the propellor blades were in the vertical position. The gun and ring sight were harmonised to hit a target ahead at the best range of 200 yards.

The CC gear consisted of two cams machined on the rear plate of the propellor hub diametrically opposite to each other and at right angles to the line of the single bladed propellor. Twice during each revolution of the propellor, when the blade was in a vertical position each cam lifted a tappet that transmitted a hydraulic impulse along an oil-filled pipeline pressurised by a spring-loaded hand operated pump. By pressing a thumb lever on the control column the pilot channelled the impulses along a pipeline to a plunger mounted on the gun casing and the plunger tripped the sear and released the firing pin to fire a round each time an impulse was received.

A drawback was that the pressure in the pipelines had to be maintained by a pump in the cockpit. If the pilot failed to operate this after each burst of firing the system became spongy in operation (like the brakes of a modern car hydraulic system that needs the air bleeding from it). The resultant lag in operation could put a few rounds through the propellor. The lag also happened at low engine speeds when the pilot throttled back to below half normal revs. One or two pilots trying to achieve high gunnery scores by throttling back and attacking the drogue at low speed found this out to their cost when they returned with perforated propellors to face the wrath of the Squadron Commander.

On the final day of the Practice Camp I was sent up to complete the last air gunnery detail of the morning before refuelling my aircraft in readiness to return with the Squadron to Worthy Down in the afternoon. It was all a bit of a rush so I finished off the gunnery in record time and hared back to the aerodrome at low level. I intended to land close to the fuelling point so that I wouldn't have to waste time all round the boggy areas. Unfortunately my approach was too low and my starboard wheel struck a grassy bank on the boundary of the field. I completed the landing on the port wheel but was unable to stop the aircraft from slewing round and damaging the starboard wing tip as it stopped. Feeling a bit of a fool I turned off the fuel switches in the cockpit and climbed out to inspect the damage. Other than the wheel and oleo and a few scrapes on the lower wing tip it didn't amount to a lot. The greatest damage was to my professional pride as a pilot in wrecking the aircraft. But it was one I walked away from.

The C.O. was waiting to give me a rocket when I reached the tarmac, understandably enraged that together with Rusty Wardell's accident on arrival he was now two aircraft short for the return trip. He decided that Paddy Flynn and I, being both technical people, should stay behind and create one serviceable aircraft out of the two damaged ones for us to fly back in as soon as possible, using whatever assistance we would get from Aldergrove technical resources. It was poetic justice for Paddy and me to watch disconsolately from the Duty Pilots' Hut as the rest of the squadron started up their engines and taxied off.

Later that afternoon we inspected the damaged aircraft, now dumped side by side in one of the hangars, and came to the conclusion that the quickest way to make one serviceable aircraft out of them would be to remove the complete set of mainplanes from my old aircraft and fit them to the other one which still had its landing gear intact. As we had no workshop manual to refer to for rigging details we had to do it all by rule of thumb. Armed with a long tape measure we went over all the lengths of the flying and landing wires and jotted down the measurements. Next morning, with the help of a couple of airmen borrowed from the Duty Flight, we removed both sets of mainplanes at the root ends, then bolted the undamaged ones in position on the fuselage with the good undercarriage. We then connected up the control cables adjusting all flying and landing wires to the measurements taken earlier. Much to our surprise all the work was finished by lunchtime and the aircraft was ready for an air test. We tossed up to decide who would fly it and Paddy won. Leaving the duty airmen to fill the fuel tanks we went off to the Mess for lunch. Over lunch Paddy suggested that if the weather was good and the aircraft reasonable to fly once it was in the air we might as well carry on back to Worthy Down. So, we collected our kits and stowed them in the back of the Gordon and arranged with the Duty Pilot to book us out to our destination if we didn't land back at Aldergrove. After take-off, apart from flying slightly one wing low the aircraft seemed fine so I gave Paddy a course for the Isle of Man and we climbed over the Irish Sea on direct course for Sealand. Over Sealand the fuel situation looked reasonable with the north-westerly wind helping to push us along, so we carried on and made it back to base in one long hop of three and a half hours.

Back at Worthy Down the weather began to warm up and I enjoyed that summer, getting in lots of flying or taking part in the many sporting and social activities that went on. We practised formations in the air, trained the air gunners under instruction in wind finding and practice bombing at Porton, practiced low level cross countries and map reading, and gave local Army personnel short trips around for air experience.

All day bomber pilots had to be able to operate at night if called upon to do so and the Squadron training programme therefore included a certain amount of night flying. The old Fairey bi-plane was a really lovely old lady to fly at night; it approached to land in a graceful manner almost hands-off and would just about land itself if the wheel of the actuating gear was wound slowly back at the right moment to round off the approach. Night flying included the usual circuit and bumps on a flarepath formed by a combination of gooseneck and Money paraffin burning flares laid out in the form of a Tee. For good measure a short triangular cross country flight was also made and occasionally night emergency landings were practised using the wing tip magnesium flares carried by the aircraft at night, a somewhat dangerous procedure. Timing was of the essence. The flares once ignited burned furiously in their holders beneath the wing tips for around two minutes and if set off too early during the approach burnt out at a critical moment of the landing leaving the pilot in utter blackness. If left too late the flares would still be burning after the landing and some fast taxying without brakes was needed to prevent the wing tips from catching fire. All in all a very dicey business!

During the long summer evenings under the guise of training for the forthcoming Station Sports we pottered around in athletic kit or hacked our way round the partial golf course laid out round the perimeter of the aerodrome; afterwards, undoing all the effort, a small crowd of us would squeeze into Amy and make the rounds of a few local pubs drinking the local Strongs Golden ales and playing darts and shove-h'apenny.

At the weekends there was always some sort of social activity taking place in the Mess or around the district. Treasure Hunts were always a popular start to the Sunday evenings, when every car available would be pressed into service ranging round the area following up silly clues and collecting a range of items that might include anything from a beer mat issued by a certain brewery to hairs from a horse's tail. The first car crew to get back to the Mess with the full list of items collected a prize. It was all good clean fun, usually ending with a bit of a party and dancing to the radiogram until the Mess Caterer decided it was time to close the bar and send everybody home.

My room was in the first block away from the Mess and had an open fire as well as central heating radiators. I had an airman to clean it out daily and do the chores, so I was in a very comfortable situation. This was a great help when I decided to have a shot at the written examination that would confirm me in my Fitter Aero Engine trade as a Senior NCO. Besides qualifying me for further promotion wilst I was still flying, this would be a form of insurance against having to revert back to junior rank. I set aside two evenings a week to prepare myself in good time to cover the syllabus, and fortunately passed at the first attempt.

In July the Station Sports Day was held in fine weather. Points given for each event were hotly contested by four teams representing the three squadrons and Station Headquarters. I took part in the three field events I usually entered for, the high and long jumps and putting the shot, with some success. I was then coopted for the Squadron team in the hurdles, the 220 yards and even the quarter mile when the other team members failed to appear. Cursing them roundly I laboured round the track on leaden feet and to my surprise managed to scrape another point or two for the team without actually winning a prize. However, my reward was to come at the end of the day when the judges totted up the points won individually for the award of the Victor Ludorum Trophy and made me the winner on the strength of those extra points. I still have the handsome silver cup to remind me of that happy day at Worthy Down.

That August all the rumours about the two Gordon squadrons being re-equipped with modern aircraft were confirmed with the announcement that Vickers Wellesleys would be delivered to us before the end of month. The RAF Expansion Plan was taking effect and the Wellesley was one of several new types of aircraft ordered straight from the drawing board and now coming off the production line, for better or for worse. Produced by Vickers at Weybridge it was a single-engined monoplane with an exceptional wing span. It had been designed by Barnes Wallis and built on the geodetic principle to give the maximum flexibility and strength. It was the fore runner of the heavier twin-engined "Wimpey" already taking shape at Weybridge.

We were getting an ultra-modern aircraft with such innovations as a variable pitch propellor and retractable undercarriage. Bombs were carried in wing pods with hydraulically operated bomb doors and containing the latest electro-magnetic bomb carriers. A forward firing Browning machine gun mounted in the wing well away from the arc of the propellor gave two or three times the rate of fire of the old Vickers gun. Powering this collection of marvels was a nine-cylinder Bristol "Pegasus" fully supercharged engine that developed twice the brake horse power of our old Siddeley Panther II's. We couldn't wait to get our hands on them.

One morning about the middle of August there was great excitement when a new engine note was heard and a strange monoplane arrived over the aerodrome to execute first a perfect loop then a three point landing. It was obviously handled by an expert; Geoffrey Quill, the Vickers test pilot was making delivery of our first plane. Pilots from both squadrons swarmed round the aircraft when it parked hoping for a chance to sit in the cockpit but there was no hope of that until the C.Os and other senior officers had their turn. As no dual aircraft had been built conversion on to type was to consist of cockpit familiarisation followed by a quick circuit and landing in the rear seat and then off solo to sort things out in the air.

In all service matters the order of pecking is based on rank so that it was some days later before I was called upon to be given my circuit behind the "A" Flight Commander, to be sent off solo immediately afterwards. I found it very easy to handle.

As the Wellesley was of a completely new design and construction using new materials, and so far had done few hours in the air, no ground maintenance schedule had yet been produced for the aircraft. To assist the technical staff, Group Headquarters decided that three aircraft from each squadron should be flown as hard as possible around the clock by the use of slip crews to achieve a total of five hundred hours flying time on each aircraft. Faults encountered during this development flying would assist the technical staffs to draw up a proper maintenance schedule.

Meanwhile, as more and more Wellesleys rolled off the production line at Weybridge, other squadrons of the RAF were being either re-formed or re-equipped with them. This in turn created another problem. At Cardington near Bedford there was a small unit of experienced pilots known as the Ferry Flight, based in the old Airship Hangar. It was their job to collect and deliver aircraft to squadrons in the U.K. The unit was finding itself hard pressed to cope with the flood of new aircraft and an appeal was sent for two pilots experienced on Wellesleys to be attached on a temporary basis for ferrying duties. Tommy Moon from "A"

Joe in the cockpit of a Wellesley bomber . . .

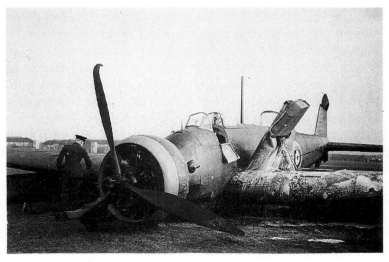

. . . And the one he walked away from!

Flight and myself from "B" Flight were singled out for the task and we left for Cardington in my little car almost at once. For a period of three weeks we had a marvellous time taking the old Fairey IIIF most mornings into the aerodrome bounded by the old Brooklands racing track, being entertained to lunch by Vickers and then returning to Cardington with a new Wellesley each afternoon. Landing there was always a tricky business as the small grass aerodrome was being fully utilised by the Barrage Balloon tenders and winches and usually bristled with inflated balloons at various heights that were always changing position.

Sergeant Thomas, the RAF champion miler, was one of the permanent staff of the Ferry Flight and I knew him from the old RAF Athletic Championships days. On two occasions when we were not required to go to Brooklands I went with him in the old Vickers Valentia troop carrier aircraft which the Ferry Flight used to pick up their pilots after delivery flights. It was too good a life to last, though, and by the middle of October the bottleneck in Wellesleys had been cleared and Tommy Moon and I returned to Worthy Down to divide our activities between flying on the development trials and normal squadron training.

While we had been away problems had arisen with the three development aircraft when on longish flights around Scotland. A fault in the fuel systems was suspected. A few days later the fault was pin-pointed when Bateman, the most experienced pilot in "A" Flight, was killed. He was trying to make an emergency landing over some trees on the approach to Abingdon after engine failure due to fuel starvation. The Wellesley, with a hefty wing-span of more than 70 feet, and main planes almost five feet thick at the root, had been designed for long range operations. With this end in view practically all the space in the wings was taken up with fuel tanks. Fuel from the tanks in both wings was fed to a common collector box via non-return valves. It then passed through a fuel cock operated from the cockpit by the pilot who was thus able to select delivery from either set of wing tanks or all at once, and finally reached the engine-driven pump that supplied fuel under pressure to the carburettor. A small header tank of a few gallons capacity was fitted in the engine bay to give a gravity feed stand by supply in emergency. The pilot could select gravity feed as a last resort and was supposed to be able to maintain the header tank in a full state by operating a small toggle pump fitted on the right hand side of his seat while controlling the aircraft with his left hand. In actual practice the big Bristol engine ate up the fuel, emptying the header faster than the efforts of the pilot on the toggle pump could supply it. It was the music hall joke about the petrol pump attendant asking the Rolls Royce owner to switch off his engine as it was beating the pump, the only difference being that it was happening in the air and costing lives. This was what had caused Bateman's death. He had changed over to gravity feed and headed for Abingdon. Within minutes the engine had cut out during the approach and the aircraft was too low to clear trees ahead.

The real nigger in the wood pile, however, was that the fuel tanks each had separate air vents on different sections of the mainplane. This resulted in differential pressures being created in the tanks that affected the flow of fuel to the collector box and caused an engine failure in the first instance. The problem was very quickly solved by the simple expedient of connecting all the fuel tanks to a common vent, and we had no more troubles with fuel after that.

Another aircraft was brought in to replace the one written off at Abingdon and the development flying carried on throughout the Autumn. On a Wednesday morning in November, when the Met reports gave dense and widespread fog over East Anglia and Lincolnshire, Tommy Moon and his crew were briefed for a long cross-country flight, overflying these areas and Scotland and returning via the West Coast in the fine weather conditions. That afternoon was a normal sports period and I was playing for the Squadron football team in a friendly match. At half-time as we sucked our lemons on the pitch we were told that Tommy's aircraft had crashed in thick fog somewhere in Lincolnshire around noon, all three crew members being killed.

This was sad news indeed, for since our time together at Cardington on the Ferry Flight Tommy and I had become firm friends. The news had shocked other Mess members as well and that evening I accompanied several of them to the "Springvale" at Kingsworthy less than a mile away from Worthy Down as the crow flies. The hotel had only been opened a few months before and was being managed by the former Signals Officer of No 207 Squadron, John Scott, who had retired earlier in the year. Tommy and I had been there a few times for, thanks to a shortcut, it was an easy place to reach.

On this evening we were all in sombre mood after the day's events and stood in the small lounge bar drinking our favourite tipple, Strongs bitter, and discussing the possible causes of the crash. At this stage Lofty Swain the Photographic SNCO who was with our party and knew the Scotts family well, caught sight of the eldest daughter Pamela and started a game of shove h'apenny with her; I had seen her with her father at the Mess once or twice but had never spoken to her before.

Pamela was beating Lofty at the game at which she was a bit of an expert and in between shots was telling him about a film that was showing in Winchester that she badly wanted to see. Lofty challenged me to play him adding that whoever won should take Pamela to see her film the next evening. Whether by design or accident, for he was a much better player than I, Lofty lost the game and the following evening I called for Pamela and escorted her to the cinema. It was to be the start of a lifetime together for us.

In the last few weeks of 1937 the squadron trained hard to become proficient in all aspects of flying. Operating the Wellesley in its day bomber role many hours were spent on practice bombing at all levels on the Porton range, long cross-country flights coupled with vertical and oblique photography, air firing using camera gun and blank ammunition and the inevitable formation flying. There was one unfortunate incident when I landed in a snow storm after an abortive high level bombing practice. As I touched down the starboard undercarriage leg collapsed and the aircraft did a frightening cartwheel turn on that leg, forcing it through the port mainplane, and rupturing a fuel tank before the aircraft skidded to a stop. Switching off everything in the cockpit, releasing the seat harness and operating the quick release box on my parachute harness I struggled to open the sliding hatch of the cockpit. To no avail, it would only open a couple of inches due to distortion caused by the impact. To make matters worse I was being showered by high octane fuel from the ruptured tank. There was a distinct possibility that I might be burnt alive if oil from a broken pipe were to drip onto a hot exhaust. To add to my fear, one of the practice bombs still in the aircraft started to discharge a white plume of stannic vapour giving the impression of a fire breaking out. I could see the fire tender belting towards me and the next moment I was practically asphyixated under a white cloud as a mountain of foam was built up over my head; seconds later a crowbar forced the hatch free and I was able to drag my body clear and join my bomb-aimer who had managed to get out by himself.

Investigation into the failure of the under-carriage leg revealed that at the time I landed the trunnion bolt securing the top of the leg to the mounting in the wing had been half-sheared through due to faulty machining of the part. The resultant collapse could have occurred at any time; it was just my luck to be piloting it when it did happen.

Just before Christmas it was decided that the squadron would be sent to Armament Practice Camp at West Freugh near Stranraer, West Scotland. Disquieting reports were already being circulated that the Wellesley was useless for any form of bombing above sea level in the winters of North West Europe, and West Freugh was to be a form of test.

My Austin Arrow was giving trouble at this time with the main bearings starting to knock and it was only a matter of time before I would have to decide whether to part exchange Amy for the new Ford then on the market, or to have a new engine installed for about the same price. I drove to Yorkshire for a weeks leave in appalling weather with the hood leaking and the interior of the car awash and came to the conclusion that for all the year round driving in Britain it was essential to have a saloon car. The day after I arrived home I went with my father to Appleyards new car centre in Leeds where we saw the very model I wanted at a knockdown price of £105. Asked about a part exchange arrangement the salesman then climbed into Amy with a pained expression on his face as he listened to the collection of noises coming from under the bonnet and did a quick circuit of the block. He returned to offer me £45 in part exchange for the Ford which I thought reasonable in view of what I had paid for her eighteen months earlier. We clinched the deal on the spot with my father standing surety, and drove home for tea in the new car absolutely delighted.

I returned to Worthy Down after Christmas making light of the journey and the weather in the closed comfort of the saloon car and was quickly caught up in the flurry of preparation for our month away in Scotland.

★　　　★　　　★

The Squadron moved after Hogmanay, flying in formation with a ground party going by train. Few of us had expected to do much flying so far north at that time of the year but we were to be proved wrong. For much of the next three weeks the weather conditions stayed good and we were able to keep to the daily programmes on the ranges. Generally speaking the gunnery details against the ground targets and the drogues towed by Westland Wallaces went off without much trouble, and firing live at these targets was enjoyed by the crews. Our problems started on the bombing ranges when, after initial low level practices at around 250 feet, we attempted bombing at heights above the freezing level.

The aircraft were picketed out in the open. When the temperature dropped at night any moisture in the air was condensed on the electrical selector switches inside the cockpit and on the external electro-magnetic releases on the bomb carriers inside the pods on the wings. As soon as the aircraft climbed above the freezing level (and at this time of the year it was usually near the ground) everything froze up and it proved impossible to operate the bombing panel switches in the air. We tried every trick we could think of, eg taking off with bombs already selected and master switch on. It made no difference. And when a few switches did work the bomb casings of the practice bombs froze in the air, then fell away on landing. Eventually we abandoned attempts to drop bombs and concentrated on gunnery, carrying out up to four or five daily sorties each on the ground screens and the sleeve targets.

Half-way through our stay at West Freugh we were joined by 101 Squadron who were still equipped with old twin engined bi-planes, Boulton and Paul Overstrands.

During our last week there Scotland was hit by line squalls sweeping in from the Atlantic and gales of over 100 miles an hour were forecast moving across the country from west to east. Under such abnormal conditions it would be impossible to ensure the safety of our aircraft if they were picketed facing into the wind because of the large angle of attack presented by the mainplanes in this position. We therefore clamped all the control surfaces and turned the aircraft tail into wind hoping that the wind pressure would push down on the upper surfaces of the mainplanes and hold the aircraft firmly in contact with the ground.

All that night we stood by on emergency and were rewarded by seeing that the plan worked, for when the high winds struck, the Wellesleys stayed firmly rooted to the ground and rode out the storm without any damage. The other squadron was not so lucky and sustained damage to several aircraft despite the use of treble screw pickets. It was the only occasion on which I ever saw a twin engined aircraft tethered to screw pickets with its wheels off the ground and both airscrews windmilling from the force of the wind. In the paper the following day we read that a complete squadron of twin-engined Heyfords at an aerodrome on the east coast of Scotland had been blown into the sea and lost without trace.

The Squadron returned to Worthy Down on the 30th January still intact and continued with the normal training programme, concentrating on long navigational cross-countries ending with low level attacks and photography. On 12 March 1938 Austria was annexed by Germany. As a precautionary measure our training was stepped up to include night flying. On 29th March after an exhausting day in the air on a long low level cross-country flight I returned to find my name on the night flying programme for the third time in a week to practice circuits and bumps. Because the prevailing wind was south-westerly the goose neck flarepath was usually laid out by the Officer in charge of night flying to give an unobstructed approach between the hangars on the right and the main camp buildings to the left and an up-hill landing and take-off run. Control of all aircraft in the air or on the ground was exercised by light signals from Aldis lamps and Verey pistol by the Officer stationed at the taxying post at the down-wind end of the flare path. The exit road from the main camp ran roughly in the same direction as the flare path for the first two or three hundred yards then dog-legged to the left towards the Guardroom; there was a deep ditch running along the aerodrome side. That night I taxied out from the hangar area, signalled my aircraft identity letter and received a green for take off. A quick circuit of the aerodrome and I again flashed my letter on the Morse key and received a green to land.

After landing on the right hand side of the goosenecks I taxied left around the short arm of the Tee past the end flare and lined up with the Christmas tree lights on the taxi post at the downwind end to give me a clear and unobstructed run into position for another take-off. Halfway there I ran into the ditch at the point of the dog leg and finished up with the aircraft on its nose. Switching everything off I climbed down to investigate and it soon became clear that O.C Night Flying had laid out the Tee flare path without realising that the dog leg of the ditch was protruding into what should be a clear taxi way. I just happened to be first man off that night and had been unfortunate. The damage to the aircraft wasn't very much, luckily.

Meanwhile Higher Authority studied the results of our Armament Practice Camp. The decision was made that the Wellesley was better suited for operations in warmer climes and all our aircraft would be sent out to the Middle East. We would now be re-equipped with another new aircraft about to come off the production line in large numbers. This was the Fairey Battle powered by the Rolls Royce Merlin liquid cooled engine.

Also, within weeks, both squadrons would be leaving Worthy Down and moving to a newly built aerodrome at Cottesmore in Rutland. Cottesmore was one of a number of new aerodromes on which work had started in the mid-thirties to house the increased number of squadrons planned in the RAF expansion. The policy now was to discard the old stations that were either too small to operate modern aircraft, or lacked the facilities, or were sited wrongly.

Rumours had been rife for some time that Worthy Down was to

be handed over to the Fleet Air Arm to be used for training Naval Air Gunners. In the second week of April, as if to confirm it, a Naval advance party arrived on the Station and strange things started to happen. Before we departed for Cottesmore on the 20th of the month the web-footed influence made itself felt in the introduction of port and starboard watches, an Officer of the Watch doing his rounds at night by the light of a horn lantern and "liberty boats" taking men ashore from the main Guard room.

The 'Phoney' War

The fateful year, 1939, started with me in a class-room at Shoreham eager to complete my Navigation training. I was impatient to get it over and done with and get back to the squadron at Cottesmore where I had lots of things to attend to before the Spring. Over Christmas Pamela and I had agreed our wedding date and we were to be married in Kingsworthy church on 22nd April; I had to make certain I could get leave, sort out a best man and all the other matters that a potential bridegroom is expected to deal with.

Otherwise I enjoyed the school atmosphere at Shoreham. The classes covered more advanced navigational techniques, meteorology and compasses than I had experienced before. I became completely absorbed working on outline Mercators charts, carrying out "dry swims" all over the Atlantic. Sadly, when it came to putting theory to practice on airborne exercises in the School aircraft from Shoreham aerodrome the whole business became a farce. Old twin engined De Havilland "Rapides" based at Shoreham were used for this purpose. The normal passenger seats had been removed and a small chart table fitted for use by two trainee navigators sharing the exercise. The only other equipment carried in the aircraft that could be used for navigation, other than the pilot's compass, was an obsolete tail drift sight. As the fuel capacity of the aircraft limited each flight to between two and two and a half hours' duration, the radius of action was around 100 miles, mostly over the sea. With no landing aids available the pilots always kept below cloud where flying conditions were least stable. On most trips the light Rapide was bounced around the sky on erratic courses that usually ended with the people in the back becoming so air sick that they had little interest in the proceedings.

The pilot, who knew every landmark in the area from experience, then made a bee-line for Shoreham and the exercise was counted as completed.

On most of the trips my pilot was Robert McIntosh, better known in Civil Aviation circles in those days as "All-weather Mac". Mac had been flying continuously since the First World War when he started with the Royal Flying Corps and was a legendary figure in flying. He went on to fly with the Royal Air Force throughout the next war. He was decorated with the Distinguished Flying Cross in his fifties for his splendid work rescuing ditched aircrew when Commanding an Air/Sea Rescue Squadron. After the war Mac returned to Civil Aviation and finally retired from active flying when approaching his eightieth birthday. What a career to look back on!

As might be expected, the maintenance of the School aircraft was minimal and at one time there was seldom more than one ground engineer available in the aircraft parking area for general handling and starting of engines. This lack of hands led to a dangerous practice springing up whereby the single engineer played the part of both engineer and pilot when starting the engines by hand swinging the propellors. It led to me witnessing a most alarming incident one lunch time.

My co-navigator and I were standing near the airport control building discussing our next exercise as a mechanic went by us to an aircraft some 20 paces away to start up. He entered the Rapide by the rear door to check that the main engine switches were in the "OFF" position, then closed both throttle levers and placed the small hand brake on its ratchet-held quadrant. He then primed each engine in turn and got out of the aircraft, and turned each propellor by hand to draw the fuel mixture into the cylinders. Re-entering the cockpit he placed both sets of engine switches "ON" then got out again to swing each propellor in turn.

The starboard engine started at once, settling down to a fast tickover whereupon he ducked round the nose of the aircraft and swung the port propellor. The engine roared into life but instead of settling down to a tickover it started to increase in revs as the throttle lever vibrated open on its quadrant. Before the panic-stricken mechanic could get into the cockpit to shut it down the turning differential imposed on the wheel brakes caused the hand brake lever to snap off and the aircraft set off in a wide arc across the aerodrome without anyone at the controls the mechanic frantically giving chase. The Rapide complete a full circle and headed directly for the open doors of the nearly hangar that was choc-a-bloc with small privately owned aircraft. Suddenly realising the danger the mechanic dashed towards the metal hangar doors and with the assistance of several others who had seemingly materialized out of nowhere managed to partially close them before the Rapide's propellors chewed into them and the aircraft stopped dead. Fortunately there was no fire or it might have been another story.

Some days later, on 2nd February I completed my final air exercise and during the next week all the students sat the end of course examination which would qualify them for the Air Navigators Certificate. The results were published on our last day at Shoreham and I was delighted to find that I had top marks. I headed for Cottesmore to get back into uniform and resume Air Force duties feeling well pleased.

★　　　★　　　★

Back at Cottesmore little had changed. The aerodrome had been under snow for a time and the grass surface was only just becoming fit for everyday flying. Parked in the hangar waiting to be taken to the Maintenance Unit for repair was a damaged Battle. Apparently during the recent heavy snow falls our newly appointed Commanding Officer, Squadron Leader Chester, had welcomed the opportunity to fly a Battle in a snow storm and had blithely taken off in a blizzard. After some desperate moments in almost blind conditions he had been extremely lucky to find his way down and make a belly landing without writing himself off.

Within days of my return the Squadron was ordered to Armament Practice Camp at short notice to fill a gap in the programme. After hurried preparations we managed to get all our serviceable aircraft off the ground and en route for West Freugh on the morning of 19th Feburary. There, despite awful weather, everyone worked hard to achieve some sort of results and make all the upset worthwhile. For my part I managed to squeeze in two air gunnery and and two practice bombing sorties in the fine intervals. The rest of the time in rain and low cloud was spent tramping around the heather-clad shores of Luce Bay with a shot gun used for clay pigeon shooting, borrowed from the Armoury, looking for anything that would add more variety to the Mess diet. We were all glad to get back to Cottesmore at the beginning of March and to concentrate on the night flying practice that day bomber squadron pilots so badly needed. Recent policy changes now insisted that the crews should be capable of full night cross-country flights and later that month I took my crew on their first long night flight of over three hours' duration.

The Fairey Battle was hopeless at night from the pilot's point of view. During take-off until sufficient forward speed had built up to raise the tail and bring the nose down, his forward view was completely blocked by the engine and his night vision destroyed by the open flames belching from the stub exhausts. The final stages of the landing approach were even worse for on throttling back huge sheets of flame licked over the cowlings turning the subsequent hold off and landing into a hit and miss affair. Many changes and modifications were made to the manifolds to overcome this problem without much success. Most of us ended up adopting a sort of "Spitfire" curved approach by night but the resultant landing was almost entirely "by guess and by God".

The date of our wedding was fast approaching and I went to see the Vicar in Cottesmore village to arrange for the banns to be read there at the same time as they would be in the church at Kingsworthy. Mike Mitchell of 207 Squadron had agreed to act as my best man. Everything had been arranged for 22nd April at Kingsworthy Church with the reception at the Springvale Hotel. I had booked our honeymoon at a small hotel in the West Country in the quiet fishing village of Looe.

After a normal days flying on Friday 21st April 1939 I changed out of uniform, loaded everything I had already checked and packed into the Ford and set off for Kingsworthy and the wedding. My parents were already at the Springvale when I got there and went off to bed early after their long journey down from Yorkshire. After a meal and a few Strongs beers I too felt tired and turned in.

Not for me a rip-roaring last night as a bachelor with a hangover to nurse through the wedding ceremony!

Next morning Mike escorted me to the church in good time, fully booted and spurred in my new Mess kit and we sat in the front pew in splendid isolation to await the arrival of the bride as the guests started to arrive. Everything went off without a hitch. After signing the register in the vestry and posing for the wedding photographs outside the church everyone repaired to the Springvale for the reception and champagne. All that is except for my father who still stuck out his teetotal principles and asked for water in his glass each time he joined in the toasts. However, it all went off so well that Pamela and I were late in leaving the reception and it was well into the evening before we got into the car and set off for the West country, covered in confetti and rice and dragging a string of old tins and assorted footwear tied to the car bumper. Out of sight of the wedding guests I stopped the car and removed the noisy attachment and cleaned off the decorative art and newly married signs.

It began to get dark as we reached the outskirts of Yeovil and by then it had become obvious that there was no hope of reaching Looe until the early hours. It had been a long day and we were both tired out so we decided to stay the night in Yeovil if we could find a room. Luckily a small inn that looked promising came into view shortly afterwards and we were soon spending our first night together in a clean and comfortable if old fashioned room.

Next morning we set off to complete the rest of our journey to Looe at our leisure; the weather was warm and sunny and the countryside looked green and fresh and we meandered blissfully along in the car with few interruptions from other road users reaching our hotel in Looe in time for tea. The days that followed were blissful too. At that time of the year few guests were staying in the hotel and there were few visitors to the West country. The roads and normal tourist sites were deserted so that we could set off each day by car or on foot over the moors and hardly see anyone all day. On the second day of our honeymoon we stopped to have tea at a little café perched by the roadside and overlooking the sea we gorged ourselves on fresh Cornish splits with home-made strawberry jam topped with thick clotted cream before returning to the hotel in time to freshen up and start a four-course dinner. We enjoyed it so much that for the rest of our stay we made a point of adjusting our daily itinerary so that we arrived back in the area to take tea at the same café every afternoon.

Apart from eating and drinking that took up so much of our time we visited the famous "rabbitries" at Looe harbour where we admired the lovely Angoras with their silky pelts, and we went one evening to a show in the smallest cinema in the country. By day in wet and blustery weather that made it much more realistic we drove out to the Jamaica Inn of Daphne du Maurier fame and lunched on "tiddy oggies" and Guinness; afterwards we wandered around the Cheese Rings on Bodmin Moor and climbed up to King Arthur's castle for the view at Tintagel.

All too soon the week's honeymoon was over and we started back to Kingsworthy to collect our few belongings prior to rejoining the squadron at Cottesmore. Our problems would start from then on for there was little or no suitable accommodation for rent in the sparsely populated farming area surrounding the aerodrome. On the brighter side it seemed fairly certain that new married quarters now nearing completion would be ready within a matter of weeks and that I would be one of the first to get one; so it was a question of finding something short term during the waiting period.

Ron McClachlan, one of the pilots in "A" Flight, was already living with his family in one of the first houses to be built on the station and they had offered to put us up for a few days while we had a good look around. Our worst fears were soon confirmed and after several days of fruitless search around Rutland and in the country town of Oakham we had to accept defeat and settled for room and board in a nondescript old inn in the main street of the town. Here we made the best of things for a few weeks with frequent visits to the local cinema, and most weekends away to break the monotony. Then at last, early in June, a married quarter became available and we quickly moved into our first fully furnished house. It was quite a relief to be living on the station within walking distance of the Squadron offices and hangar and to be able to join Pamela most days for a lunchtime snack.

I felt much happier when I went off each day for flying duties knowing that she was surrounded by lots of other service wives and families some of whom we had known for quite a time.

It was even more re-assuring after we had been living there some weeks and Pamela began to experience morning sickness; a joint visit to the Station Medical Officer confirmed the fact that she was going to have a baby the following Spring.

As that summer of 1939 progressed, Chamberlain now began to realise the treachery of the Munich Agreement made evident by Hitler's invasion of Czechoslovakia in March, followed by Mussolini's take over of Albania the following month. Following these acts the Anglo-Polish treaty had been signed in London on 25th May and in July the Prime Minister re-affirmed the British pledge to Poland. As the European situation worsened the Royal Air Force struggled against the odds to achieve some degree of operational readiness with untried aircraft and crews for whatever might lie ahead. A steady flow of newly qualified pilots and Air Observers were leaving the training schools to be teamed with W.Op/A.Gs and fly as crews on new aircraft with newly-formed squadrons on newly-built airfields. In this situation it was no wonder that most squadron training at that time was something of a hotch potch and totally dependent on the state of the weather. The only blind landing systems available were experiental Lorenze ones installed at Boscombe Down and Martlesham Heath, where a few Anson aircraft had been fitted with the receiving equipment. The rest of the Royal Air Force pilots had to rely on their skill and map reading abilities to get down in bad weather. Meantime they practiced assiduously on the Link Trainer simulating the climbs and descents on instruments followed by holding patterns and final landing procedures which they should have been doing daily in the air if only the aircraft and aerodromes had been equipped with the necesary receivers and transmitters.

By far the greatest activity was taking place on the ground. At most aerodromes civilians worked overtime, blacking out every window with removable felt screens or heavy curtains. Camouflage netting was draped from the external walls of the huge hangars to soften and conceal the stark vertical outlines from the air. Circular gun emplacements built of sandbags appeared overnight at key points designated for aerodrome defence, and underground air raid shelters were everywhere.

In the air, as might be expected, silly and stupid incidents were taking place all around. One newly joined Pilot Officer with a poor reputation for flying who was generally disliked for his high-handed attitude and lack of patience with his crew set off for Scampton one afternoon. In the rear seat, as ballast, was a young inexperienced Wireless operator under training. Before the passenger had time to stow his parachute pack and other equipment and plug in to the intercom system the pilot ran up the engine, waved away the wheel chocks taxied out and took off without bothering to establish contact with the unfortunate airman. It so happened that the WOP had failed to push his earphone plug into the socket fully so that when the pilot had settled down on course and tried to speak to him he was unable to get a reply. After several attempts the pilot lost his temper and waggled the control column from side to side rocking the aircraft violently to attract his passengers attention. Unfortunately for him this action only served to panic the passenger into thinking that an emergency had arisen and the aircraft was out of control so he promptly buckled on his chest parachute pack and dived out of the aircraft, pulling the ripcord as soon as he was clear. The pilot blissfully unaware that he was now alone in the Battle gave up trying to contact his passenger and carried on to Scampton intending to give him a rocket after landing. On switching off the engine he stormed out of the cockpit and down the catwalk on the wing root to vent his wrath. When he realised that the rear seat was empty he almost had a fit on the spot. However, in the middle of reporting the loss of his passenger to the Station Commander in Lincolnshire, Police phoned in to say that they had picked up a parachutist in RAF uniform and were bringing him over for identification. After that incident a very relieved pilot never again left the ground without first making sure that he was in communication with his crew.

One of the pilots in "A" Flight was a red-haired Irishman notorious for his bright green sports jackets and dash but with little idea of things mechanical. The throttle quadrant on his aircraft could easily have been replaced with a stop/go type of engine control for there was no in between fully open or fully closed position and he never bothered to look at engine instruments. One day he returned at full throttle from a flight to Ringway. It was a hot July afternoon and he was completely unaware that the engine had developed a coolant leak and the aircraft was streaming a white cloud of glycol in its wake. Flying low over the aerodrome he pulled up to circuit height and came in to land still oblivious of the fact that his temperature gauge must by then have been off the clock and the Merlin engine on the point of seizure. As he taxied towards the tarmac in front of the squadron hangar the usual crowd of onlookers had materialized from nowhere and tried to draw his attention to the cloud of steam he was trailing by pointing and gesturing but he just waved at them. Then, suddenly, the penny dropped as he realised the something was wrong. He switched off the engine, undid his safety straps, slid down the catwalk on the wing, dropped to the ground and started to run. As he got clear of the area the radiator blew up in a scalding blast of steam.

Earlier, while practising for an Empire Air Day Display, the leader of a small formation of Battles from a nearby aerodrome led the flight through a bumpy cumulus cloud that lay ahead. A photographer from "Flight", the aircraft journal, was a passenger in one of the aircraft taking photographs for publication. As the formation entered the turbulent cloud the number two aircraft lost his station and crabbed into the leader the huge three bladed metal airscrew ripping open the thin fuselage with the ease of a tin opener. At that split second the Air Observer in the aircraft was crawling on hands and knees along the interior of the fuselage to pass a written code message for transmission by the Wireless Operator; as he reached up to hand the form over he was decapitated by the blades of the airscrew his head falling at the feet of the horrified WOP. Despite the terrible damage to the controls of the leading aircraft and the damaged airscrew on the other both aircraft managed to get down safely emphasising the one good quality of the Battle; it was so robustly constructed that it would have made a better tank than a day bomber aircraft!

Other newly-formed squadrons at nearby aerodromes who flew Blenheims also had problems. Smithy, who had been at Netheravon with me, hit the news headlines when he was court-martialled and reduced to the ranks. He set off one morning on a training flight to Aldergrove in Northern Ireland and got into difficulties flying on instruments through a thick and turbulent front cloud system over the Pennines. Firmly believing that the aircraft was in an inverted position and out of control he gave the order to abandon and left through the top hatch. For some reason the observer sitting alongside him stayed put and when the aircraft righted itself and emerged into clear weather conditions shortly afterwards he managed to get it down on a belly landing in a large field; Smithy never flew again as a pilot, the observer was awarded the B.E.M.

★　　　★　　　★

By the end of July, despite Chamberlain's 'piece of paper', the general feeling grew that war with Germany was unavoidable and was only a matter of time. Preliminary moves of key personnel were already taking place and some pilots had been given special sealed orders effective from the announcement of hostilities starting. In this charged atmosphere the annual Home Defence Exercises were brought forward to the second week of August; once they were out of the way, if nothing started up, I was hoping to have a few days leave and take Pamela home to Kingsworthy for a break.

I flew with the squadron in the Exercises on the 7th, 8th and 10th making daylight attacks on various targets.

On 10th August Cottesmore was placed on standby to accept emergency night diversions should expected bad weather make landing at some aerodromes in East Anglia impossible. A young and enthusiastic pilot who had only recently joined the squadron had been detailed for Duty Pilot in the temporary wooden Watch Tower alongside the signal square of the aerodrome that night. With commendable zeal and foresight he proceeded to site his emergency flarepath of paraffin goosenecks early in the evening so that if called upon he could light it quickly. He also placed a charge in the breech of the maroon signal mortar and laid out the firing cable and toggle in readiness for an emergency firing. When the call for assistance came in the early hours of the next morning he rushed out on to the aerodrome to light the flare path only to lose himself in the fog that now blotted out visibility in all directions. Eventually he managed to find and light the goosenecks and struggled back to the Watch Hut to find the Station Commander standing near the signal mortar calling for someone to fire it off immediately. Panicking in this august presence the duty pilot yanked at the firing toggle and the resultant blast as the mortar went off almost removed the Station Commander's trousers and gave him the fright of his life. Once he had recovered his composure the C.O stalked off breathing threats of courts martial and the young Duty Pilot spent the rest of that night worried sick about what lay in store for him next morning. However, he need not have bothered, for first thing next day a signal arrived from Group expressing their appreciation and thanks for the invaluable assistance given and the matter of the signal mortar was conveniently forgotten.

Despite the growing international tension annual leave had still not been cancelled so that Pamela and I were able to leave for Kingsworthy at the end of the Defence Exercise. Pamela's father had "green" fingers and in the kitchen garden at the rear of the Spring-Vale he had a fine crop of old-fashioned red shallots ready for lifting. I am very partial to them when pickled and I spent several hours preparing enough to fill three large jars to take back with us for home pickling when we returned.

For the rest of our ten days we lazed around most of the time trying to forget the news which got gloomier each day; we returned to Cottesmore to find the station in a state of turmoil. Germany and Russia had signed a non-aggression pact on 23rd August and with the invasion of Poland the RAF was being placed on a war footing. A number of pilots had already left the Station to take up their war appointments; the remainder were to move as a squadron to Cranfield the following day, 25th August. The squadron would provide replacements for those earmarked for the British Expeditionary Force to France should they suffer casualties.

This was the "crunch" in my estimation, and there was no way, war or otherwise, that I was going to leave Pamela behind at Cottesmore to fend for herself. In the few hours now left I arranged for a hurried departure from the quarters that had been ours for a mere two months. Stewart who had been flying with me

114

most of the time I had been with the squadron and was in a similar position, also handed over his house. We then decided that as soon as the two of us took off for Cranfield by air the two wives would leave by car in convoy and would find temporary accommodation in Cranfield village until the situation was clear.

On the morning of the 25th both the cars were loaded in readiness and Stewart and I left for the hangar to check our aircraft. The last act before leaving the house was to present the astonished milk delivery girl with three large jars of pickled onions. An hour later I took off in a Battle with Stewart in the back and landed for the first time at Cranfield. Shortly afterwards I was ferried back to Cottesmore to pick up a second aircraft and this went on most of the day until all our serviceable machines had left Cottesmore. Meanwhile the two wives had driven over and had managed to find a room for the night. That evening, as we had arranged, Pamela waited for me in the car outside the main gate of the Camp. I had nothing new to tell her other than the fact that I had to sleep on the Camp while the emergency was on. The main thing was to find something suitable for her in the area until the situation was clearer. We drove around the district for a while looking for a likely village where we could make enquiries and eventually came to Sherington, some two miles from Newport Pagnell, which boasted an old fashioned pub, The White Hart, where we decided to stop for a breather. We were shown into the sitting room away from the public bar where we sat and chatted with the landlord's wife, while he went down the cellar steps to draw my beer from the wood. The Simmonds's were a lovely old couple straight out of a Dickens book. Alf was a shy and retiring character who had been coachman to the Duke of Bedford at Woburn in his youth. Volunteering for service in the Boer War he had been badly wounded in the leg and was unable to return to his old job when he came back. He had then married a little apple-cheeked cook from the Duke's staff and they had scratched a living at the inn ever since.

The White Hart was a period piece in itself; a high four storey building on one side of a courtyard with outbuildings and coach house on the other two sides and deep cellars beneath where the beer was kept at the right temperature. Every room was cluttered with patriotic pictures and mementoes of Alf's Boer War service and his previous service as a coachman, all kept in spotless condition. They seemed such a nice old couple that we decided to ask if they would put Pamela up for the time being and to this they readily ageed. We finished our drinks and drove back to Cranfield to pick up the luggage. The state of emergency in being meant that I had to be available for duty at Cranfield day and night. For the next week we worked out a routine whereby Pamela picked me up in the car at the end of the day's flying, we spent the evening together and she then delivered me back to sleep at Cranfield while she returned to her room at the White Hart. At least it was better than being completely separated.

★   ★   ★

The squadron was still carrying on its reserve role and putting in lots of hours in the air training newly posted observers and gunners. The European situation was becoming more critical by the hour and there was no surprise when the British Fleet was mobilized on the last day of August. The following day, German forces invaded Poland whereupon Great Britain and France mobilized all their Armed Forces and issued an ultimatum calling on Hitler to withdraw his invasion troops. On Sunday, 3rd September at 11 a.m. we packed into the Mess to listen to Neville Chamberlain's broadcast. No reply had been received to his ultimatum to Hitler and a state of war existed between Britain and Germany. It was a sombre moment but at last something definite after all the manoeuvring of the past months. With the grim prospect of a long struggle now facing us there was an even more vital need to get on with our training of gunners and in particular to give them some live firing practice as opposed to the camera gun work to which they were limited in the Cranfield area. On 7th September I left for Weston Zoyland near Bridgewater with a small detachment of aircraft and most of our air gunners to give them much needed practice on the ranges in the Bristol Channel. Ever since war had been declared we had been expecting some action by enemy aircraft. When, therefore, over the Cotswolds the huge and distinctive shape of a Fokker Tri-motor shot across my path heading towards Bristol my first thought was that it must be a German and my second one to get after it and have a go with the Browning front gun. I turned and followed and soon caught up with the slower Fokker but on drawing abreast I was able to see the pilot waving a white handkerchief and noted that there were no Luftwaffe markings on the fuselage, so I turned away and resumed my course. On reporting the incident after landing at my destination I was told that it was one of two aircraft bought by Imperial Airways and being ferried by their pilot to Bristol. It should have been notified through RAF channels no wonder the Captain panicked when I came on the scene; he was lucky that I didn't open fire first and ask questions afterwards!

During the next week I gave all our gunners practice firing at towed targets on the Watchet Ranges. I returned to Cranfield on the 15th passing over the White Hart during my landing circuit to signal to Pamela that I was back. She got the message and was there to meet me with the car that evening. During my absence it seemed that she had become something of a local heroine for when the Brewery had failed to deliver the beer supply and the White Hart was on the verge of closing she had volunteered to take Mrs. Simmonds to collect two barrels from the brewery in Newport Pagnell saving the day for the thirsty locals who had much appreciated her initiative.

After a fortnight of being at war but with as yet no war-like activities taking place the early restrictions on staying out of Camp overnight were relaxed. The shortage of petrol was already causing difficulty in getting to and from Sherington so we decided to try for accommodation closer to the aerodrome, within cycling range if possible. This time we were lucky for we chanced on a pleasant couple by the name of Joyce who lived with their small son in a detached house about a mile away. They were quite happy for us both to live there "en famille" so having made the arrangements we moved in without further ado. We quickly established a satisfactory routine whereby I left the house early in the morning for the aerodrome, returning in the evenings for an evening meal, after which we sat in front of the fire playing cards or listening to the radio. I shall always remember the delicious pickled walnuts Mrs. Joyce often produced for us during those evening meals.

117

This situation dragged on into October when the rain started. Since our arrival in August there had been little or no rainfall in the area and we had been able to operate the heavy Battles on the hard clay and grass surfaces of the aerodrome without any difficulty. With the coming of the rain the disadvantage of Cranfield's position in the middle of a clay bowl became apparent. To build the landing area a number of fields had been compulsorily purchased from local farms and estates under the Emergency Powers Act. Over centuries of farming individual drainage systems had been developed to suit the crops and keep the heavy clay soil workable.

When the aerodrome contractors took over, all the old drainage pipes were torn up by the bull-dozers and an overall system, as yet untried, was introduced. The local sons of the soil shook their grey heads over it and forecast dire problems when the winter storms arrived and sure enough, within a week the whole area became a quagmire. Any aircraft trying to taxi was soon bogged down to the wheel axles and all flying operations came to a grinding halt. This situation went on until well into November when snow and fog added to the general misery. By then weeks of squelching through clay puddles to attend to aircraft which could not be flown, widely dispersed around the perimeter of the aerodrome, had reduced morale to a low ebb. To combat boredom one of the Ralph Reader "Gang Shows" arrived to perform on a temporary stage erected in one of the empty and unheated hangars. It was without doubt the worst show I have ever seen and the audience had drifted away long before it ended.

After the snow came a cold spell freezing the ground hard and allowing limited flying to take place if we could start the Merlin engines. This proved difficult as the few starter trollies we had were soon flattened and the hand turning operation too slow to achieve starting in such weather. Eventually we had to resort to erecting canvas tents around the engines and prior to starting connect up a hot air supply from a pre-heating pump for some minutes before removing the tent and using the starter trolley. It was a long and cumbersome procedure to get any aircraft into the air.

On one of the few occasions that I got into the air during the cold spell I was leading a Vic formation of three around the area when the pilot of the outside aircraft allowed his aircraft to slip inwards on the turn, damaging my tailplane and causing the starboard elevator to jam; I had a few anxious moments making a straight-in approach and landing at Cranfield using engine and trimming tabs to control my descent.

By this time the aerodrome was in such a state that it was decided to stop all flying from it until hard runways had been constructed and once again the squadron was on the move, this time as a temporary measure to Bassingbourn, a newly built station recently vacated by Blenheim squadrons. Not knowing of the situation there and not wishing to leave Pamela by herself at Cranfield the only answer seemed to be to take her back to Kingsworthy until things settled down. The baby was expected at the beginning of March and we could arrange for Pamela to book into a good nursing home in Winchester then.

The weekend before the move to Bassingbourn took place I obtained a 48 hours pass and contacted the local black market operator who filled the tank of my car with some sort of fuel of doubtful origin. No questions asked, but the price was exorbitant. I then packed Pamela in the car with all our bits and pieces, said good-bye to the Joyces who had been so kind to us, and drove to Kingsworthy. Next day I returned to Cranfield to play my part in the forthcoming move happy in the knowledge that Pamela was being well looked after.

On 7th December we started ferrying all our serviceable aircraft to Bassingbourn and by the 13th the move of all aircraft, personnel and equipment was completed; we then carried on flying in the training role as before. Conditions at the new aerodrome were much better than at Cranfield and in the colder weather which we were now experiencing we kept on plugging away, giving the new arrivals as much time in the air as was possible.

The "phoney war" situation was still dragging on. There were no casualties amongst the squadrons of the B.E.F. in France to be replaced, and we were literally kicking our heels waiting for some sort of action to start. One compensation was that over Christmas I was given a few days leave and was able to get over to Kingsworthy again. By then the baby was really making its presence felt, it was very much alive and kicking.

★ ★ ★

The beginning of 1940 brought more snow, followed by an extremely cold spell. The temperature fell so low that the nearby river Ouse froze from bank to bank for the first time in many years. At this time I was flying a lot in the rear seat of the dual Battle, the trainee pilot being under the hood in the front cockpit practising instrument flying while I acted as safety pilot, looking out for other aircraft and ready to take over control if he got into difficulties under the hood. For structural reasons the rear seat was installed well back along the fuselage in the W/Op Air Gunner position so that to be able to see anything ahead the occupant had to raise the seat as high as it would go and sit with his head and shoulders well into the slipstream. Being used to a closed cockpit I had not bothered to ensure that my leather flying helmet fitted snugly and was draught-proof and after several flights in the very cold and draughty conditions I developed a sinus condition on the left side of my face, with a badly inflamed ear drum. Reporting sick next morning I saw the temporary Medical Officer who turned out to be an aged RAMC Major with First World War ribbons called up from the Reserve, and from his manner more used to dealing with sick animals than RAF pilots. He peered into the offending ear through his optical torch and prodded around for some time. Then he gave me a scare by pronouncing that I had a perforated drum and would be grounded forthwith. For the next month I had to stick around the Flight Office making myself useful and feeling quite miserable at the possibility of not being able to fly again. Much to my relief the ear returned to normal of its own accord and when I saw the Major again he could find no trace of a perforation, and he passed me fit for full flying duties.

It was only just in time for, on 10th February, the squadron was on the move again, this time to Upwood a few miles north of Huntingdon. There we were to re-equip and convert on to Blenheims and would then join with No. 90 squadron to form a new Operational Training Unit to be based there. Our live wire C.O. Squadron Leader Chester was delighted at the news for he was a Q.F.I. and relished the idea of giving dual to all the pilots in his squadron. As soon as we moved over to Upwood he commandeered the first short-nose dual Blenheim allocated for our use and spent the whole of the next month converting each and every pilot until they had soloed. My turn came on 6th March when I was given two short periods of instruction flying from the now deserted aerodrome at Bassingbourn. Next morning I practiced solo take-offs and landings in a newly arrived long-nose and from then on plunged into the deep end, trying to become operationally efficient on all aspects of flying the twin engined aircraft. Alongside all this activity new aircraft were constantly arriving and the Battles flown out, much to everyones relief. It was an aircraft that no pilot would want to go to war in!

In one flight with Terry King we carried for the first time ever live 250 lb GP bombs. These were released on a bare mountainside with the unpronounceable name of Transfynydd in Wales. On landing I was sent for by the Adjutant and told to report next day to the PMRAF Hospital at Halton for a full medical board. This was a preliminary to being commissioned. I had been interviewed by Squadron Leader Chester before leaving Cottesmore and recommended for a commission. But that had been before the outbreak of war and I had heard nothing further and so had assumed that in the several moves and resultant dislocation of files since, then the recommendations had been 'lost'.

Reported to Halton next day I found myself in the company of a number of other N.C.O. pilots also being boarded. We were soon dealt with by the Board's specialist medics and by mid-afternoon I was on my way back to Upwood with a small medical form certifying that I was fully fit to be commissioned. It had all happened so unexpectedly that I had to take it out of my uniform pocket several times on the journey back to reassure myself that it had really happened, and that very shortly I would achieve the reward I had always hoped for during the eleven years of my RAF service.

Back at Upwood I was kept busy on the training programme with squadron crews on our long nose Blenheims and in between flying Ansons on navigation training by day and night. I also had to do my share of extra duties on the ground. On 8th March after a full day's flying I began duty as Station Orderly Sergeant, parading the duty airmen and defaulters before the Station Orderly Officer on the barrack square as the RAF ensign was lowered. After that I reported to the Watch Tower to take charge of the crew of a ground Vickers machine gun deployed in a sand-bagged emplacement which formed part of the aerodrome defence against occasional low flying intruder aircraft. Relieved from that duty at midnight I returned to the Mess for some well-earned sleep to find a copy of a telegram from Pamela to let me know that I was now the father of a seven pound baby daughter, born that afternoon in the Nursing Home somewhat earlier than had been expected. This really caught me on the hop for there was no way I could get off duty until six p.m. And I still had some work to do to make the car serviceable before I could leave. Everybody was most helpful however and I eventually left on a 48 hour pass the following morning, having finished working on the car by the light of a torch under a tarpaulin after dark.

I arrived at the Nursing Home in Winchester that afternoon still in a bit of a daze to find Pamela looking the picture of health, sitting up in bed and tucking into tea and cakes. Nearby was our new arrival sleeping off her last intake of calories and in all probability dreaming of the next one, a perfect baby. As yet we had still not decided on a name and much of my visit was spent wading through books and lists of Christian names. Eventually we agreed that she should have the same initials and second name as her mother so that limited the scope and she was named Denise Pamela, which we both liked.

On return to Upwood I found that Squadron Leader Chester had pulled strings to get himself posted to an operational Blenheim squadron and our new C.O. was Wing Commander Hurley. My commission had not yet materialised and I was kept busy flying on training flights and in the office. On 22nd April when on a navigation training trip I lost all oil pressure on one engine, but switched it off before any damage was caused and carried out a single-engined emergency landing at Harwell. Nobody on the Duty Flight was available to deal with the trouble, so I borrowed some tools and removed the cowling of the troublesome engine to find that the main pressure pipe from the engine oil pump had fractured and half the oil in the tank had been lost. Fortunately no other damage had been caused. I removed the two halves of the fractured oil line and took them along to the Station Workshops, where I managed to get a sleeve brazed over the break. I refitted the pipe, filled the oil tank and replaced the cowling, then started the engine which ran perfectly. So I promptly started the other and took off without more ado, one of the few occasions on which I had to do my own servicing.

★   ★   ★

Back in the Flight Office I found that my long awaited commission had come through with effect from 1st April 1940 and the Adjutant had already put in train action under Kings Rules and Regulations to discharge me from RAF service at 23.59 hrs on 31st March and to bring me on the strength as a Pilot Officer. I was disappointed however, to find that the permanent commission I had been recommended for in the first place had now been changed to "duration of hostilities only". Goldsmith from 90 Squadron had also been commissioned from the same date so we joined forces and decided to drive to London to be kitted out at the Moss Bros establishment next day. The scale of Officer kit and allowance had been drastically reduced on the outbreak of war and the £50.00 now authorised barely covered essentials. However, some two hours after parking outside the shop in Covent Garden, Goldie and I emerged dressed in Pilot Officer uniform for the first time. In the gathering dusk he hailed a taxi and left for his home in North London while I drove cautiously through central London until I found the Basingstoke road and headed for Kingsworthy to surprise Pamela. It was a proud moment for me when I arrived and it was marvellous to see how well she and our babe looked; now a month old, Denise was as fat as butter and putting on weight rapidly and gave little or no trouble to her mother.

I had to be back at Upwood on the Sunday as I still had to sort out my new sleeping quarters and make my debut in the Officers Mess. I left earlier than I would normally have done and parked the car outside the Mess around six o'clock. Signing in, the Mess Sergeant informed me that I had been given a room on the ground floor of the nearest Officers' married quarter, long since evacuated, and arranged for an elderly civilian batman to show me the way and take my kit. While he unpacked and stowed my things away I had a quick wash and brush up then walked back to the Mess to have dinner. As I entered the strange Mess anteroom I was spotted by Rusty Wardell who had been my Flight Commander for the past three years, and he came charging over with Bill Keighly and Scotty Russell to buy me a welcome drink and take me in to dinner some time later; it was all a new experience for me.

I quickly settled down in my new surroundings; there was little change in my flying duties but on the ground I now shared the Flight Commander's office with the others. Walking daily between the Officers' Mess and the Flight it was gratifying to be saluted, and the quality of life and the higher standards generally were a great improvement. Financially, however, I found myself much worse off and was hard put to get by for some time.

★ ★ ★

At the end of April Goldsmith and I were sent to the School of Air Navigation at St Athans for the month long Astro-Navigation course. Before leaving Upwood we were warned that the Welsh station was bursting at the seams and that we would have to bring our newly-issued Officers' Camp kits with us and be prepared for hard lying conditions. On these grounds we obtained petrol coupons to travel to St Athans in my Ford saloon where we soon experienced the hard lying we had been warned to expect. Four of us slept on camp beds in one small airless room of an empty airman's married quarter, there was no heating and black-out screens were permanently in position. We had a good half-mile walk to reach the Officers' Mess for meals and as there were several sittings in the dining room we often had long waits for our food. Coffee was taken standing up as one could never find an empty chair on which to sit. All in all it was a most uncomfortable and crowded existence. During the first week we spent many hours in the classroom as we assimilated the mysteries of spherical trigonometry and the movement of planets, mastered the use of the bubble sextant and practised identifying the stars in the night sky with the planisphere whenever they could be seen from the ground. After the first week of ground work we started to put the theory into practice in the air in the Schools Anson aircraft.

While we were on the course the Germans invaded the Low Countries and in a very short time the British Expeditionary Force was encircled and in desperate trouble. On 13th May Winston Churchill made his famous "blood, toil, tears and sweat" broadcast to the nation and on 23rd the evacuation started from Dunkirk resulting in over 300,000 of our troops being recovered against all the odds.

As history was being made in the Channel, Goldie and I found it difficult to concentrate on academic lectures or on air navigation exercises. We were flying these over the Bristol Channel and the Western approaches, as far south as the Channel Islands which were soon to be occupied by the Germans. Partnering each other and sharing the navigational duties, we clocked up some 40 hours in the air by day and night and usually ended the flights on D.R. navigation with a visual reference to the distinctive shape of Lundy Island. Even using the latest continuous reading bubble sextant it was almost impossible to obtain star sights or even accurate sun shots from such an unstable platform as an Anson at a few thousand feet altitude and half the time the weather was such that we were unable to see any heavenly bodies for cloud. I rapidly came to the conclusion that something better was urgently needed to replace the combination of dead reckoning and map reading used by our bomber crews. The old adage of "by guess and by God" just about summed it up.

On the night of 29th May we flew on the last navigational exercise of the course, the aircraft being piloted by the C.O. of the Navigation School; on this flight we tried out the new Astrograph designed by Kodak and now undergoing trials in conjunction with the continuous reading bubble sextant. Although I could visualize its use in future air liners crossing an ocean or other desolate regions where no other facilities could be provided, and possibly in Coastal Command aircraft operating far out at sea, I couldn't see Bomber Command crews flying over enemy territory being able to make much use of it. That trip marked the end of the course for us and we returned to Upwood. It was good to get away from the appalling conditions of living at St. Athans; the few shillings or "hard lying" allowance that we were later able to claim in no way compensated for the miserable time we had.

★   ★   ★

During our absence many changes had taken place at Upwood as 35 and 90 Squadrons had lost their identities and had merged together to form No. 17 Operational Training Unit. I found myself in a new role as a Staff Pilot in "B" Squadron of the Training Wing. We heard that Squadron Leader Chester who had moved heaven and earth to obtain a posting to a front-line squadron had gone missing on his first operational flight. "Rusty" Wardell followed him shortly afterwards and ended in a P.O.W. Camp for the rest of the war. Bill Keighly joined No. 82 Squadron on 20th June and on 29 July was shot down on his ninth operational sortie attacking oil refineries at Hamburg.

No. 17 O.T.U. was getting into full swing by now and I was getting in quite a lot of flying in Blenheims and Ansons both by day and by night. At times our routine was interrupted by single German raiders in Dorniers or Heinkels who came in low over the coast to avoid being picked up by our radar and bombed airfields and other targets before returning the same way to Germany. Whenever such raiders appeared in the area plans either to disperse aircraft on the ground to emergency landing grounds, or to stay in the air until the danger was over, would be put into effect. Our most popular landing ground was a big grass field adjacent to a well known Cambridgeshire hostelry, "The Caxton Gibbet," and on some occasions when I had to take an aircraft there during a raid warning there was a greater concentration of aircraft in the field and pilots in the bar than at the aerodrome we had left. Another puzzle was that the recall message never seemed to reach us by telephone and I strongly suspect that the landlord had a hand in seeing that it didn't while his bar was filled with customers...

Late one night after completing a night flying detail I had my first taste of enemy bombing on the ground. I had just got into bed when a German intruder aircraft roared over at low level releasing a stick of bombs along the still lit flarepath. The first two bombs straddled the building, the blast shattering a few windows and waking me up. As I sat up in bed and heard the explosions of the rest of the bomb load getting further and further away the door of my room was flung open and a young trainee from one of the upstairs rooms appeared and dived under the bed yelling "Air Raid". I stayed where I was and a minute or so later he emerged from under the bed looking sheepish, apologised for his behaviour and disappeared upstairs again. That was the first and last time I ever ran into him but I can still remember his silly face.

Other than sporadic raids of this nature nothing much happened during the weeks following the drama of Dunkirk as the country braced itself for the expected invasion. The OTU carried on as usual with its programme of training, the only change being that the nearby Wainfleet gunnery ranges could only be used on a restricted basis. To overcome this problem it was decided to detach a small number of aircraft to Squires Gate near Blackpool where unlimited firing could take place over the Irish Sea and on 23rd June I flew there as part of the detached Flight. A small boarding house nearby was used as a Mess and the empty golf club house and buildings on the aerodrome became the Flight Office. Each morning and at intervals throughout the day we took off with a batch of trainee gunners on board, and headed for the massive bulk of Blackpool Tower, turning above it on a compass course out to sea and keeping clear of any shipping in the area.

Here we would be joined by the towing aircraft streaming the target flag or drogue, and after an exchange of visual signals the gunnery would start, each gunner taking his turn in the turret. On completion we returned to Squires Gate to pick up another batch of gunners while the next detail joined the towing aircraft over the sea. Most days the programme ran as smooth as clockwork but it was a repetitive and boring form of flying from a pilots point of view, and after a couple of weeks I was fed up to the teeth. To make matters worse there was a sudden influx of thousands of Poles, both officers and men from the Polish armed forces who had found their way out of Nazi occupied Poland, and overnight they took over all the empty hotels and other accommodation, some even being packed into our small hotel.

At this moment came a bolt from the blue. On the morning of 4th July I took off on the early morning detail with the usual load of trainees on board and landed at Squires Gate to pick up the next lot some 40 minutes later. As I taxied the Blenheim towards the waiting group of airmen the C.O. of the Detachment came haring out of the Clubhouse and signalled to me to switch off the engines. As soon as I left the aircraft he came up to me and told me that an Anson was on its way from Upwood to collect me and that I had to fetch all my kit from the hotel where I was billeted and get back as soon as I could. He had tried to find out more for me and come up against a blank wall – all he could tell me was that I was leaving that day on a special posting to a new unit whose origin was shrouded in secrecy. It all sounded most intriguing – or perhaps ominous might be a better description. Later as I sat in the back of an Anson with my kit piled around me all kinds of awful possibilities kept passing through my mind. Back at Upwood I was told to clear from the OTU within the hour and be ready to fly to Boscombe Down near Amesbury for special duties. At 4 p.m. I was unceremoniously dumped outside the small Watch Office at Boscombe Down and my kit passed to me; the aircraft then took off in haste as if it might get caught up in something if it stayed around. Feeling lonely in the strange surroundings I gathered my kit together and staggered towards the rear of the building where I found a small crowd of people who must have been flown in a few minutes earlier. I knew several of them and paused to greet Roger Reece, Pat Hennessey and Goldsmith and to ask if they knew what all the flap was about. It was clear from their replies that none of them had the faintest idea. A common factor seemed to be that, with the exception of Goldie and myself, all had passed through the Blind Approach Test and Development Unit set up at Boscombe Down under Wing Commander Bobby Blucke shortly before the war.

Flying The Beams

The course at the Blind Approach Development unit on which most of the pilots assembling at Boscombe Down in July 1940 had attended had been to train them to fly on the German Lorenz beam, using it to land in poor visibility in conjunction with the outer and inner marker beacons that formed the full Blind Landing system. The beam transmitter was still in use at Boscombe Down, one of the few places in England to have the installation, so putting two and two together it looked as though we were going to have something to do with beams. More pilots were turning up by the hour including Bobby Sage, Canadian George Grant, Vic Willis and Butch Cundall both ex Cranwell, then Munro Johnny Bull and Harcourt-Powell, all very experienced people. The acting C.O. of this mixed bunch was Hal Bufton and the unit he was forming was to be given the title of: "Wireless Intelligence Development Unit (WIDU)".

Bufton addressed us all later that evening. He was unable to give the full story but he did impress us by saying that the unit was being formed on the direct orders of the Prime Minister himself. The operations we would be engaged on must be cloaked in the utmost secrecy as they would be directed against a German bombing threat that made use of radio beams for guidance to the target in all weather conditions. Our aircraft, Ansons, Whitleys and Wellingtons, were being made available on top priority and would be arriving within hours. On arrival the interiors would be fitted out with racks and special aerials that were necessary to mount and operate big American Hallicrafter S21 and S27 receivers for searching the wavebands. As well as the normal aircraft crews we would carry special operators for this task, most of whom had been selected from dedicated radio 'hams". Because of the chronic shortage of experienced navigators, Goldie and I had been press-ganged to fill gaps in the crews and initially we would fly as navigators, later reverting to piloting as required. At least we now knew the answer to the odd-man-out questions that had been puzzling us.

During the course of the next few days we were made aware to a limited extent of the events that had led to the formation of the W.I.D.U. Dr. R. V. Jones, a young scientist working for Air Intelligence had pieced together German radio signals intercepted by the RAF "Y" service referring to "Knickebein" (Crooked Leg) that he suspected to be a system of blind bombing based on intersecting radio beams. Corroborative proof had been provided by a technical examination of a Heinkel III shot down in the Firth of Forth, and from a prisoner of war. On the strength of this evidence a search aircraft had been sent into the air on 19th and 20th June but had failed to detect a beam. The next day, however, Hal Bufton returned from a search flight flying north from Wyton and reported the existence of two beams in the area.

This final proof resulted in a number of urgent decisions being made. First of all Wing Commander Addison, a Signals specialist, was given the task of forming No. 80 Signals Wing with the full backing and authority of the Prime Minister to be given any personnel and equipment he might need. The Wing was to be set up in a large mansion at Radlett not far from the Handley-Page factory and aerodrome. From here W. Cdr. Addison was to direct and control the day-to-day search for beams. Whenever the searches provided evidence of a particular target his field operators would jam the signals. Telecommunications Research Establishment at Swanage would design the specialised equipment for "jamming" purposes.

From Boscombe Down our newly-formed unit would carry out the airborne search and provide the day-to-day intelligence needed by 80 Signals Wing to enable radio counter measures to be taken. It was hoped that by giving warning of intended German targets it would be possible to pre-position Jammers, and to deploy ARP, Fire and Ambulance services into the target area and perhaps even evacuate people. In some cases it might also be possible to start dummy target fires nearby to attract bombers away from the real target. This was the set up for the early detection and partial frustration of Knickebein, then known only to a few, which was to prove an early and major British victory in the Battle of Britain.

During the next few days the first of our aircraft, mainly Whitleys and Ansons, began to arrive. They then had to be fitted with I.F.F. and special racks with power sources for the radio receivers we were to use. In some instances it was necessary to ferry the aircraft to St Athans or to Christchurch to get the job done quickly and much air testing was required before everything worked satisfactorily.

Dudley Saward, then a Flight Lieutenent, had been posted to the unit from a Flying boat squadron. Having done most of his flying from water and so being out of touch with land-based aircraft, he went off one morning to take a new Whitley to St Athans to be fitted with special equipment. He returned in the Whitley next day and came gaily in to land in the same direction from which he had taken off without bothering to check on the signals square outside the Watch Hut for the direction of landing. The net result was that he landed down wind at a rate of knots, overshot the aerodrome limits and disappeared from view into the open part of the entrance to the bomb dump some fifteen feet down. The aircraft fitted like a glove into the excavation and no one was hurt. The expression on our Engineering Officer's face when confronted with the problem of recovering the aircraft was however, something out of this world!

At the start of the beam finding operations I found myself teamed up and flying as navigator with Bobby Sage, a diminutive but experienced Flight Lieutenant from Doncaster. We got on well together and quickly developed a mutual trust of each other in the air that was so vital in the peculiar circumstances under which we operated the searches. At first the Knickebeins in the 30 megacycles band occupied our full attention, being related to the day battles in the air that had been going on since the second week of July, largely against coastal shipping. Then on 12th August the German attack switched over to our radar stations and aerodromes, leaving us wondering whether Knickebein would soon be used on a large scale for night attacks. In readiness for such a move and to cover the target areas of the Midlands and North West England Bobby Sage I were sent to Wyton with a small detachment of aircraft and crews on 17th August, and from the following night we began beam-finding operations over Eastern England as far north as Spurn Head. There were successive heavy attacks on Liverpool on the last four nights of the month but by then 80 Wing was in a position to bring countermeasures into play in the shape of high powered transmitters designed by T.R.E and coded "Aspirins" to counteract the beams which had been code-named "Headaches". On 7th September 1940 the Luftwaffe concentrated on London and the city was bombed by day and night continuously. The climax of the daylight attacks came on 15th September when both Fighter Command and the Luftwaffe were stretched to their limits. From then on the Germans concentrated on attack by night.

During these first weeks of September, Intelligence sources heard mention of a new X Gerat equipment as distinct from that used to pick up the Knickebeins. This was being fitted to certain Kampf Gruppe aircraft. About the same time new beams operating at 70 megacycles were identified on the Cherburg peninsula and also near Calais and near Brest. On 20th September intercepted German signals specified the settings of certain of these beams to the nearest five seconds of a degree, thus implying an accuracy of something like 10 yards at a distance of 200 miles. However, with the combined information supplied by our airborne searches and signals intelligence, the X-beam set-up was soon pieced together and "Bromides" with which to jam the X-system were quickly devised.

The KG 100 aircraft flew along a beam that was laid directly over the target (usually from the nearest beam station to that target) known as the Director beam, and had to release its bombs at a point a little short of the target to allow for trajectory. The information needed to compute this release point involved the height and speed of the aircraft, the type of bomb used and the distance from the target. This information was obtained in the X Beam system by laying two further beams across the main Director beam so that they crossed it at pre-determined distances before the target. The first of these, the Main Signal crossed five Kms before the target and the other, the Fore Signal at twenty Kms. Thus when the KG 100 pilot flew his aircraft along the Director beam, either listening to the audio signal or watching a directional indicator to keep his position on the beam, his bomb aimer listened on another frequency for the cross beams. The time interval between crossing through the two beams was the time taken to cover the distance of 15 Kms thus giving the speed of the aircraft over the ground; the Main signal also told the pilot that he was 5 Kms from the target. To determine the bomb release point a small mechanical computer involving a stop-clock was started by the bomb aimer on crossing the Fore signal and stopped as he crossed the Main Signal. If the correct height information from the altimeter had been fed in the "bombing clock" mechanism would work out automatically the exact moment of the release of the bomb load.

On 26/27th September a factory in Birmingham was bombed by the use of X beams and by the end of October, KG 100 aircraft were acting as primitive Pathfinders by dropping flares over the night targets for small forces of bomber units. By early November the X beam stations had become so adapt at setting up their beams on British targets that KG 100 aircraft were able to mount attacks on two targets in quick succession on the same night. Using this method attacks were made on Birmingham and Coventry on 4th November, Coventry and Birmingham on the 5th, Liverpool and Birmingham on the 8th and Liverpool and Coventry on 12th November. These activities culminated in the "Moonlight Sonata" blitz on Coventry on the 14th and the "Regenschaum" blitz on Birmingham on the 19th/20th November. Both before and during many of the attacks Bobby Sage and I covered the target areas on our beam investigational flights and were helpless spectators of the bombing.

During this period we lost Goldie who had been with me on the St Athans Navigation Course and, like me, was acting as navigator on our second aircraft. His aircraft hit balloon barrage cables in the Midlands and all the crew were killed. One night I flew with HP (Harcourt-Powell) who was standing in for Bobby Sage. After searching for beams in the Lowestoft area we returned to Wyton to find mist and low cloud and came in to land on the beam. HP must have been a bit off that night for we hit the Chance light with our starboard wing, losing about four or five feet of the mainplane in the process, but it could have been a lot worse. I remember being very impressed by the repair job done by the AVRO representative who came one afternoon carrying his toolkit and a large tin of cold water glue. In a very short time he trimmed off the damaged main spar, spliced on an extension by means of a simple angle joint applied glue to the face and then clamped it in position to allow the glue to harden. By the following afternoon it was set and a loading test carried out by inviting a number of onlookers to hang from the end of the new extension; it passed the test with flying colours much to my astonishment and after some further carpentry the aircraft was passed fully serviceable and was flown the next day.

While I was busily engaged flying by day and night and spending long hours on stand-by for instant take-off for the special investigational flights, problems were arising on the domestic front. Earlier that year my father-in-law, who had only retired a year ago, had been called up from the RAF Reserve for active service — this despite the fact that he was medically unfit, having lost one lung and developed a duodenal ulcer during his previous long service with the Royal Navy, R.N.A.S. and Royal Air Force (he was a founder member of the RAF). Apparently it now seemed that his specialist Signals knowledge and experience was indispensible to the war effort and all objections on medical grounds were brushed aside. Initially he was posted to the Coastal Command Group H.Q. at Mountbatten, Plymouth. But within a matter of weeks he was moved to Squires Gate near Blackpool, now a Coastal station and the place I had left in such a hurry in July. Pamela's younger brother, "Bill" as everyone called him although he was christened John, had also left home. He had volunteered for aircrew training for the RAF straight from school at Peter Symonds, Winchester and on reaching the age minimum had gone to Initial Aircrew Training Wing, Torquay to await pilot training. With only her youngest daughter Fay and Pamela and Denise left at Kingsworthy, Pamela's mother decided to store her furniture and join her husband in Blackpool, taking Fay with her. Pamela and Denise had no option but to leave for Yorkshire to stay with my parents until something could be sorted out. My father, into his sixties, had also volunteered for Naval service but had been turned down by their Lordships, so he turned his energies towards the Local Defence Volunteers, later to be the Home Guard, and in running a Citizens Advice Centre.

It wasn't long, however, before this miserable situation changed for the better. Quite unexpectedly my father-in-law was moved from Squires Gate to North Coates now a fully operational Coastal aerodrome from which Beaufighters attacked German shipping in the North Sea. On arrival to take over as Station Signals Officer he was offered the immediate tenancy of a fully furnished bungalow within a few yards of the Camp gates and my mother-in-law and Fay were able to join him there almost immediately. A few days later he had a second stroke of good fortune when he attended a sale of missing aircrew effects and bought a Morris ten saloon car that was in excellent condition.

In this car a week or so before Christmas he was able to drive over to visit Pamela and Denise at Knottingly and take them back to stay in the bungalow at North Coates over the holiday or until such time as I could get leave from Wyton to join them there.

This took some of the pressure off as Pamela had not been very happy in Yorkshire. While the Germans continued the air blitz I was unable to get leave. I could only keep flying on investigational flights with Bobby Sage, and whenever possible as a pilot, against the day when my navigation skills would no longer be needed. Christmas Day was spent flying, and in the days leading up to the New Year there were rumours of major changes taking place in the Radio Counter Measures organisation back at Boscombe Down leaving us wondering what effects they would have on our small detached unit.

1941 started with enemy beam activity over East Anglia necessitating a number of special flights to be carried out in the Lowestoft area. At the same time a new German threat appeared in the south in the shape of a different form of bombing attack on the Army Camp at Bovingdon. This used new "Y" Gerat equipment in conjunction with a single directional beam operating in the 40 to 50 megacycles wave band. The new type of equipment enabled the pilot to lock on to the beam by using a visual indicator without having to listen to audio signals, the aircraft then being ranged to the target along the single fine beam. Aircraft for KG 26 used this single station beam and ranging system on several bombing raids throughout January.

On 15th January a long awaited weeks leave was at last approved. That morning I took advantage of a practice flight over Lincolnshire to land at North Coates and surprise the family at lunch with the good news before hurrying back to Wyton with the night "stand-by" aircraft.

That night it started to snow heavily and kept up for the next two days. By the time I eventually cleared from Wyton on the 18th and set off on leave in the Ford heading along the Great North road towards Newark, the conditions were appalling and the car was skidding all over the road. Eventually I reached Newark and turned on to the Sleaford road where the going was even worse with the road obscured by deep drifts. As I tried to pick my way along the edge of Cranwell I missed a turn and shot into an eight foot deep snowdrift, almost disappearing from view. I crawled out and climbed on top of the car, cold and miserable. In that position I could be seen if a vehicle came along, but nothing was moving in the white wasteland surrounding me. After some 20 minutes it was getting dusk and I was considering trying to cross the aerodrome to seek sanctuary at the Camp. But then the screened headlights of a heavy lorry appeared. When it stopped it turned out to be from a local brewery and was returning to Sleaford. It was equipped with all the tackle needed to pull the car back on the road and I was soon on my way again in the gathering darkness. Driving slowly and carefully I crawled through Sleaford and Horncastle and started the steep climb over the escarpment. I was now driving in a single track between six foot banks of snow and when the track petered out and I ran into a solid wall of whiteness I knew I was beaten. Before some other unfortunate came up behind me I reversed the car almost blindly and eventually arrived back in the darkened main street of Horncastle. I stopped outside the outline of the biggest building in the street hoping it was a hotel. As I got out of the car a chink of light appeared at a window as the curtain was pulled back, and my mother-in-law's face appeared. I often wonder who was the most surprised at the time! I was soon fixed up with a room and was able to phone Pamela at North Coates where she was alone in the bungalow except for the baby. Then I thawed out in front of the log fire and joined my in-laws in a hot meal in the dining room. It turned out that my father in law had been to a meeting at Cranwell that morning and had taken Bym, his wife, along as far as Sleaford where she had spent the day with some old friends. On the return journey, like me they had found the road impassable, and had returned to Horncastle and booked into the hotel only half an hour or so before me. After a good night's sleep we rose bright and early and set off in a two car convoy, making a long diversion and sticking to major roads on the level. We arrived in time for lunch with a relieved Pamela.

It was great to be together again as a family. In the evenings, after drawing the black-out curtains to shut out the sounds of enemy activities in the nearby Humber area, we tucked Denise in bed and sat around the fire playing cards or listening to the radio, forgetting the war going on outside the door. I wandered into the garden for a breath of fresh air after supper one evening and called the others out to witness a text book attack on Hull, most likely the work of our KG 100 enemies; the whole of the Humber was lit up by parachute flares drifting slowly down with the flash and noise of exploding bombs as bombers found their target. Single attacks by lone aircraft on the aerodrome also took place and one day just before lunch a Heinkel made a low pass towards the camp over the bungalow. Bym was in the garden and took no notice of the approaching aircraft until its guns started firing then she cleared the fence to the safety of a shelter like a two year old. The worst incident occurred one day as we sat down to lunch. A new consignment of magnetic mines, which Beaufighters were laying in large quantities in enemy sea lanes, had been delivered that morning. The Armaments staff were preparing them for the night's operations when the whole lot went up in a tremendous explosion that rocked the house to its foundations. We crawled out from under the dining table where we had all taken shelter, thinking it was an enemy bomber, to hear that most of the armaments staff had been killed in this one accident. It was a sobering experience.

★   ★   ★

All too soon it was time to return to Wyton where changes were in the air. Enemy beam activity was now on a reduced scale and the powers-that-be had decided that we should return to Boscombe Down immediately where the W.I.D.U. was to become No. 109 Squadron under a new C.O., Wing Commander Willie Hebden. "A" Flight was still to be on investigational duties combined with development work under Vic Willis. Hal Bufton was to take over "B" Flight using the Wellingtons to back-track along the "X" beams and bomb the transmitting stations using whatever methods could be devised for the purpose. Back at Boscombe I was allocated a ground floor room in one of the old brick O.M.Q.s, quite a long way from the Mess. The sole heating was from a small open grate fire with a two hour ration of coal that barely took the chill away before it ran out. In the Officers Mess itself the service was still of a peace-time standard as the mess staff were nearly all of long standing civilian status. They were getting on in years but endeavoured to give excellent service to the A&AEE officers including interlopers like us who interfered with the routine by flying at night. Afternoon tea was still served as a ritual with an individual choice of a small pot of China or Ceylon tea with toast and an assortment of pastes and jams, this after eighteen months at war. The Commandant still hankered after his Sunday morning sherry parties and dining-in nights. Unfortunately two New Zealanders belonging to our Squadron helped themselves to the Commandant's special bottle of claret that had been set out on the table opened "to breathe" prior to one of the dining-in nights and emptied it in record time. The incident did not make us popular.

I reported to the Squadron offices at the back of the old Watch Hut at Boscombe to join Vic Willis and sort out my new duties. One familiar face was missing, that of Flying Officer Munro who had acted as Adjutant when the W.I.D.U. was formed six months earlier. Returning from an investigational flight at night in thick fog his aircraft had crashed killing all on board – a sad end to a flying career spanning many years.

The need for using me as a navigator had now ended. With the influx of trained navigators to make up the Wellington crews and I was now able to go ahead and form my own crew, working them up to operational efficiency for what lay ahead.

"Duggie" Morrison became my navigator, "Gerry" Hoey, Wireless/Operator and Sewell and Sandifer the two gunners. Special set operators were in short supply so I had to take whoever was available. The crew were all newly promoted aircrew Sergeants, Duggie was a Scot, Gerry an Irishman, Sewell a fellow Yorkshireman while Sandifer, who sported the Auxiliary Air Force Efficiency Medal on his tunic, who came from Essex. After a few trips together in the Wellingtons, Whitleys and Ansons we quickly came together as a team in the air and acquired a mutual trust in each others abilities.

We were still being called upon for some investigational beam flights by H.Q. 80 Wing but by the beginning of March 1941 the indications were that the battle of the beams was as good as won. Although some bombing had to be endured, the three main beam systems on which the Luftwaffe had relied for their bombing offensive, Knickebein, and the X and Y Gerats had been defeated by our search and counter-measures operations. With the last major raids in April and May the German Air Force was not only experiencing difficulties in locating their targets, but were also beginning to encounter losses on a large scale. However the general situation was still grim as the easier targets of the major ports were still being heavily attacked and an invasion in the summer still seemed a possibility.

Meantime further investigational flights had to be made into the operation of the recently installed German radars used for the defence of the homeland – the Freyas and the Wurzburgs – so that the counter-measures could be developed to assist our bombers.

Up to now Bomber Command had always maintained that the use of astro-navigation and radio beacons together with dead reckoning was adequate to reach the target. By the summer of 1941 however, enough evidence was available from photographs of bomb release points to prove that only one tenth of our bombers came within five miles of their target. A drive was at last started to develop radio navigational techniques, and as most ideas were to germinate at T.R.E. it was obvious that our aircraft should be used for whatever development and testing was needed in the air.

The first of the new radio-navigational aids to be developed was the idea of R. J. Dippy at T.R.E. and was soon to become available. The system involved sending out synchronised pulses from three transmitting stations in Britain. From the differences in the times of arrival of the three pulses received by an aircraft, the navigator could plot his position on a lattice chart.

Next came "OBOE" a method of using pulses to determine distances from two transmitting stations and to measure the range of an aircraft. A. H. Reeves and F. E. Jones of T.R.E. with some assistance from Blanchard of the Post Office Engineering Department were working on two versions at centimetric wave lengths. Because of the curvature of the earth, the range of the system was limited by the operational height of the aircraft being used. To extend the range to be able to use the system against the furthest German targets, it was proposed to use repeater aircraft, and Wellington VIs with pressurised cockpits capable of operating at then extreme heights were on order from Vickers. In the event the high flying Mosquito superseded the Wellington. The OBOE was eventually developed to be the most accurate radio bombing system produced in the war. George Baillie was also working on the narrow directional "Jay" beam system that was to prove useful in many future operations and would be a help to returning bombers. Meanwhile the Wellingtons in Hal Buftons Flight kept up the good work of harrying the X beam operations staff by laying sticks of bombs along the beams in the transmitter areas and achieving some success.

With all these activities going on there seemed little chance of being moved away from Boscombe Down at least for some months. However, restrictions on being on the Camp every night were being lifted and limited petrol on coupons was becoming available more readily where there was little public transport. Salisbury, some fifteen miles away, offered the best chances of finding rented accommodation for Pamela and Denise, but the whole area of Salisbury Plain for twenty miles around was crawling with Army Units and nothing vacant was advertised. Undaunted, however, I

140

drove to the outskirts of Salisbury one evening, parked the car near the remains of Old Sarum castle and worked along the larger houses bordering the main road asking if anyone knew of accomodation available. Eventually the approach paid off and I was asked indoors for a cup of tea and a chat by the man of the house. He was obviously trying to help and, after some discussion as to how things might be worked if we came to live there and share the kitchen and other facilities, he agreed to have us, and we fixed a date on which to move in.

Pamela and Denise travelled down by train a few days later but we only stayed at the house for a couple of weeks or so as sharing facilities proved difficult, but it did help us to get a foothold in the area and we soon heard of a place nearer to the city centre. The house had a small garden and was in a quiet backwater. It belonged to a widow whose two sons had been called up and who was out at work all day so we virtually had the place to ourselves. We moved in immediately and quickly arrived at a routine that suited everybody. Meandering through the hamlets around the outskirts of the town one afternoon we established contact with a farm in the village where A. G. Street, the Wiltshire author of farming repute lived, and from then on there was no shortage of fresh farm eggs for us. Our stay lasted out the end of the year, and in the garden that summer Denise started to walk, first by hanging onto and pushing a tubular chair on wheels to get the idea, and then in no time at all she was a sturdy young miss running around on long legs.

By the start of November 1941 changes were once again in the offing and "Willie" Hebden was replaced by Wg.Cdr. MacMullen, another Signals Specialist. Boscombe Down was even more crowded by now as new types of aircraft flowed in for evaluation and moves were afoot to change the Squadron by splitting it into specialist Flights and moving them to other locations around the area. Hurn, a new airfield being constructed in the New Forest, was having its runways and hard standings completed and I was sent there with a Wellington for a couple of nights to assess the operational possibilities. The whole area was a sea of frozen mud. The Nissen hut offered as sleeping accommodation had no heating or lighting other than a single hurricane lamp, and I was lucky to get away without double penumonia. I arrived back at the house in Salisbury to find Pamela *hors de combat* in bed with a bad knee and no one to help her or look after Denise. It was fortunate that I had got back so quickly and was able to look after them for a while, particularly as within the next forty-eight hours I would be fully occupied with Operation TRINITY against Brest.

★　　　★　　　★

Throughout the year the Admiralty had made strong pleas for bomber squadrons to be used against U-boat bases and especially against the German capital ships based on Brest; *Scharnhorst*, *Gneisenau* and *Prinz Eugen*. On nights when weather conditions permitted, bombers attacked these major targets. Broadly speaking ten sorties were made against Brest to each attack on the U-boat pens being constructed along the Atlantic coast of France, the priority being dictated by their Lordships at the Admiralty.

So far most of these attacks had been made by the ageing Whitleys and Wellingtons dropping smallish bombs of 1000 lbs and less from heights of around 10,000 feet, with little effect against the heavily armoured decks of the ships. Even when new aircraft started to come into service in the middle of the year they had proved a great disappointment. The twin engined Manchesters with the Rolls Royce Vulture engines proved unreliable on early operations and had to be withdrawn and the aircraft re-designed as the Lancaster. The four engined Stirling, dated already, was capable of carrying a heavy bombload but could not accept the 4000 lbs H.C. bombs in its long and narrow bomb cells. It was thus limited to the less effective 2000 lbs bomb. The four engined Halifax when first introduced needed modification in many respects to improve its performance. A number of them were lost over the target area not through enemy action but due to loss of control when making a diving turn out of the area. The fault was remedied by increasing the rudder surfaces by one third.

The intention now was to have a real crack at Brest with Stirling carrying 5 × 2000 lb Armour Piercing Bombs. They would be guided to the target using the Baillie beam and OBOE, with modified IFF sets in the aircraft, for measuring range. The decision made preparations were soon under way. George Baillie set up his beam array on a suitable site at Predannock in Cornwall aligning the fine beam over the ships in the docks. On the 8th November 1941 I flew F. E. Jones and Blanchard of the OBOE development team to RAF Oakington where a start was made on installing modified IFF sets (coded BROOD HENS) in Stirlings of No 7 Squadron then commanded by Wing Commander Bobby Graham. These sets were to supply the signals required by the Oboe ground stations for ranging purposes. Similar installations were also carried out in Stirlings of No. 15 Squadron based at RAF Wyton.

As only one aircraft at a time could be handled by the OBOE team time and spacing on the beam was of the utmost importance. Accurate flying along the beam maintaining set height and airspeed was vital on the run-up to the target. To ensure this our experienced beam pilots would be included in the crews and would take over control and fly the aircraft during the final stages of the attack.

On 12th November I spent 45 minutes in the air at the controls of a Stirling. Then, on 15th I took part in a simulated operation designed to practice all but the final stages of the attack. Unfortunately we were unable to pick up the special frequency beam due to technical trouble at Predannock and had a wasted journey. On returning to base at Wyton we found that the operation was postponed until the following month, and we were sent back to Boscombe Down. A few days later I made an investigational flight to bring our knowledge of the German radar defences on the Brest peninsula up to date, taking a Wellington to St Eval and making the night trip from there and returning to base next morning.

Three weeks later Operation TRINITY was mounted once again and on 21st December all the 109 Squadron pilots taking part were ferried by Anson to Oakington and Wyton. Neither station had any accommodation for us as the influx of new aircrew to make up the full complement of the Stirlings had left the messes bursting at the seams and we were accommodated at St Ives hotel for the duration of the operations. After the Japanese attack on Pearl Harbour followed by the sinking of *Repulse* and *Prince of Wales* on 10th December we could hardly wait to have a go at the German ships. Much to our delight no further practices were to be carried out and the first attacks were to be made the following night as planned. Next day my name appeared on the 15 Squadron battle order flying with the young Pilot Officer Deville and his crew, recently joined from the Heavy Conversion Unit at Waterbeach. We took off in daylight climbing laboriously with our 10,000 lbs bomb load to operational height and headed for Predannock, with nothing more than an occasional adjustment to the exactor controls to keep the engine revolutions in phase. Shortly before reaching the target area I changed seats with Deville and tuned in to the Baillie beam frequency easing the aircraft to port and then starboard through the beam to get an idea of the width before settling down to fly along the beam itself. Right on time approaching the northern coast of the Brest peninsula the OBOE ground station ranged our position from our I.F.F. transmission. We approached the target with bomb doors open heading into a welter of searchlights. Flak filled the sky all around with greasy black puffs and the smell of cordite penetrated the aircraft with the occasional tinkle as we flew into or were hit by pieces of shrapnel. Concentrating on maintaining airspeed and height in the beam I felt the aircraft lurch upwards as the stick of five tons of bombs was released on the OBOE signal. I allowed time for a photo to be taken on the heading before closing the bomb doors and making a diving turn out of the area, where I changed seats with Deville and settled down for the trip home. On arrival in Wyton we ran into low cloud and heavy rain and were diverted to nearby Alconbury where we "crabbed" along the runway in a strong crosswind to a safe landing and were transported back to Wyton for de-briefing. Next morning operations in the Brest area were cancelled early because of weather.

Before leaving Salisbury I had arranged that Pamela and Denise would travel by train to join her mother and father at North Coates for Christmas where I would try to join them if possible. I checked the times of trains in the Orderly Room Bradshaw and found that if I could get to Peterborough station by three p.m. I would be able to meet them on the incoming train and see them off on the last stage of their journey, a nice surprise. An Anson was available at Wyton for ferrying purposes in connection with TRINITY and I persuaded Fernbank to drop me off on Peterboro' aerodrome after lunch and wait there until I returned around 3.30 p.m. It worked like a charm and really surprised the family. The following day, Christmas Eve, operations were again postponed until the night of the 27th and I was given leave of absence until the morning of the 26th; one of the Ansons had to pick up some spares from Scampton in the afternoon so I got the Aussie pilot to drop me at North Coates. Fernbank agreed to pick me up again on the morning of Boxing Day so I was able to spend most of Christmas with the family away from all thoughts of war and felt much better for it.

Back at Wyton again, the weather conditions forecast over Brest on the night of the 27th were good and once again Deville and I were on the battle order flying in the same aircraft; approaching the Brest peninsula it was quite obvious that the Germans had redeployed guns and searchlights in depth along the track. We were flying in on the beam and as soon as we crossed the coast were met by a heavy box barrage of AA fire, and had to fly through it all the way to the target to the usual accompaniment of shrapnel tinkling against the metal skin of the aircraft as it hit or was hit by them. I was happy to feel the upward lurch of the Stirling as we parted company with our lethal load and were able to get the hell out of the area and head for a more friendly shore.

The weather over the next two days precluded further operations; and on the last day of 1941 operations were cancelled at mid-day. I asked if I could take on a ferry trip in one of the Ansons to Boscombe Down returning to Oakington and then take it on to North Coates where Pamela and Denise were still staying and return the following morning. Permission was given and once again I surprised the family by walking through the door in time for tea without any warning, and being able to stay over New Year's Eve.

The following morning the North Coates weather was living up to its reputation with thick clammy coastal fog blotting everything from view and visibility zero. I checked with Wyton who assured me that the beam there was working and the weather improving slowly; the only snag was that the C.O. at North Coates would not let me take-off until mid-morning. I landed on the beam at Wyton in poor visibility, the only aircraft in the air that morning, to find that my efforts were all in vain. The night's operations had already been cancelled.

Next day the weather improved and again I joined Deville's crew on the battle order for TRINITY operations and a late afternoon take-off. Over the target area the barrage of flak and the searchlights were worse than ever and we completed the final run in held by a cone of lights and expecting a fighter attack. We escaped from the area having suffered only minor flak damage from shrapnel and enjoyed the run back to Wyton, landing in time for a beer before the bar closed in the mess.

Operations were on again the following night but this time I was sent over to Oakington to be crewed up with a Pilot Officer Pilling. By the time we had been briefed and ferried out to the aircraft it looked as though we had trouble on our hands as the ground crew were still working on one of the engines. Time was of the essence as if we failed to arrive in the beam during the OBOE ranging period allocated to our aircraft our sortie would be cancelled. At that moment we had 20 minutes grace which by juggling the speed and cutting corners could be extended to 30; we entered the aircraft and took up crew positions and sat waiting for the thumbs up from the ground crew clustered around to the No. 3 engine as the minutes ticked by. When this came after a further 15 minutes of nail-biting, Pilling started the engines so quickly that the airmen on the wing were almost blown off by the slip-stream. Waving away the wheel chocks he taxied the aircraft at speed along the peri-track towards the take-off holding point for the main runway running through the take-off cockpit checks with the Flight engineer as he went along. The runway controller in the caravan flashed a green and without more ado Pilling lined the Stirling up on the runway, opened the throttles fully, and we began the laborious business of gathering speed with a heavily loaded and under-powered aircraft.

Unlike the three previous take-offs this one appeared extremely sluggish to me and as the end of the runway came into view and we were committed to taking off without having reached unstick speed, I suddenly realised why. Pilling had switched the flaps

146

control to down intending to put on the normal one third to assist take-off, but in his haste had failed to stop them in the one third position, and the flaps were now fully down and could not be retracted until the aircraft reached a safe height. I yelled a warning to Pilling on the intercom not to touch the flaps as he operated the boost override and the extra surge of power for emergency use got us a few feet into the air, enabling the engineer to start raising the huge wheels and reduce some drag. By now the cylinder heads were all but glowing and the temperature gauges off the clock as we ploughed on below two hundred feet on the verge of stalling. Eventually we were able to take off a degree or so of flap at a time and to build up a little more speed and height all the time praying that the engines would take it. After a hectic few minutes we achieved a safe height with the flaps fully up and the engines settling down to normal cruising conditions. Pilling, however, called up control and aborted the sortie and we were instructed to jettison our load safely and return to base. Somewhere in the shallow depths of the Wash those five monsters must still be rusting to this day.

That proved to be the final night's operation on TRINITY and all our beam pilots returned to Boscombe Down the next day. I never saw the P.R. photos of Brest afterwards but I understand that our beam bombing proved a qualified success. I like to think that the dash up the Channel under low cloud cover by the three ships that took place on 11th and 12th February was a direct result of our efforts. The great pity is that having been holed up for a year or so in Brest, events combined to take us by surprise when they finally came out and a great opportunity was thrown away.

More changes were in the air during the first weeks of 1942. New ideas for promoting the radio counter-measures war and using our limited resources to the best advantage were bandied around, and both Tempsford and Hinton-in-the-Hedges began to figure in some aspects of our development flying. Our days at Boscombe Down were clearly numbered.

Towards the end of February a separate unit to be known as

No 1473 Radio Counter Measures Flight was formed to be commanded by George Grant with the rank of Squadron Leader. Both Roger Reece and myself, now Flight Lieutenants, were to be in the unit which would operate under the direct control of No 80 Wing at Radlett and would initially be based as a lodger unit on the Wellington OTU at Upper Heyford, where suitable facilities would be provided until a more permanent home could be found. We were to move out of Boscombe Down the first week in March so once again I had to face the problem of moving Pamela and Denise, this time to Yorkshire, until I could look for accommodation in the Heyford area. Two factors helped to make the move bearable. Firstly, relations with our landlady were becoming more and more strained. Secondly, as a result of an accident on an icy road the Ford was barely roadworthy; also petrol was becoming impossible to get hold of in the area. Having seen my family off from Salisbury and returned to Boscombe Down to play my part in the move to Upper Heyford, I was faced with leaving the car behind or accepting its scrap value from one of the A&AEE officers. I chose to take up the offer at the eleventh hour.

By 8th March after much to-ing and fro-ing we had moved our complement of aircraft to Upper Heyford and set up 1473 Flight offices in wooden buildings erected for us in the dispersal area, well away from the main hangars and lecture rooms of the Wellington O.T.U. Station Commander Group Captain Sheene, and the Chief Flying Instructor "Drain" Lowe, were most co-operative. The last time I had seen "Drain" was just before the outbreak of war when he was celebrating the move of 49 Squadron from Worthy Down and had ended up driving his little MG Midget through a plate glass window in Winchester High Street.

As we settled into the everyday routine of the station and began to mix with the O.T.U. staff I had the most amazing piece of good fortune. I was chatting to a Squadron Leader who had just received notification that he was being sent to the United States on a P.R. tour within days. Before the war he had been an architect living with his wife in a modern flat in Central London but they had been bombed out in the Blitz. Looking around the Heyford area for a safe place for his wife and the remains of his furniture, he had stumbled on a pair of old Cotswold stone farm cottages long disused and only a couple of miles from the aerodrome, and he had promptly rented the best one from the farm owners for a matter of a few shillings a week. Using local handymen, he managed to get the cottage into habitable shape within days and moved in with his wife and furniture. Now, with his imminent posting to America, his wife had decided to stay with relatives until he returned and he was looking for someone who would live in his cottage and look after it for the time being.

This was an opportunity not to be missed and I immediately volunteered, subject to seeing the cottage and assessing its suitability. That evening he drove me over, showing me a farm *en route* where fresh milk and eggs could be obtained. Entering it was like stepping inside a West End flat, most of the furnishings being of a tubular chromium steel nature and very modern. There were snags. Lighting was provided by oil lamps and candles, heating and cooking was by a small coal fuelled range supplemented by an oil-lamp-type oven used in caravans, and water had to be fetched in buckets from a stand pipe 50 yards away with all hot water boiled in pans or kettles on the coal range. Against these obvious disadvantages were many good points; the cottage looked warm and cosy, it was within easy cycling distance of the aerodrome, it was going to cost very little and with summer coming along it should be pleasant living the rural life. So without more ado I agreed to take over on the basis that I would have my family live there and pay the rent (a matter of seven shillings a week) and any small running expenses subject to my staying at Heyford. If I was moved before he returned from the U.S.A. I undertook to lock up the cottage and hand the keys for safe keeping to the farm owners. With that we shook hands and returned to Heyford for dinner in the Mess; as events turned out I never met him again afterwards.

A week later on a ferrying trip to Ringway I took along a second pilot who dropped me off overnight at Snaith, where I hitched a lift home to join Pamela and Denise for a few hours and detail the arrangements I had made for them to travel to Oxford where I would have a car to take them the last few miles to the cottage. Everything went as planned and by the end of March they were settled in and enjoying a rural existence in the Oxfordshire countryside as if they had been born to it.

★　　　★　　　★

By now at Upper Heyford 1473 Flight had implemented satisfactory stand-by arrangements and agreed procedures for priority take-off day or night at short notice from their dispersal area, without interfering with the day to day work of the O.T.U. Through the agency of a small Operations and Intelligence Room set up under a newly-appointed Intelligence Officer with a direct telephone link to H.Q. 80 Wing at Radlett, we were able to maintain day and night standby crews who could be airborne within minutes in the event of enemy beam action; the crews could only stand down on the authority of 80 Wing. Other crews carried on with development flying of new jamming aids for Bomber Command and special investigational flights against German radar. When on 23rd April the German Air Force started the "Baedeker" raids using KG 100 aircraft to lead small bomber forces against Exeter, Bath, Norwich, York and Cowes, we were ready for them. The raids fizzled out by the 4th May, never to be repeated.

On 22nd February Air Marshal Harris had taken over Bomber Command, pledged to operate a much more aggressive bombing policy than hitherto. It came as no surprise then that the Baedekar raids were replied to by the first 1000 bomber raid against Cologne on 30th May 1942. To achieve the required number of aircraft Harris had to draw on training aircraft and crews from the OTUs and several aircraft from Upper Heyford took part. We unsuccessfully appealed to 80 Wing to include our Wellingtons but were refused on the grounds of security. I shall always remember my frustration, watching the OTU aircraft taking off for Cologne that evening on the first large scale operation against Germany and wishing like hell that I was among them. Nevertheless I was kept very busy, leaving the cottage early each morning on the heavy service push-bike come rain or shine to put in a full day's flying or a long stand-by period. In the meantime Pamela and Denise led an isolated existence. Milk and water had to be collected from the main farmhouse each morning a few hundred yards away. Shopping meant a long foot-slog either to the next farm half-way to Steeple Aston Village where they could get eggs and cream and were always welcome, or to the village shop armed with ration books to obtain the weekly rations. But they were both thriving on the fresh air, exercise and good food. Five elderly and unmarried brothers and sisters lived in the huge three-storey building. They ran the farm and most of the other businesses in the area, such as the coal merchants and the corn chandlers, like a Mafia family. On our arrival we were regaled with tumbler-sized pourings of cowslip and parsnip home-brewed wines brought up from the cellars deep below where they must have been increasing in potency over many years; we only just made it back to the cottage afterwards.

★　　★　　★

It had always been a condition of 1473 Flight's stay at Upper Heyford that we would move out as soon as a more permanent operational base could be made available in the area. However, after some eight months of flying from the O.T.U., the unit had adapted to the routine and become well-established in its little corner of the airfield, and thoughts of a move away had receded into the background. So it came as something of a shock when towards the end of November we learned that a new home had been found for us nearby. We were to move to Finmere, a new satellite airfield being built for the Blenheim and Mosquito O.T.U. currently based at Bicester. Bicester, a pre-war grass aerodrome, was too small to be laid with hard runways for the Mosquito aircraft now replacing the Blenheims, and the runways at Finmere were already being used for Mosquito conversion. Our new base was a matter of 15 miles from Upper Heyford and alongside the main Bicester-Buckingham road, near the village of Tingewick.

Once again I was faced with the dreaded wartime problem of finding a new home for my family, for there was no way they could carry on living in the isolated farm cottage on their own once I had moved. Even if I did manage to get over from Finmere on occasions it would mean a 30 mile round trip under dark wintry conditions on the heavy service bicycle. A move closer to Finmere was necessary, with a return to Yorkshire as a last resort if all else failed.

I had a word with our unit Adjutant, Flying Officer Frazer-James, who had been a solicitor in civilian life and knew the area well from his school-days when he had been a boarder at nearby Stowe Public school. He too had family problems arising from friction with his in-laws at Torquay, where his wife and young baby were living, and needed to find accommodation for them in the Finmere area; so when he went to the new airfield to earmark accommodation for the unit he made a preliminary recce of the surrounding area returning late that evening in happy mood. He had found wonderful accommodation for both our families in a large country house only a mile from the perimeter of the airfield. The address was Finmere Warren and it was owned by Vere Gosling who came from a well connected county family; his brother, Major Gosling was the MFH of the Bicester Hunt and lived not far away in the family home. Vere's wife was apparently happy to have people live in parts of the rambling old farmhouse as her small contribution to the war effort. Besides that, Vere was still running a Ford V. 8 shooting brake on petrol obtained on the grounds of farm business, although he had let the farm acreage and other buildings to a local farmer. He had volunteered to fetch us and our belongings to the Warren as soon as Mrs Gosling had made our rooms ready.

This was fantastic news coming just at the right moment, for the next day the move of the Flight started and we were kept busy shuttling our ground personnel, equipment and serviceable aircraft over to their new quarters at Finmere while still maintaining our standby's at readiness. It was a week before the move was completed and during that period I cycled the 15 miles from Finmere to the cottage in the dark after being stood down, returning in the dark before dawn to a full flying day. In that week I developed leg muscles like a champion athlete and a hatred of all service bicycles from then on. It came as a relief when we heard from Mrs Gosling that our accommodation had been sorted out at the Warren and that Vere would pick us up in the shooting brake the following afternoon and deliver us there in time for tea. The following grey and miserable November afternoon we sat in the

152

cold cottage, having let the fire die down, with our few belongings piled around us waiting for the car and feeling like refugees facing the unknown. Right on schedule across the huge field between the cottage and the main road came the shooting brake, meandering slowly and scattering the sheep in its path, and out stepped a tall angular man with an old trilby on the back of his head who introduced himself as Vere. All our bits and pieces loaded, we locked the cottage door and handed the key in at the farm, then took our seats in the brake and were off. The 30 minute drive to our destination was made mostly in silence, each of us busy with our own thoughts as to how our "blind" move was going to turn out. The car turned off the road and approached the house along a drive flanked by over-hanging chestnut trees, finally coming to a stop at the rear of the building. There we were greeted by a chorus of barks from three small dogs and warmly welcomed by Vere's wife. I felt that all was going to be well, and so it turned out.

In a remarkably short space of time, routines had been worked out and adapted to suit the three families now living at the Warren and we had made friends with the three dogs, Gussie the Sealyham, Gretel the long-haired Dachshund and the Corgi bitch who loved nothing better than to be taken out shooting around the farm fields. To watch the three of them trying to chase a rabbit or hare across the furrows of a ploughed field and hitting every furrow top with their long bodies and short legs and enjoying every minute was a scream; they never succeeded in catching anything, needless to say. On those dark winter mornings Frazer-James, F.J. for short, and I would cycle to the perimeter fence of the airfield about a mile away where a well disguised entry/exit gap gave us access to the taxi-track, enabling us to complete our journey to the Flight Offices within the airfield boundary. There was little beam activity although we still maintained standby crews. There was, however, plenty of development flying to be done on the other projects. One of these was the fitting out of a Whitley V as a prefabricated signals communication and homing ground station. It was to be used in the Italy campaign, the idea being to crash land it near to the front line and for it to be fully operational within a short space of time for use by our tactical aircraft. Several trials of the equipment were made on the deserted airfield at Bradwell Bay and the idea proved a great success when later used operationally.

At the beginning of September orders were received to move 1473 Flight to Feltwell. A new group was to be formed and known as No 100 (Bomber Support) Group under the current C.O. or 80 Signals Wing Group Captain E. B. Addison, who would be promoted to Air Commodore. To it would be posted the radio countermeasures squadrons and several Mosquito fighter squadrons, a tactical development that was to enable Bomber Command to directly control the Intruder and Serrate effort in the forthcoming Battle of Berlin.

Hard on the heels of the news of the move I was informed by "P" Staff that a suitable replacement for me had at last turned up, Flight Lieutenant Moore DFC, a veteran of the North African desert campaign and an experienced Wellington pilot. Now on leave he would be taking over the unit after the move to Feltwell was completed and would join us there for the hand-over. After that I and the four other members of my volunteer crew would be released to join the Pathfinder Force. I passed this information to Hamish Mahaddie at 8 Group who agreed to initiate the postings on the first day of October. All crews joining PFF were obliged to attend a week-long course at the N.T.U. Upwood to be brought up to date with the latest Pathfinder navigational techniques, and before joining a squadron, and my crew would be no exception to the rule and would report there initially.

The Movement Order covering the move to Feltwell over the period 12th to 14th September was quickly produced with everyone in the unit working flat out to ensure maximum serviceability of equipment and aircraft overall, while maintaining standby aircraft and crews at readiness right up to the moment of departure. Also at short notice came strong representations from all sections to hold a farewell party and dance locally to repay in some small way the friendliness and hospitality shown to the members of 1473 Flight over their year-long stay in the district. Fraser James the Adjutant was happy to take on the arrangements, and was the best man for the job having enjoyed more hospitality than most and knowing the area well from his schooldays. The main public rooms in Buckingham's Town Hall were booked for our last Saturday night at Finmere and arrangements for a drinks licence and bar made. Service Transport was laid on and a good band booked from nearby RAF Bicester. Everything that could be adapted for use as decoration was pressed into service. Particularly successful was an endless supply of large teazles found in a nearby field; sprayed with different coloured paints they were ideal decoration for a large hall. The technicians from the Electrical section also came up trumps with a huge "head" setpiece with flashing eyes overlooking the proceedings which would add to the gaiety of the occasion.

Much of my time during the early part of the month was taken up "toing" and "froing" between Finmere-80 Wing, Radlett-Hinton-in-the-Hedges and Feltwell, attending to the many problems occasioned by the move and for these journeys the tiny Leopard Moth was invaluable as a time saver. There was also a further problem on the domestic front, for the Goslings now announced their intention of selling Finmere Warren and moving to the edge of Dartmoor near Chagford in the West Country. It was fortunate for us that the Reverend Armstrong, the ageing Vicar of Finmere who lived alone with his snuffling Pekingese in the rambling Victorian Rectory adjacent to the Church came to the rescue, and Pamela and Denise moved into part of the huge building soon after the unit moved to Feltwell and shortly before the Goslings departed for pastures new on Dartmoor.

The farewell party in the Buckingham Town Hall was duly held on the Saturday night preceding the start of the exodus to Feltwell and proved an unqualified success. Invitations were sent to all the local dignitories the only refusal was from the Head of the Buckingham Police. He had a reputation locally for his surly manner and uncooperative approach towards any form of entertainment or function being held within the confines of the town where a licensed bar was permitted. Thus, it came as no great surprise to me, when half-way through the evening when everyone was enjoying themselves and making the most of a few hours away from their Nissen huts at Finmere, I received a message that the Chief of Police was downstairs and that he would like to have a word with me.

Excusing myself from the guests I was with I went downstairs to the entrance hall and made myself known to the senior of a small group of police officers standing there. He immediately launched into a series of compaints about the noise from the band, the fact that several couples were sitting with drinks on the staircase and he wanted to know who would take care of any misbehaviour breaches of the peace that might occur through the effects of drink when the party ended. I replied that in my opinion there were no grounds for anyone to complain about noise or behaviour and that as soon as the party ended, service transport would arrive and all the unit personnel would be checked on board by SNCOs and leave immediately for Finmere. He appeared to accept my assurances and refusing my invitation to look in on the festivities upstairs departed with his henchmen, leaving me to rejoin my party. There were no further interruptions during the rest of the evening. At midnight the band stopped playing and departed, all our people were shepherded on to the now waiting transports and returned to camp, and the Town Hall was handed over to the waiting Mrs. Mopps who were to clean and polish and generally restore the areas that had been in use to their usual pristine condition. At that stage the remaining officers and SNCOs departed, having voted the party a huge success, to get on with their job of winning the war against Hitler.

The move to Feltwell started on 12th September 1942 and was completed on the 14th, it falling to my lot to ferry the two Halifaxes and a couple of Ansons over in between supervising the rest of the personnel settling into their new accommodation and keeping standby crews and aircraft on call as required by 80 Wing Operations. Flight Lieutenant Moore had arrived at Feltwell by now and until the last day of the month I spent all my time and energy on handing over the unit to him and briefing him as well as possible on what would be expected of him by the operations staff

(Editor's note: Joe Northrop was awarded the Air Force Cross in recognition of his contribution of the Battle of the Beams).

at Wing Headquarters. Finally I flew him to Radlett in the Leopard Moth to see Group Captain Addison and formally handed over command of No 1473 Flight to Moore.

Joe and his Halifax crew 1943

Pathfinder

Joe's manuscript covering his time in No 83 Squadron of the Path Finder Force is not continuous, possibly because of the enormouse strain he was under at the time. The story is, however, held together by his flying log book, some pages of which are reproduced. They tell of nine months intensive flying in the course of which he took part in raids on nine different German targets and visited the hardest nut of all, Berlin, no less than eight times. The remainder of this chapter is largely Joe's own words, drawn from a number of sources and held together by the minimum of continuity provided by the editor.

As arranged with 'Hamish' Mahaddie, posting for myself and the four volunteers who were going with me had now arrived. After first attending a week-long course at the Navigational Training Unit (NTU) at Upwood we would be joining No 83 Squadron at nearby Wyton to become operational as a crew on Lancasters. On the last day of September I borrowed an Anson from my old unit and flew the short distance to Upwood taking with me Charles Burdett, Ron Foster, Ronnie Weston and Gerry Hoey as the nucleus of my crew. On arrival at Wyton I would be able to recruit a Flight Engineer and additional gunner to complete the crew and to get in a few hours flying together on a spare aircraft until considered fully operational on Lancasters. The only other option would have been to spend up to three months passing through a Heavy Conversion Unit from scratch in order to achieve the same objective. The short training course at the NTU proved extremely useful. The first three days we carried out dry runs as a crew practicing the latest Pathfinder techniques for navigation, timing and target marking. These methods were then put into practice in the air during three specially designed cross country exercises during which I was able to familiarise myself with the Lancaster cockpit.

On 10th October, having completed the course, we left Upwood and travelled the few miles to Wyton where accommodation had been reserved for us. In the Squadron Office I was welcomed with outstreched hand by 'Honest John' Searby who, like myself, had started his RAF career as a Halton apprentice in 1929 with the 19th Entry. I had last seen John at Worthy Down in 1937 when he flew in for a fleeting visit from Hucknall in a Hawker biplane. After passing through Navigation School he had been commissioned early in 1940 and had attended the Astro-Navigation Course at St Athans. John had then been sent to Canada for the Specialist Navigation Course while I had ended up on special duties investigating the German beam systems of bombing.

One of the attacks listed in Joe's log book was the infamous 'Black Thursday' raid on the night of the 16/17 December 1943. This was carried out in bad weather conditions to give protection from the German fighters. In this it was successful although 25 Lancasters were lost to anti-aircraft fire. The price of this 'success' was that 30 Lancasters were lost in crashes in the UK on return. Joe's aircraft, "F, for Freddie", was very nearly numbered among these. In a post war contribution to a book about the Lancaster Joe recorded how on return: –

We had a fair amount of fuel in reserve and I planned to start my approach on SBA well above the fog layer, the top of which was around 1,200 ft. Then, with all cockpit checks done apart from final flap, I would be able to concentrate on flying the aircraft accurately on a straight approach and let down. The stack of aircraft dwindled slowly until I was No 1 to land. At this time Control warned me to watch out for an unidentified aircraft in the circuit attempting to land visually. I acknowledged and alerted the crew to keep their eyes peeled as I flew the aircraft well out from the outer marker beacon, carrying out landing checks on the way and started a procedure turn to bring the aircraft on a straight approach to the main runway. When lined up in the center of the

Pathfinder Training Group at Warboys
(Joe seated 4th from left)

beam I let down the aircraft into the rather turbulent layer of fog and mist at a constant rate of descent until the altimeter read 600 ft: at which stage I applied power to maintain height until the outer marker signal was heard. I then continued to descend keeping in the centre of the beam and listening for the inner marker signal. At this moment with the altimeter showing around 200 ft, we received the full impact of the slip stream of another aircraft which suddenly crossed our path from the port side in a steep turn, its port wingtip almost scraping the mid upper turret and nearly causing the gunner to throw a fit. Our aircraft plunged madly and lost height (we found afterwards that it had actually ploughed through the upper branches of some trees) and I slammed the throttles fully open to emergency boost to keep us from hitting the ground. For what seemed ages 'Freddie' literally hung on its props. Then, as the the engineer retracted the undercarriage and the speed began to build up, it started to climb through the murk to temporary safety.

The other aircraft, one from Joe's squadron, crashed. Joe climbed to 5,000 ft and remained there until he had regained his composure to allow him to land safely after a flight of eight hours. Another flight of which Joe left a record was one on the 15/16 March against Stuttgart, it was the heaviest of the war up to then: –

I remember it well for I was lucky to get back from it. Planning for the attack was based on a Met forecast that a frontal system would clear the target area by our time on target leaving clear skies for a visual marking to be carried out. I carried an additional crew member for the trip, our most experienced visual bomb aimer (Warrant Officer Gray), his task being to identify the aiming point by the light of 4.5 flares dropped by an Illuminator aircraft just ahead of us. He would then mark it accurately with the huge green TIs we carried in addition to dropping our bomb load. Other Pathfinder aircraft would then back up our initial markers with further greens thus providing an unmistakeable aiming point for the main force of bombers as it approached the target. All was going well as we approached the target after an uneventful trip above heavy clouds; then the cloud started to break up as forecast and we gradually lost height to 8,000 ft and positioned the aircraft in readiness for the final run up, carefully checking our position and timing. Up to that moment there was no reaction from the ground defences ahead although we had run into the downwash of an aircraft several times and assumed it must be our Illuminator. Usually, such a reaction either meant that AI fighters were operating in the vicinity or the AA guns and searchlights were tracking us and lying 'doggo' until they were sure of a good fix. Now on the last stages of the run up I opened the bomb doors and listened to the set operator doing the count down to the time of target illumination. With only seconds to go the aircraft ahead of me was suddenly 'coned' by searchlights and the heavy flak below opened up into the cone. They must have scored a direct hit with the first shells for the aircraft disintegrated in a vast sheet of flame lighting the whole area momentarily then dying away as a thousand pieces of burning debris appeared to float down in our path, colliding with our aircraft in a series of bangs and crashes.

The smooth synchronised notes of the four Merlins changed as the engines vibrated badly in their mountings indicating airscrew damage. The aircraft had a decidedly port wing down attitude and an icy gale was blowing through the cockpit from breaks in the front turret and damaged perspex on the pilots clear vision panel. To make matters worse the searchlights then held on to us and shells were bursting all around as the guns gave us their undivided attention. I called to Gray the bomb aimer to hang on to the TIs but to let the bombs go and felt the aircraft lurch as they went and he closed the bomb doors. For the next few minutes I twisted and turned and lost height as I tried to shake off the searchlights. Suddenly we were in darkness as they looked elsewhere for another victim. I asked the navigator for a direct course for home and checked the crew to see if they were all OK; meanwhile the engineer juggled with the throttles and pitch controls and managed to cut out some of the vibration.

We were now at around 6,000 ft and fast approaching the solid wall of cloud over which we had flown on the way in. I got Foster, the Australian flight engineer, to use the Aldis lamp to check for serious damage to the engines and wings before we entered the clouds. He reported damage to the leading edge of the starboard wing and a large piece of Lancaster fuselage jammed into the port wing causing the drag and the left wing down attitude. Happily there seemed to be no damage to the engines so the vibration must have been caused by bent or damaged airscrew blades. After a nightmare journey flying through thick clouds in freezing conditions we eventually broke cloud over the North Sea and limped into Wyton nearly seven hours after take off.

★   ★   ★

By now Joe had been promoted to Wing Commander and was the Commanding Officer of No 83 Squadron. This was part of No 8, the Pathfinder Group, under the command of Air Vice Marshall Donald Bennett and Joe was very happy with that. He records that; –

The Australian born Bennett was, at 32 years of age, the youngest and certainly the most efficient member of the RAF to achieve Air Rank. His contempories in the other Bomber Groups were of a generation earlier and thus lacking in up to date flying experience; Bennett on the other hand had been in the thick of flying operations since the war began. In the early stages, as a Civil Airline Captain, he had been used on special duties and played a major part in the organisation and early operation of the North Atlantic Ferry Service. Recalled to the RAF from the reserve he then took over command of a night bomber squadron in Yorkshire with the rank of Wing Commander. During an operational flight over Norway in mid- winter his Halifax had been shot down but he escaped over the mountains to neutral Sweden and internment before returning to the UK to carry on with the war.A dedicated professional flier and a strict teetotaller, Bennett was a humourless man who did not suffer fools gladly and on this score he made many enemies outside No 8 Group. Within his own group, however, by his example and ability in all matters concerned with flying he was able to demand the highest standards from his flying crews and under his guidance and leadership a fine 'esprit de corps' built up. This was reflected in the 'press on' attitude of the largely volunteer Path Finder Force crews, the pride with which they wore the coveted eagle gilt badge that set them apart from other main force crews, and their professional rivalry with others, in particular No 5 Group which they scornfully alluded to as 'Cochranes Independent Airforce'.

All was to change. On the 23rd of March came the news that 83 Squadron and two other squadrons were to come under the operational command of No 5 Group: –

Although we would still be administratively responsible to No 8 Group and would retain our Pathfinder badges and ranks from henceforth we would be operating with the 'Independent Air Force' under the orders of its AOC, the Hon. Ralph Cochrane. The news came as a bombshell to everyone and cries of anguish rose all round the messes. Bennett's remonstrances were brushed aside by Command and on the morning of the 17th of April 1944 the Squadron took off from Wyton for the last time and landed shortly afterwards at Coningsby, an airfield deep in the heart of the No 5 Group airfields in Lincolnshire, where they were to join up with No 97 Squadron moving from Bourne.

As soon as the unhappy and disgruntled crews tumbled out of their aircraft the station Tannoy loud speakers were in action blaring out a summons to all the new arrivals to report at once to the Operations Briefing Room for an address by the Base Commander, Air Commodore Bobby Sharpe. This turned out to be not so much a welcoming speech to brothers in arms as an harangue against them based on the necessity for crews to shed all the bad habits they had picked up in No 8 Group and to concentrate on becoming proficient in the No 5 Group methods of target marking. Needless to say this was not very well received by the audience and there were a number of catcalls and hoots of derision. At the end, when Sharpe instructed the Squadron Commanders to initiate a training programme right away, tempers were at boiling point and the resentment could be felt.

Training started right away although the 'Illuminator' role we were to play was really child's play after the many marking techniques we had practised in No 8 Group. However, we buckled down to the situation with as good a grace as we could muster. Between training flights we waded through the masses of flying orders and Air Staff Instructions issued by the Group on every subject from the patter to be adhered to in the air by crew members to the colour of the toilet paper to be used in the aircraft Elsan if caught short over the target. Cochrane had procedures on paper for every eventuality and woe betide the hapless crews who dared to address each other by their Christian names in the heat of battle, or forgot the correct reporting drill. He even went to the lengths of having black box recorders installed in some aircraft with the intention of monitoring the attitude of aircraft throughout each operational flight, and voice recorders to record the crews conversations on intercom and R/T transmissions. None of these innovations served to endear our new Group Commander to us; rather they confirmed what we already thought. What a lousy set up we had been pushed into against our wills.

The much vaunted technique that No 5 Group had developed under the aegis of Leonard Cheshire and in which we were to play a role was intended to provide pin-point identification, marking and controlled bombing of small and vital 'Pre-invasion' targets. It involved using smaller forces than those used by the Command when saturation bombing German cities. The aim was to to ensure the maximum concentration around the aiming point and thus to minimise civilian casualties in the surrounding areas, most of whom would be friendly nationals. Railway centres and many of the explosives and fuel dumps and aircraft repair factories set up in the occupied countries came into this category.

Basically, the method required 'Blind Illuminators' finding their way to the target and lighting up the whole area with strings of 4.5 flares dropped blind on H2S. The Controller, in the area by now, would broadcast the standard wind setting for the main force to set on their bomb sights and would then send in Mosquitoes at low level to mark the aiming point with red spot fires. If the marking was accurate enough it would be backed up by other marker aircraft called in by the controller. At this stage aircraft of the bombing force would be orbiting a point nearby to be called in a few at a time to bomb the markers using their special bomb sights. The Controller could stop the bombing and have the aiming point re-marked if he was not satisfied with the accuracy of the attack. On occasions the aiming point might be away from target and false settings put on the bomb sights to enable 'off-set' bombing. The advantage of this was that there was little chance of the marking being obliterated if bombs hit the target. Using these techniques it was hoped that a steady and continuous stream of accurate bombing would concentrate damage to the small target area rather than saturate the area around as well, as in the major attacks on German cities. Whether the night fighters of the Luftwaffe would allow us the time and freedom of action over the target to achieve results without heavy losses remained to be seen.

In addition to their role as 'Blind Illuminators' the senior members of the ex Pathfinder Squadrons were to be used as Controllers and deputies when required in support of the No 5 Group Controllers. These would normally be Leonard Cheshire from No 617 Squadron at nearby Woodhall Spa, and Willie Tait and Bill Jeudwine, both on Sharpe's Base Operartions Staff at Coningsby.

Meanwhile Bomber Command carried on its saturation attacks on selected targets and included us in the major forces despatched over Germany. On the 22nd of April we were part of a force of between 700 and 800 heavies that attacked Brunswick. Poor visibility in the target area resulted in reverting to 'Parramatta' H2S blind marking for the attack. First impressions at the de-briefing were that it had been highly successful. Only later when full photo reconnaisance results were available was it found that most of the bombing had been concentrated on an industrial estate away from the city itself. The marking had gone astray because the metal roofs of the industrial estate had misled the H2S operators.

The failure of the marking on this attack influenced Command into trying the No 5 Group technique on Schweinfurt on the 26th of April and on this occasion I acted as Deputy Contoller for the first time. It was a long haul to the target and by the time we arrived in the area and dropped the illuminating flares smoke from ground generators blotted out the town. The Mosquitoes bravely went into the murk below at low level but after several abortive tries the Controller called them off and sent in the Lancaster Blind Markers. After several dangerous runs to back up the markers with more greens the main force, impatiently hanging around, were called in to bomb on these and clear the area. We landed back at Coningsby after almost nine hours in the air, exhausted and extremely critical of the whole operation which was a complete flop.

Undaunted by this set back Cochrane next obtained approval to try the marking technique on a French target and two nights later an almost identical force headed towards St Medard en Jailes in the Bordeaux area. Once again I found myself acting as Deputy Controller. And once again the Mosquitoes at low level had trouble in pin pointing the aiming point with their red spot fires and the operation turned out to be a dismal failure.

On 1st May a strong force of No 5 Group aircraft went to Tours, the target being a Messerschmitt repair factory housed in hangars on the airfield. This time I was to be the Controller. During the morning planning in the Base Operations Room Bobby Sharpe had drawn me aside and told me that he would be flying with me on the trip as a passenger. However, up to the time of going out to the dispersal area on the crew bus half an hour before take off nothing further had been said about it and by the time we arrived at our aircraft, 'D Dog', I had given him up.

As I began to carry out the external checks on the aircraft, the crew already having gone inside to do theirs, a large American staff car flying the Base Commanders pennant drew up nearby. I carried on with my checks and presently the driver came over and told me that the Air Commodore was in the car and would be coming with us but that he first wanted me to line up my crew and present each member to him. Eventually, after much cursing, I managed to get the crew out again and line them up in front of the aircraft where-upon Sharpe, who was in full American type bomber kit acquired no doubt during his years in Washington, moved over and was introduced to them one by one. The formalities over he then entered the aircraft through the rear door and succeeded in blocking all other movements of the crew until he had reached the navigator's table. By then the engineer and I had entered the aircraft by the ladder and front hatch and were in process of starting the engines.

We took off dead on time and Sharpe stayed with the navigator until we climbed away from base on our first course, maintaining radio silence. He then decided for some reason to carry out a test transmission on the Controllers frequency with a 'Monday, Tuesday, Wednesday — are you receiving me?' type of broadcast to the force, thereby breaking the strict silence normally observed. He received in reply a number of fortunately unrecognisable voices telling him to belt up and keep quiet. That didn't please him at all.

The weather was fine with some moonlight by the time we reached the target area and, apart from the possible threat of night fighters arriving in the area, it looked as though we would have few problems marking. The only ground defences consisted of some 20 mm light AA that opened up at us each time we went low across the airfield. The Illuminators lit up the airfield like day and there was no difficulty in marking the hangars and backing up the marking from around 6,000 ft whereupon I called in the main force in batches to bomb and watched the hangars disintegrate as the attack progressed. We circled round the target for about half an hour with small strings of 'flaming onions' from the light flak rising towards us and shooting past the wing tips at speed. There was little chance of being hit but Sharpe didn't care for it very much and in the end I climbed the aircraft a little to keep him quiet. Eventually the last few bomb loads that by now were just stirring up the smoking rubble were dropped and we set course for the English Channel and Coningsby without having seen any fighter activity.

Six hours after take off we touched down on the airfield where the Air Commodore hurriedly left the aircraft and was whisked away in his car without a word to the crew or the offer of a lift to de-briefing. We waited for the aircrew bus and were shuttled to the Operations block some twenty minutes later where we found Sharpe deep in conversation with Cochrane, the AOC. His account of the operation must have been good, for the next day an immediate DSO came through, for him. Not one of the crew who carried him on his arduous passenger trip over France was invited to have a drink with him at the subsequent celebration.

Possibly heartened by this success a larger 'Independent Air Force' drawn from Nos 1 and 5 Groups (but not including 83 Squadron) with Leonard Cheshire controlling in a Mosquito aircraft was sent on the night of 3rd May to attack the Panzer Training Unit at Mailley le Camp. This time there were delays in marking the aiming point aggravated by a partial communications failure in the Mosquito and this resulted in the main bomber force being held in the vicinity of the target in moonlight long enough for the night fighters to get among them. Of the 346 aircraft despatched 42 were destroyed, mostly by the fighters. This had a sobering effect on those who had been calling the French targets a piece of cake and not worthy of full operational status.

After a short leave to see my family in Norfolk I returned to Coningsby in time to pay a repeat visit to Tours on the 19th of May. This time the target was the rail centre and marshalling yards. There was only light flak and no fighter opposition and we were able to bomb accurately with few losses. Despite the disaster at Mailley le Camp (after that night No 1 Group practically refused to operate with No 5 Group) and the failure at St Medard en Jailes this second successful attack on a French target encourage Cochrane to risk another crack at a German one. So three nights later, on 22nd May, Brunswick became the target for the 'Independent Air Force', just a month after the failure of the 'parramatta' blind marking attack on it.

At the briefing for the attack the AOC announced that Bill Jeudwine would be the Controller, flying in a USAF P40 Lightning single seater fighter that Sharpe had borrowed for the purpose. I was to be the Deputy Controller in Lancaster 'M Mike'. Jeudwine was new to the group having been in the Far East for the early part of the war and I doubted if he had sufficient experience of European conditions to be able to navigate to Brunswick at night alone in a Lightning. There was another problem for, as the details of the attack were thrashed out, I became aware that we would be crossing the Dutch coast in the false twilight at operational height and would be vulnerable to night fighters. I therefore queried it with Sharpe, suggesting that the timing should be set back half an hour. Much to my surprise he slapped the suggestion down and made it worse from my point of view by adding that he wasn't asking me to do anything he wasn't prepared to do himself. My worries were fully justified. As we approached the Dutch coast, struggling to reach our operational height of 20,000 ft, other aircraft in the vicinity were clearly visible to me as they would be to the fighters now climbing to attack or orbiting their beacons under GCI control. Before we had even crossed the coast visible below the attacks started and I had to carry out some rivet popping corkscrews with 'M' to shake off three attacks by Junkers 88s. There was visible evidence of the force being harried on all sides and behind as we pressed on towards Brunswick. I was listening out on the Controller's frequency for the usual check from him but I heard nothing and got no reply to my transmissions to him. Twenty minutes from the target I decided that I would have to take over and I broadcast the wind setting for the bomb sights and informed the Mosquito leader of the situation. With the time lost trying to shake off the fighters we would be a little late on target and the Mosquitoes were to go ahead and do their stuff as soon as the Illuminators dropped their flares. Still hoping against hope that Jeudwine would turn up I saw the flares drop and light up the sky ahead and heard the Mosquito spot fire markers as they dived to ground level and searched in the murk for something to identify. There were many searchlights and heavy guns in action now as well as some fighter activity and it was getting very unhealthy around the target area. Time was getting on and the Mosquitoes were unable to see anything down below because of the smoke and the main bombing force, holding off a few miles away, was coming under attack from fighters. Too much time had already been wasted without achieving anything. I therefore gave the order for the 'Backer Up' aircraft carrying green TIs to do a run over the target and drop them on H2S and for the main force to bomb the markers and get the hell out of it. Nothing loath they unloaded their bombs and headed home and I brought up the rear. We landed back at Coningsby six hours after take off to find Jeudwine looking sheepish. Apparently he got off in the Lightning alright but managed to lose himself and ended up somewhere south of Paris from where he had been able to get back to base. There was no sign of Sharpe who had retired to bed with a cold after receiving some of the de-briefing reports indicating that the raid was a failure and the losses high.

★   ★   ★

June 1944 saw the launching of the second front and Bomber Command was called upon in the tactical role to destroy enemy opposition in advance of our ground forces whenever they were held up by the Germans. Joe's squadron, still under the operational control of No. 5 Group, played a full part in this: –

During the second week of June most of my crew became tour-expired and left for pastures new to sit out the rest of the war in training establishments. They had flown odd extra sorties filling temporary vacancies in other crews due to sickness or for other reasons, on nights when Laurie Deane went on the battle order and I took over as Squadron Commander on the ground. One by one my crew left on their well-earned end-of-tour leave with recently awarded DFC ribbons under their brevets. (*Joe was himself awarded the DFC in June in recognition of his contribution to the battles over Germany. Ed*) I then formed a new crew from the unfortunate 'odds and sods' who for various reasons were not permanently crewed up with a captain. On the night of the 14/15 of June we were called upon by the army to attack a large concentration of German Panzer units dispersed around Aunay-sur-Odon and E'vrecy near Caen. These raids were prepared and executed in great haste because of the fluidity of the situation. I flew as deputy Controller for the Aunay raid using a scratch crew and taking with me the Senior Medical Officer (Flying) of Bomber Command, Wing Commander Ewens, along for the ride. The weather in the target area was clear, the aiming point cross roads identified and marked accurately, and the area obliterated by the force of 337 heavies bombing the markers. No aircraft were lost. Later photographs showed the highest concentration of bombing achieved on a target of this nature.

Between such operations I spent some time welding my scratch crew together, practicing bombing on the nearby Wainfleet ranges from various altitudes, combined with navigational exercises. My navigator was now 'Sandy' Galbraith, a red haired Kiwi, and he flew with me on the night 14/15 July when I was the Controller of a force of 242 Lancasters and a dozen Mosquitoes attacking the railway yards at Revigny and Villneuve. The raid on Villeneuve was successful but that on Revigny was abandoned as the Mosquitoes were unable to pinpoint the railway yards. Seven of the Lancasters were lost when German fighters arrived on the scene.

Just as my new crew had come together, working as one, 'P' Staff at HQ Bomber Command annotated my record as 'tour-expired' on heavies and told Group to arrange a non operational posting for

YEAR 1943		AIRCRAFT		PILOT, OR 1ST PILOT	2ND PILOT, PUPIL OR PASSENGER	DUTY (INCLUDING RESULTS AND REMARKS)
MONTH	DATE	Type	No.			
—	—	—	—	—	—	— TOTALS BROUGHT FORWARD
DEC.	12	LANCASTER	"D" EE201	SELF.	6 CREW.	"Y" TRAINING — BOMBING RUNS
DEC	12	OXFORD.	"S"	W/O DOUGLAS	SELF	S.B.A. PRACTICE.
DEC	13	LANCASTER	"D" EE201	SELF (C)	6 CREW.	FIGHTER AFFILIATION AND HIGH LEVEL BOMBING · WHITTLESEY.
DEC	16	LANCASTER	"F"	SELF (C)	F/LT FORSTER	OPERATIONS — BERLIN. (15)
					F/O BURDETT.	(5 × 2,000LBS HC DROPPED)
					F/O FOSTER.	10/10 CLOUD OVER TARGET.
					F/O WESTON	BOMBED ON SPECIAL EQUIPMENT.
					W/O HOEY	
					F/LT WESLEY.	
DEC.	30	LANCASTER	"F" JB453	SELF (C)	6 CREW.	FIGHTER AFFILIATION AND "Y" TRAINING.
					DECEMBER 43	LANCASTER
					83 SQUADRON.	OXFORD.
		J. Mathick R. W/CDR OC 83 SQUADRON.			1ST. JAN 1944 J. Mathick S/LDR	
1944 JAN.	1	LANCASTER	"F" JB 453	SELF (C)	F/LT FORSTER	WAR OPERATIONS — BERLIN. (16)
					F/S MARTIN	(1×4,000, 3×1000, 4 B.T.L.S)
					F/O FOSTER.	10/10 CLOUD TARGET, BOMBED ON
					F/O WESTON	SPECIAL EQUIPMENT. BACKED UP.
					W/O HOEY	
					F/L WESLEY	

GRAND TOTAL [Cols. (1) to (10)]

1719 Hrs 05 Mins.   TOTALS CARRIED FORWARD

Log. 1.

172

SINGLE-ENGINE AIRCRAFT				MULTI-ENGINE AIRCRAFT						PASS-ENGER	INSTR/CLOUD FLYING [incl. in cols. (1) to (10)]	
DAY		NIGHT		DAY			NIGHT					
DUAL	PILOT	DUAL	PILOT	DUAL	1ST PILOT	2ND PILOT	DUAL	1ST PILOT	2ND PILOT		DUAL	PILOT
(1)	(2)	(3)	(4)	(5)	(6)	(7)	(8)	(9)	(10)	(11)	(12)	(13)
					2.30							
					.40							
					2.00							
483 Lang	25 6sf.							8.05				8.05
					2.50							
					7.20			8.05				
						.40						
				TOTAL FLYING FOR MONTH : 16 HRS. 05 MINS.								
421 Lang	28 6sf.							7.25				7.25
6.20	542.55	1.35	24.35	11.20	748.55	103.10	—	128.15	92.00	41.15.		
(1)	(2)	(3)	(4)	(5)	(6)	(7)	(8)	(9)	(10)	(11)	(12)	(13)

Log. 2.

173

YEAR 1944.		AIRCRAFT		PILOT, OR 1ST PILOT	2ND PILOT, PUPIL OR PASSENGER	DUTY (INCLUDING RESULTS AND REMARKS)
MONTH	DATE	Type	No.			
—	—	—	—	—	· —	—— TOTALS BROUGHT FORWARD
MARCH	3	OXFORD.	X	SELF.	F/L COLLETT. T.	BACK BEAM APPROACH.
MARCH	6	OXFORD	X	F/O SKITCH.	SELF.	WYTON — FINMERE.
MARCH	14	LANCASTER.	J.	SELF	2 CREW.	REFRESHER
			NO 499	F/L McDONALD.		CIRCUITS & LANDINGS.
MARCH	15	LANCASTER	"D"	SELF (c)	W.O GRAY	WAR OPERATIONS: STUTTGART. (25)
			ND 529		F/L BURDETT	VISUAL MARKER.
					F/L FOSTER	CLOUD 10/10 OVER TARGET — REVERTED
					F/S EARNSHAW.	TO VISUAL BACKER UP. A/C
					W/O HOEY	DAMAGED OVER TARGET BY ANOTHER
					F/L WESTON	MACHINE BLOWING UP AHEAD ON RUN UP
					F/L WESLEY.	HEAVIEST RAID OF WAR TO DATE.
MARCH	22	LANCASTER	"D"	SELF (c)	P/O TAYLOR.	WAR OPERATIONS: FRANKFURT (26)
			ND 529		F/L BURDETT	VISUAL MARKER.
					F/L FOSTER	CLOUD 10/10 OVER TARGET. — BOMBS
					F/S EARNSHAW	ONLY DROPPED VISUALLY ON T.Is.
					W/O HOEY	MUCH FIGHTER ACTIVITY AND MANY
					F/L WESTON.	SEARCHLIGHTS.
					F/L WESLEY .	VERY SUCCESSFUL RAID.

Northrop For W/CDR.
O.C 83 SQUADRON.

Summary for MARCH 1944
Unit 83 SQUADRON Aircraft
Date 1ST. APRIL 1944 Type.
Signature Northrop W/C.

1. LANCASTER III
2. OXFORD.
3. ———
4. ———

GRAND TOTAL [Cols. (1) to (10)]
1797 Hrs. 45 Mins.

TOTALS CARRIED FORWARD

Log. 3.

174

SINGLE-ENGINE AIRCRAFT				MULTI-ENGINE AIRCRAFT						PASS-ENGER	INSTR/CLOUD FLYING [incl. in cols. (1) to (10)]	
DAY		NIGHT		DAY			NIGHT					
DUAL	PILOT	DUAL	PILOT	DUAL	1ST PILOT	2ND PILOT	DUAL	1ST PILOT	2ND PILOT		DUAL	PILOT
(1)	(2)	(3)	(4)	(5)	(6)	(7)	(8)	(9)	(10)	(11)	(12)	(13)
						.20						
						.25						
						.30						
863 a/c		37 a/c Post						6.10				6.10
816 a/c		33 a/c Post						5.05				5.05
						18						
						.30		11.15				
						.45						
					TOTAL FLYING FOR MONTH: 12 HRS. 60 MINS							
6.20	542.55	1.35	24.35	11.20	757.05	106.25	—	195.30	92.00	41.15		
(1)	(2)	(3)	(4)	(5)	(6)	(7)	(8)	(9)	(10)	(11)	(12)	(13)

Log. 4.

YEAR 1944		AIRCRAFT		PILOT, OR 1ST PILOT	2ND PILOT, PUPIL OR PASSENGER	DUTY (INCLUDING RESULTS AND REMARKS)
MONTH	DATE	Type	No.			
—	—	—	—	—		— TOTALS BROUGHT FORWARD
					Summary for APRIL 1944	1. LANCASTER
					Unit 582 SQUADRON Aircraft	2. _____
					Date 1st MAY 1944 Types	3. _____
					Signature _____	4. _____
MAY	1	LANCASTER	"D" ND529	SELF (c)	F/LT BURDETT	WAR OPERATIONS : TOURS (30)
				AIR COMMODORE SHARP.	F/LT FOSTER	AIRCRAFT REPAIR FACTORY. OVER TARGET
					F/LT WESTON	AT 5,000', CONTROLLING FOR 50 MINS
					P/O EARNSHAW.	VERY SUCCESSFUL RAID
					W/O HOEY	FACTORY BUILDINGS COMPLETELY
					W/O MATTHEWS	OBLITERATED.
MAY	18	LANCASTER	"D" ND529	SELF (c)	6 CREW.	PRACTICE RUNS ON 184 AT 17,000 FT.
MAY	19	LANCASTER	"D" ND529	SELF (c)	F/L BURDETT.	WAR OPERATIONS : TOURS. (31)
					F/L FOSTER	RAILWAY YARDS AND STORAGE.
					F/L WESTON	2ND. DEPUTY CONTROLLER . TARGET
					P/O EARNSHAW	MARKED SUCCESSFULLY AND BOMBED.
					W/O HOEY	FAIRLY GOOD RAID. VERY LITTLE
					F/L WESLEY.	FLAK OR FIGHTER ACTIVITY.
MAY	22	LANCASTER	"M" JA705	SELF (c)	F/L BURDETT	WAR OPERATIONS : BRUNSWICK. (32)
					F/L FOSTER	ASSUMED CONTROLLER OVER TARGET.
					F/L WESTON	ATTACKED BY FIGHTERS 3 TIMES - MANY
					P/O EARNSHAW	SEARCHLIGHTS CONES AND HEAVY FLAK.
				F/S HARRISON.	W/O HOEY	UNSUCCESSFUL RAID - WIDESPREAD

GRAND TOTAL [Cols. (1) to (10)]

1342 Hrs. 30 Mins.

TOTALS CARRIED FORWARD

Log. 5.

SINGLE-ENGINE AIRCRAFT				MULTI-ENGINE AIRCRAFT						PASS-ENGER	INSTR/CLOUD FLYING [incl. in cols. (1) to (10)]	
DAY		NIGHT		DAY			NIGHT					
DUAL	PILOT	DUAL	PILOT	DUAL	1ST PILOT	2ND PILOT	DUAL	1ST PILOT	2ND PILOT		DUAL	PILOT
(1)	(2)	(3)	(4)	(5)	(6)	(7)	(8)	(9)	(10)	(11)	(12)	(13)
					3.20			22.55				
					TOTAL FLYING FOR MONTH : 26 HRS 15 min							
46 hours + 4 mins. No Passes								5.55				5.55
Share suicide immediate D.S.O. for this passenger trip												
					1.10							
113 hours 4 mins No Passes								5.25				5.25
Bill ... should have completed this attack when for the first time a USAF. Single ... at Lockheed Lightning Fighter. the ... ... up ... Pan Am. Force ... Dutch Coast in near ... and ... heavy ...								6.00				3.00
6.20	542.55	1.35	54.35	11.20	761.35	106.25	—	235.45	92.00	41.15		17.35
(1)	(2)	(3)	(4)	(5)	(6)	(7)	(8)	(9)	(10)	(11)	(12)	(13)

Log. 6.

me. At this time Air Commodore 'Bobby' Sharpe, the Base Commander at Coningsby, was looking for a base Operations Officer on his planning staff and offered me the post. I was apparently still in his good books from the occasion when he had been awarded the DSO for flying as a passenger with me on the very successful attack on the Messerschmitt factory near Tours. I had no wish to finish the war on his staff and without being too obvious was making up excuses to wriggle out of the offer when a miracle happened! In the middle of the night I was called to the telephone and found myself talking to Donald Bennett from No 8 Group. Never one to waste words he told me that Wing Commander Lockhart, the CO of 692 Squadron, had failed to return from operations over Berlin and he offered me the job. The only proviso was that I would be limited to two or three operations a month in view of the fact that I had only just finished on heavies. I accepted at once and was told to clear from Coningsby and get down to Graveley that afternoon to take over. Before I could thank him he rang off.

I was on cloud nine as I sat down to an early breakfast after which I went round obtaining clearance from the few sections of the station which mattered and saying cheerio to my friends in No 83 Squadron. Sandy Galbraith was particularly cut up at the news and asked if I would take him as my navigator on Mosquitoes. I promised to try and arrange it with P Staff and he perked up a bit at that. By mid day I had packed the last of my kit into my current car (a 1926 Austin 7 I had acquired for £20 while at Wyton) and set off towards the main station gates and the Boston road. Air Commodore Sharpe's office window had a clear view of the traffic entering and leaving the Camp so he would almost certainly see me leave. I decided, therefore, that it would be polite to call in on him and the Station Commander Evan-Evans but I would make my farewells as short as possible. I popped in to see Evan-Evans first and was warmly welcomed by the large and cheerful character. Because he had been a station command since 1940 and was very overweight he rarely flew although he badly wanted to be one of the boys. (Sadly, on the night of the 21/22 of Febuary 1945 he was allowed to take an 83 Squadron aircraft for an attack on the Mittelland Canal and was lost with all but one of his crew who were drawn from 97 Squadron). My call on Air Commodore Sharpe was much shorter and in a frostier atmosphere. He was obviously annoyed I was going but made no attempt to put a spoke in my leaving for Graveley. It was only a matter of minutes before I drove out of Coningsby for the last time. My car coasted merrily along the deserted Fen roads apparently as happy as I was to be escaping from No 5 Group and returning to the Path Finder Force.

Mosquito Leader

Graveley in 1944 was a typical wartime airfield created to a standard pattern from the rich farmlands bordering East Anglia that lie between Huntingdon and St. Neots. It was off the beaten track and well hidden from casual view. It was the operational base for No 35 (Madras) Squadron, now a Pathfinder marker squadron equipped with Lancasters. My new command, No 692 Squadron, was equipped with Mosquito XVI's modified to carry the 4,000 lb "cookies" and formed part of the Light Night Striking Force. Reporting to the Station Adjutant's Office I was ushered in to see the Station Commander, Group Captain Menaul DFC, AFC. I had known Paddy Menaul earlier in the war at Wyton where he had been Flight Commander on 15 Squadron flying first on Blenheims and later on Wellingtons. Like me he had started his RAF career as an Aircraft Apprentice at Halton and on passing out had been selected for a Cranwell cadetship; he now warmly welcomed me to his Station.

After a short chat over a cup of tea, during which he made it quite clear that I would only be allowed to do a limited number of operational sorties during my stay at Graveley, and that he would personally see that I kept to the letter of the law, he whisked me off in his service car for a quick tour of the main sections on the Station introducing me to most of the heads. At the end of the tour he drew up at a motley collection of Nissen huts of various sizes housing the offices and crew rooms of No 692 Squadron, introduced me to Flight Lieutenant Northover, the bespectacled Adjutant with the air of a bank manager (it turned out later to be his profession) and left me to put all the pieces together. That night, 19th July, 1944, the squadron was sending 16 aircraft as part of a force of 36 Mosquitoes of the Light Night Striking Force

181

attacking Bremen. I arrived at the briefing in time to hear most of what was said by Sqn.Ldr. Saunderson, the acting C.O. The other Flight Commander Sqn.Ldr. McBain was on the battle order. (Both Flight Commanders were rapidly approaching the end of their tour of 50 operations and I would have to go into the question of their replacement before long). Later that evening after dinner I drove around the dispersal area with Saunderson checking the crews and aircraft for any snags before moving to Flying Control to watch the take-off. Here I met "Pop" Hemming the Senior Control Officer who sported RFC wings and first world war medals. "Pop" wore a black eye patch permanently over one eye and with his now white hair it gave him a distinctly raffish air. I never found out how he lost the eye. The 692 Squadron aircraft were soon taxiing onto the perimeter track and queuing behind each other at the holding point before getting a green on the Aldis lamp from the Runway Controller, and turning to line up on the long runway. A quick run up of the engines on the brakes. Then brakes off and a slow build up of speed until the tail came up giving full control by the rudder. The aircraft lifted off just before the runway ended, missing the red danger light on the SBA transmitter before starting the long climb to operational height. All 16 aircraft were on their way towards the target within a matter of minutes and from now on, other than in an emergency, would maintain radio silence until after they had crossed the East Anglian coast on the way back in around three hours time. I returned to the Officers' Mess and browsed through the periodicals for a time before dozing off in one of the armchairs. Saunderson woke me up to tell me that the first aircraft had called up and would be landing in a few minutes so I went with him to the Control Tower and watched the squadron land, afterwards looking in at the de-briefing. All the aircraft got back safely and there was nothing untoward reported by the crews. It had been a long day for me and I was glad to crawl between the sheets in the early hours and forget my problems for the time being.

Despite the lateness of the hour in getting to bed I was up bright and early and one of the first in to breakfast, and soon afterwards was in my office trying to familiarise myself with the hundred and one problems of Mosquito operations which I would be expected to deal with from now on. One of my first priorities was to renew my short experience with the Mosquito cockpit of some 15 months earlier at Finmere. There I had taken the opportunity to put in three or four hours of circuits and landings in one of the Bicester O.C.U. aircraft making use of the hard runways there. Those three hours didn't seem a lot when considered in relation to the 50 or so hours flying given to crews passing through the Mosquito Conversion Unit before joining an operational squadron. And I had to squeeze in my flying between Squadron operations as quickly as possible so that I could safely put myself on the battle order and lead the squadron by example. My next priority looking ahead was for a navigator bomb aimer, and I was quickly on to "P" Staff at Group headquarters nearby with a request for them to arrange for Sandy Galbraith to join me from Coningsby as a matter of urgency. I was promised that it would be done right away.

By mid-morning, leaning heavily on Northover, the Squadron Adjutant, I had cleared most of the outstanding paperwork in the trays, gone quickly through the files and was wading through the pilot's handbook for the Mosquito in the hope of doing some flying later on. 692 Squadron was equiped with the Mk XVI (B), the bomber variant of the PR XVI, the bomb bay having been modified to carry a single 4,000 lb HC or MC "cookie" fitting snugly in the underslung belly of the aircraft. One in ten of the total production of 7,500 Mosquitoes built in wartime were of this type; more than 800 in all. When the squadron had first formed at Graveley in January 1944, it had been equipped with MK IV type aircraft. They had their bomb bays modified the following month and had the distinction of being the first Mosquitoes to drop "cookies" on German targets. Mosquitoes carried a much greater bomb load to Berlin than the USAF Flying Fortresses and moreover did it in half the flying time and with minimal losses. The two powerful Rolls Royce engines hoisted the heavily laden aircraft to heights of 30,000 feet and above, at a speed that gave the Luftwaffe night fighters little chance of interception. At that height they were clear of most cloud conditions and out of range of all but the heaviest Flak. In addition, 50 or 100 gallon drop tanks could be carried on the underside of the wing tips to increase the range as necessary. They made a formidable addition to the Light

Night Striking Force which operated within 8 Group as a "Force within a Force" having its own H2S and Oboe marking squadrons and weather aircraft.

My hopes of flying on my first day at Graveley were rudely shattered by the arrival of the Group teleprinter orders for the night's operations, 692 being included as part of a force attacking Hamburg. This was to be my first briefing of the squadron and as such a red letter day. It was also the day on which news filtered through about the unsuccessful attempt on Hitler's life at his Headquarters in East Prussia. Once again it turned out to be a day on which I was kept fully occupied and given no opportunity of climbing into a Mosquito cockpit. Once the briefing of the crews had started all actions were geared to a timetable. Routings were detailed in the operational order and arrangements made to load the bombs. All 16 aircraft on the battle order finally took off returning without loss some three and a half hours later. Next day the 21st July the squadron formed part of a force of 33 Mosquitoes sent to Berlin. The following night the Squadron enjoyed the luxury of a "stand-down", one of the two nights in each month officially given off to each squadron in the Light Night Striking Force in rotation. The break in operational routine gave me the opportunity I needed and I was able to squeeze in two half hours of practice circuits and landings and a further two to three hours of general flying and SBA practice. I now felt that I could safely put myself on the battle order as soon as Sandy Galbraith turned up at Graveley. I was about to chase up "P" Staff to hasten the posting when matters came to a head in a most dramatic fashion.

At the crack of dawn next morning the 'phone near my bed rang and a very shaken and agitated Sandy was on the line from Coningsby, pleading with me to do all I could to get him away from the place quickly before he was killed. The night before he had been co-opted as navigator for a makeshift Lancaster crew and placed on the battle order to make up the numbers for 5 Group. Take-off at night had started off as normal with full bomb load but some sixth sense had kept Sandy standing forward of the navigator's position with his chest parachute pack still clipped on as the aircraft climbed away from the runway. So, when a few seconds later at a height of a few hundred feet all four engines cut dead Sandy was the only member of the crew in a position to leave the aircraft before it stalled and hit the ground. With great presence of mind he dived for the front escape hatch, operating the release that jettisoned the hatch, and fell through the opening pulling the rip-cord of his parachute almost in one movement. He had got out of the aircraft at such a low altitude that the parachute canopy had not fully opened when he hit the ground but he got away with only bruises and a damaged ankle and was the only survivor from the crew. Sandy was still in a state of shock and I calmed him down after a while and ended by promising that as soon as he had finished with the enquiry that was certain to be held at Coningsby I would make it my business to fly there and bring him back.

Before I received the all clear from Group I had briefed the squadron for attacks on the synthetic oil plants at Wanne Eickel and Castrop-Rauxel, and further sorties on Cologne and Berlin. Then at last on the morning of 11th August I climbed into Mosquito "M" and set course for Coningsby to pick up Sandy and his kit and bring him to Graveley as promised, with his posting properly authenticated.

The target that night was again Berlin and I had intended to carry out a few night circuits and landings once the aircraft on the battle order had taken off. However, as no spare was available I had to wait until the next night when, while the squadron was winging its way to Kiel, Sandy and I were in the circuit at Graveley practicing night take-offs and landings, the last hurdle before putting ourselves on the next battle order. This happened to be as part of a force of 30 Mosquitoes attacking Hanover the following night. It was 13th August though I cannot recall whether it was a Friday.

Taxiing from dispersal, strapped side by side in our seats and encumbered by our operational gear of parachute and dinghy packs, Mae Wests, helmets and oxygen masks, it seemed to be an exceedingly tight fit in the cockpit after all the room in the Lancaster office. But by the time I had reached the holding point before turning on to the runway and completed cockpit checks I began to feel at home. In response to the green flashed at me by the Runway Controller I turned on to the take-off heading, synchronised the directional gyros and ran the engines up against the brakes. Then the brakes were released and the aircraft kept straight by differential throttle control as it picked up speed down the runway. We used every inch of the 2000 yards runway and the red obstruction light on the SBA transmitter seemed very close as we cleared it and started the long slow climb to operational height, heading towards the East Coast and across the North Sea before turning on a dog-leg to cross the enemy coast. At a height of 29,000 feet I levelled out and checked everything in the cockpit and confirmed our height, airspeed and course with Sandy. He wasn't feeling too good so after checking that his oxygen supply was O.K. and that he was plugged in properly, I told him to go into the bomb aimers position in the nose and have a lie down. I would use my pilot's flight plan giving changes of course and times and would confirm our positions by the sky markers being dropped at the turning points before Hanover. Sandy thereupon squeezed down into the nose position and after confirming that the bombsight was switched on and he was properly plugged in took no further interest in the proceedings until I woke him up a few minutes before our time on target. As we approached the target the target markers from our marker aircraft ahead blossomed out on the ground and I opened the bomb doors and followed Sandy's instructions on the bombing run until the sudden involuntary leap of the aircraft upwards told me that our two-ton monster was no longer with us. I kept on course to ensure that the photo-flash would take the aiming point photograph beneath, then closed the bomb doors and put the Aircraft in a diving turn to port away from the heavy flak shell bursts now all around us. Sandy was still feeling pretty bad in the nose so I told him to stay there and headed for the coastline to the east of Bremen intending to let down over the sea to an altitude at which oxygen would not be necessary. In my haste I strayed over Bremen itself and was instantly coned by searchlights and engaged by the heavy guns firing into the cone. Going into a steep diving turn to get away from them my reaction was that of a ham-fisted "heavy" pilot at the controls and the amount of aileron control I suddenly applied was enough to barrel-roll the aircraft three or four times and scatter Sandy's maps and equipment, not to mention Sandy who wasn't strapped in, all

Joe briefing his Mosquito Squadron.

around the cockpit. By the time I had everything under control we were out of the danger zone and over the North Sea. The rest of the trip was uneventful and we touched down at Graveley having clocked exactly four hours flying time; all 30 aircraft sent to Hanover returned safely.

Having achieved operational status on Mosquitoes I could now catch up on the background of the Squadron and get to know the personnel, both flying and ground, much better than I had so far managed in my three weeks at Graveley. The Mossie made such a superb night bomber operating at heights and speeds far in excess of the Lancasters and Halifax's, that flying times to all the major targets in the Third Reich were literally halved. During the short summer nights when the heavies had to confine their attacks to short range targets to keep within the hours of darkness and acceptable loss rates, Mosquitoes of the eight squadrons of the Light Night Striking Force hit Berlin and all major German cities at will, keeping the air raid sirens wailing night after night throughout Germany. Only the very worst of bad weather grounded them and this high intensity of operating, together with an extremely low loss rate became so routine that the normal tour of operations was set at 50, as against 30 on the "heavy" squadrons. Even so there was a big turnover of tour-expired crews and the Mosquito Operational Conversion Unit was hard put to churn out sufficient crews to meet the needs of the squadrons. In the winter months it was often possible to fit in a sortie between afternoon tea and late dinner in the Mess, and have a drink afterwards before the bar closed. It was quite common for crews to complete their full operational tours within three months of first joining a squadron.

On the following two nights I briefed the crews for operations on Berlin, followed by a 'shortie' on Mannheim and then another Berlin trip. I was keen to get on the battle order again after what I considered was a decent interval, but at this stage the weather turned really bad, and for the next three days no operations took place.

This gave me a chance to learn of more of the short history of the squadron. One difference between 692 and other squadrons was that it was equipped with aircraft bought for the Royal Air Force by a South American organisation calling itself the 'Order of the Bellows' by virtue of its mission to raise the wind. This connection was acknowledged by the addition of the letters S.A. in brackets after the squadron number, viz No. 693 (S.A.) Squadron. The sole object of the Fellowship which had branches in most of the South American countries was to raise money for the purchase of aircraft for the Royal Air Force, and the MKXVI (B) Mosquitoes on the squadron had been provided by the Argentine branch. A squadron of Whirlwind aircraft had already been provided for Fighter Command by the Chile Branch. There were also 'perks' in the form of fresh coffee beans, sugar, sweets, and furnishings for crew-rooms, all much appreciated. On first entering the Squadron crew room I had been impressed by the furnishings, carpets underfoot, pictures scattered around and fresh coffee and biscuits instead of the normal stewed tea in a cracked NAAFI cup! Now it all became clear to me as I delved into the background of the Squadron.

The Fellowship of the Bellows was started by British Nationals and other pro-British residents living in the Argentine and other South American countries as their way of making a useful contribution to the British war effort. On enrolling, new members paid an entrance fee, for which they were issued with a badge, a small enamelled bellows emblem usually worn in the lapel or other prominent position so that it could be recognised by other members. (Only recently I came across one of these lapel badges tucked away for posterity in my stud box, hidden by a mountain of now unused cufflinks.) They also undertook to pay an agreed amount for each German aircraft shot down by the RAF from that date onwards. When a member had paid for 100 such 'gains' he was elevated to the next grade and issued with a differently coloured badge. The grades were roughly based on the Beaufort Wind Scale values, so that a new member started as a "breeze", becoming progressively a wind, gust, gale and so on to hurricane and typhoon with the possibility that he might ultimately graduate to be a full member of the Order of the Bellows. By that time of course he would have paid quite a bit voluntarily towards the war effort.

All in all it was a bit of a lark and treated as such by ex-pats in the South American countries who supported the fellowship through their pockets with great enthusiasm, feeling that they were helping in a practical way. By the end of the war the various branches had handed over an enormous sum of money to the British Government, all of which had been used to purchase aircraft for the Royal Air Force. The prospectus given to new members and outlining the rules to be observed symbolises the spirit in which it all began. It outlined the procedure to be followed whenever fellow-members recognised each other by sight or badge when passing in the street. It ruled that "Each member should bring his right hand with index finger fully extended downwards in a diving movement followed immediately by an upward movement simulating a Spitfire victory roll and ending with the arm and index finger in a straight line pointing upwards". The mind boggles at the thought of staid and respectable business men saluting each other in this manner under the mid-day sun in Buenos Aires or elsewhere to the astonishment of the natives or whatever.

On 23rd August the weather cleared and operations were laid on for that night; I put Sandy and myself on the battle order in "T" Tommy and we squeezed in a 20 minute night flying test during the morning in readiness. Around dusk we took off as part of a force of 46 Mosquitoes attacking Cologne and returned some three and a quarter hours later with an excellent aiming point photograph after an uneventful trip. Later reports mentioned the heavy damage caused to the city by our 4,000 lbs bombs.

Berlin was the target for the following two nights after which weather conditions were such that we were switched to the Ruhr attacking first Mannheim then Essen. On the 29th conditions were again favourable for the Big City and I lost no time in placing Sandy and I on the battle order once more. As our force of 53 Mosquitoes bombed Berlin, to the north and east the heavies were attacking Stettin and Königsberg at extreme range and suffering quite heavy losses. My flying time for the Berlin raid amounted to four hours and twenty five minutes, the easiest and fastest operation I ever made against the capital city. The last trip of the month was against Frankfurt with no losses whatsoever for the squadron during the whole of August.

Squadron operations were running like clockwork by now and on several occasions the A.O.C. brought visiting VIPs to Group Headquarters at nearby Castle Hill House, Huntingdon to our briefings. There was never any warning given. They simply arrived and left as soon as it was over. Because of the intensity of operations my two Flight Commanders Sanderson and McBain, were both rapidly approaching the end of their tours of operations set at 50 trips and I would have to earmark suitable replacements for them by mid-October at the latest. I had not yet felt able to take the end of tour leave due to me on leaving Coningsby but with everything going so well I decided to squeeze in one more operational flight during the first week in September and then take a well-earned week's leave with my family in the Cottage at Heacham where Pamela was now living, and forget the war for a while.

In the early hours of 1st September, Dusseldorf was attacked with two aircraft lost from the force as a whole and the next night Bremen was hit without loss. Bad weather held up further operations until the night of the 4th when 43 aircraft attacked Karlsruhr and returned safely from the Battle of the Ruhr in miniature.

Sandy and I were already on the battle order by the time the target came through next morning, a somewhat longer trip to Hanover and my third raid on the city. The flight was uneventful, all 43 aircraft bombing the accurately placed markers and returning without loss. The main difference on this trip as compared to our first operation with the squadron against Hannover was that we kept clear of the Bremen defences thereby reducing the flying time for the night's work by some 15 minutes.

The following afternoon I left the squadron in the capable hands of Sqn Ldr Sanderson for a while and headed for Heacham in the Austin 7 to spend a few days near the sea with Pamela and Denise. As with most operational aircrew who were married with a young child, I hoarded the bars of chocolate and barley sugar sweets issued as flying rations whenever we flew on operations. By the time I was due for leave I usually had a good stock of "goodies" to take along and this time was no exception. Life in the little Norfolk cottage was quiet and peaceful with Denise occupying our attentions throughout the day. In the evenings after she had gone to bed we played card games most of the time with cups of tea at frequent intervals and forgot about the war. At the end of the week refreshed in mind and body after the change in routine and the sea air I set off on the Sunday afternoon to return to Graveley.

During my absence the squadron had been kept busy and had flown on operations on every night with the exception of the 14/15th September. After Karlsruhe on 7th and Nuremburg and Brunswick on the 8th and 9th good weather over Eastern Germany had the LNS at full stretch attacking Berlin for the next five consecutive nights with a loss of three aircraft; 692 Squadron came through without loss.

The intensity of operations was such that throughout each month there was a steady trickle of tour-expired crews leaving the squadron to be replaced by crews from the Mosquito Conversion Unit, many for their first operational tour. Unlike the newly trained crews joining the heavy squadrons from the Heavy Conversion Units with less than two hundred flying hours under their belts, as they did a year before, many of the pilots had two or three thousand flying hours in their log books, the result of several years flying as Staff pilots at Air Navigation Schools or on SBA training. One such crew had arrived on the squadron during my absence and appeared on the battle order for the first time the day following my return. The effect of the huge 4000 lb cookie slung low down in the modified bomb bay between the undercarriage legs could cause the aircraft to swing with a pendulous motion in the early stages of take-off when the tail was on the ground and rudder control non-effective. Unless the aircraft was kept straight by differential use of the throttles until the tail came up and full rudder control was achieved, any swing that developed at this stage could not be corrected by rudder or brake operation and if attempted usually ended in the collapse of the undercarriage. That evening as I stood beside Pop Hemming in Flying Control and watched the squadron taking off for Brunswick the new pilot provided us with a perfect demonstration of how not to do it. Having allowed a swing to start by incorrect use of the throttles the aircraft oscillated from side to side along the first six hundred yards of runway without rudder control at which point the pilot used his brakes in a desperate effort to straighten up. This caused the undercarriage legs to collapse sideways and the aircraft carried on some distance on its belly in a shower of sparks, finally coming to rest and starting to burn. In the light of the flickering flames there was no sign of the occupants leaving the wreckage so I hurtled out of the building and into the staff Hillman and started towards the crash which was now well alight. Halfway there the bomb went off; fortunately most of the blast went away from me in the direction of 8 Group Headquarters where it accounted for a number of broken windows. The crew were interested spectators from the safety of a ditch to which they had sprinted after leaving the aircraft by the top hatch — I certainly didn't find it quite as amusing as they did!

Next night Bremen was attacked without loss with Berlin once again the target on the following night. The fine autumnal weather we had been experiencing generally was now breaking up and the Light Night Striking Force was stood down for once after Berlin. The night of 19/20th September was memorable for one incident;

Wing Commander Guy Gibson of "Dambuster" fame was killed while flying as Master Bomber on a 5 Group raid on Munchen Gladbach/Rheydt. He had taken over the Base Operations post at Coningsbury that I so nearly had and was flying a 627 Squadron Mosquito at the time. His aircraft crashed in flames in Holland before crossing the coast on the homeward flight over the North Sea.

Over the next 48 hours rain and low cloud followed by widespread fog over England kept Bomber Command on the ground but by 23rd operations against targets in the Rhuhr were possible and the squadron was briefed for a dusk take-off for Bochum. Sandy and I headed the battle order and during the morning we managed to get in a quick night flying test on "C" Charlie before it was bombed up. Dead on time that evening and all checks carried out I started up the engines and taxied along the perimeter track for take-off on the main runway in an east-west direction. This involved quite a long period of taxiing around the end of the short runway before turning left parallel to the main runway and the take-off point at the eastern end. After the heavy rain of late the grass verges bordering the perimeter track were like Irish bogs. Picking my way carefully towards the left bend and keeping a watchful eye on the brake cylinder pressure, I applied a little differential pressure through the rudder controls to start the turn and with no warning the pressure dropped to zero and the heavily laden aircraft, now uncontrollable, ploughed straight on becoming stationary as it sank into the grass surface up to the wheel axes. Cursing our bad fortune I called Flying Control to inform them of the situation and asked for transport to collect us and take us to the spare aircraft bombed up and ready for such an emergency in the dispersal area. As I fumed and waited, the rest of the squadron took off in quick succession leaving me with less than 20 minutes to get airborne in the spare, otherwise Group would veto the sortie. Within minutes the Flying Control van appeared, and throwing our parachutes in the back we hared off towards the squadron dispersal area, only to find that the armament staff, having watched the full quota of aircraft taxi out, had already started to disarm the spare and had winched down the cookie on to the bomb trolley now standing beneath the open bomb doors.

Seeing us approaching the armourers realised their mistake and in a burst of feverish activity reconnected the two hoisting cables to the bomb and started to winch the ungainly canister of high explosive upwards into the empty bomb compartment. This was always a tricky operation with the aircraft in the "tail down" position on the ground, as the clearance fore and after in the bomb bay was minimal; having first raised the bomb until the rear face was level with the rear face of the bomb compartment it was then necessary to winch up the front, thereby tilting the bomb until it started to enter the bay, being manhandled by brute force and kept steady as the two winch operators applied even lift to draw it slowly upwards and connect it to the bomb carrier. Sandy and myself and several ground crew were in the process of applying the brute force required to keep the bomb tilted when the rear cable snapped throwing the full load on the front cable which also snapped, and two tons of high explosive hit the dispersal pan within inches of my feet with a shattering crunch. After that little episode I was in no state to pursue the matter further and retired from the unequal combat with the gremlins to the Officers Mess bar for a stiff drink to restore my shattered nerves.

The squadron returned without loss some two hours later and landed safely in far from ideal conditions. Next day most of Western Europe was covered in thick cloud and the Light Night Striking Force was stood down; a small force of heavies was sent to bomb German positions in the Calais area using Oboe-aimed sky markers, but only half of them bombed. The welcome break from night operations proved a bonus for Sandy and I for early next morning "C" Charlie was serviceable and we were able to cram in some practice bombing runs on the range at nearby Whittlesea, and an S.B.A. landing during our night flying test for the as yet unknown night operations.

That eventually came through after we landed, a force of 48 Mosquitoes on Mannheim. The weather was still pretty bad as we took off from Graveley that night and climbed eastwards through nearly 20,000 feet of thick cloud before reaching clear conditions. The operations went off as planned and we returned to an SBA assisted landing at base three hours and forty five minutes later to find that the squadron had suffered its first casualty since I took over command. The crew in question was an experienced Warrant officer pilot and SNCO navigator who had only recently returned from leave and all the indications were that the pilot had lost control climbing through cloud, possibly through engine failure, and had spun into the ground with his bomb load somewhere to the east of Norwich. After notifiying the next of kin and putting in train the standard procedures regarding kit etc, operations went on as usual with the squadron being briefed for Frankfurt that night. Soon after arriving in my office next morning I received a telephone call from the Warrant Officer's father. After a long preamble he asked if he could visit Graveley the following day to see me about a personal matter concerning his son. He also asked permission to bring along the boy's uncle, his brother, to meet some of his friends in the Sergeant's Mess. I explained that the squadron would most likely be preparing for the night's operations and everyone would be busy, and that I might not be available, but he persisted with his request. Eventually I arranged with the Adjutant to have them picked up at the railway station at Huntingdon at noon, brought to Graveley for lunch and a quick visit to the crew room, returning to the rail station afterwards to catch the Birmingham train.

The LNSF was operating at full intensity at this period and that night I briefed the squadron for Kassel. The evenings were drawing in with the approach of October and on these shorter trips with a dusk take-off the first aircraft would be landing back at base around eleven o'clock giving a reasonably early night for most of us. By the time my two visitors were brought in to see me just before lunch next morning, preparations for that night's attack on Brunswick were well advanced and I was able to give them a little time. My sympathy for them in their loss soon evaporated when it became clear that the main object of their visit was to get their hands on a Post Office Savings book showing a healthy balance and a wallet containing money, both items now in the safe custody of the Officer appointed to safeguard the W.O's kit. I informed them that these items would be dealt with by the Disposal Board and forwarded to the next of kin in due course and that I could not interfere with the process at this stage. They then brought up the subject of the funeral arrangements to be held in Birmingham and asked for representation from the Squadron. I said that I would send an officer and two SNCOs and wreaths would be sent by the squadron and station. I added that I would like to send a floral tribute personally and they agreed to arrange it for me with a local florist up to a cost of £5 and to have the bill sent on to me later. After a short tour of the crew room and an aircraft they were whisked off to have the odd drink and lunch in the Mess and then returned to Birmingham.

Some days later the funeral took place in the afternoon and on his return the Flight Lieutenant who had represented the squadron at the ceremony told me how it had gone. His party had arrived at the house in Birmingham half an hour before the cortège assembled to find that a wake had been going on for most of the morning and many of the mourners were already drunk. The Fl. Lt. also commented on the magnificent floral tributes and in particular one of white Arum lilies made up in the form of a Mosquito aircraft that dwarfed the rest. Even then the penny didn't drop until some days later when I recieved the bill from the florist for £21, the best part of a month's pay, and realised that I had been taken for a ride over this solemn occasion. Never again.

The squadron was having a busy time at this period, the weather over NW Germany being generally fine, and on the next five nights attacks were made in strength on Karlsrhur, Hamburg, twice more on Brunswick and lastly on Kassel all without loss. We were then stood down for a night on 4th October and the forecast for the next 24 hours was gloomy.

For some weeks I had been trying to squeeze in a long standing visit to De Havillands at the invitation of Major Hereward de Havilland to see the latest progress on modifications being incorporated, and this seemed to be a good opportunity to visit Hatfield. By now both of my Flight Commanders were within two or three trips of finishing their tours and were taking it in turn to be on the Battle Order. So, leaving Sanderson to look after things in my absence I set off after breakfast to drive to the Hatfield works, being met there on my arrival around eleven o'clock by the Major himself. After an interesting morning discussing various problems and being shown around some sections dealing with them we went out of the gates to the Comet hotel, so named after the success of the DH Comet aircraft in the London — Singapore air race in the early thirties, where luncheon was laid on. I was about to raise the glass containing my first drink to my lips when I was called to the phone. It was the A.O.C. wanting me back at Graveley as quickly as possible, as the squadron was on a special operation that night. There was nothing for it but to make my apologies to the De Haviland people and hare back along the Great North Road as fast as the service Hillman could take me, sans lunch.

Back at Graveley the target for that night turned out to be the Kiel Canal; the Navy had produced a new type of mine for use in shallow waters that was virtually unsweepable, and nine aircraft of 692 Sqdn were to lay these mines at low level at specific points along the canal, helped by the moonlight conditions and clear skies forecast for the area. Sanderson had detailed the aircraft and crews in my absence and had included himself and the other Flight Commander. Air tests had been carried out and each crew had practiced low level runs along the nearby Forty Foot Drain during the tests. The light Ack Ack defences strategically placed along both sides of the canal were the greatest danger to low flying aircraft and I briefed the crews carefully on the latest positions from Intelligence sources. Strangely enough on this occasion the positions of the guns proved of great assistance and little danger because of the weather conditions in the Jutland area. It was a clear moonlight night with the ground temperature falling rapidly through radiation and creating a layer of ground mist that blotted out all sighting for the gunners. This radiation mist rolls down the hillsides and lays in the valleys, following the contours of the countryside. It thus clearly delineated the line of the canal. So, although the crews could not actually see the surface of the water, they had an accurate guide to its whereabouts while the Germans manning the guns, who could only fire blind through the mist, unwittingly gave away the release points for dropping the mines. All the aircraft arrived back safely after what proved to be a highly successful operation.

All shipping to and from the Baltic was held up for a period of over three weeks until the mines were eventually exploded in situ and repairs to the canal could be undertaken. The A.O.C. was highly delighted with the operation and passed word to me that he would be favourably inclined towards any recommendations I might put forward for awards. I forwarded citations for DSOs in respect of McBain and Sanderson, the two Flight Commanders, both of whom were within a couple of trips to completing their tours of 50 operations. To my great delight they were approved immediately and they left shortly afterwards.

They were replaced by Brodie and Wadsworth, two able and experienced pilots who were promoted to fill the vacant posts.

After the successful mining operation there was a short lull for the next 48 hours mainly due to weather conditions over the area. On 9th/10th October the town of Wilhemshaven was the target for 47 Mosquitoes, a force that included Sandy and I in 'C' Charlie. The target was obscured by cloud but the markers put down by the H25 aircraft were bombed successfully and all the aircraft returned safely albeit to land in poor weather conditions at base.

As I lay in bed in the early hours and mused over the three months I had been with the Squadron I could not help thinking how lucky things had turned out for me so far. Over the period something in the region of 50 major German targets had been bombed by an average nightly total of 16 aircraft from No 692 Squadron for a loss of one aircraft and crew and that was not caused by enemy action. What a difference to Lancaster operations in the early part of the year when losses each night were often 40 or more aircraft carrying 5 or more crew. Mulling over these matters I soon fell asleep.

Next night Cologne was the target and once again all our aircraft returned safely from the short trip. Everything was running so well that I just felt in my bones that something would go wrong soon, and sure enough it happened the next night. I had briefed the crews for Berlin and watched the aircraft take off in swift succession from the warmth of the Flying Control room before returning to the Officers Mess to have dinner. Three and a half hours later I returned to Flying Control in time to watch the first aircraft back touch down on the main runway closely followed by the other aircraft waiting in the circuit for the Control Officer to call them in to land. The third aircraft to touch down experienced a sudden and complete loss of brakes and had no alternative but to carry on along the runway and into the soft grass overshoot area, where it came to a stop, bogged down to the wheel axles and creating an obstruction to other aircraft landing. As it would take some time to drag it clear and there were still a dozen aircraft to get down, all with a low reserve of fuel it was decided to change over to the short runway at this point, and all pilots were informed and warned to exercise care in landing because of the changed circumstances. The first aircraft to land was piloted by one of my most experienced Flight Lieutenants who had logged almost 3,000 hours of flying and should have had no difficulty in bringing down his now lightly-laden aircraft on the 1,600 yards runway. On this occasion, however, his initial approach was too high and he touched down half-way along the runway. Realising that not enough runway was left in which to pull-up he decided to go round again and opened up the throttles fully on overshoot procedure. Conditions were clear and "Pop" Hemming and I watched the aircraft identification light as it lifted clear of the runway and climbed away. At this point the pilot should have selected undercarriage "UP" to reduce drag and increase speed. The next step would have been to raise the landing flaps gradually a little at a time until fully "UP".

To our horror the light suddenly dipped and there was a flash followed by an explosion and a ball of flame as the aircraft stuck the boles of a row of trees half a mile from the end of the runway. Either the pilot had inadvertantly selected the flap lever to "UP" in mistake for the undercarriage or had operated the lever to raise the flaps in one go. Either way there would have been no second chance at that height. The sudden loss of lift at minimal speed meant that a crash was inevitable. The crash fire-tender crew were on their toes and the vehicle was already heading the shortest way round the perimeter track towards the nearest emergency exit gate in the wire fence. Quickly pin-pointing the position of the crash on the large-scale map in the control room it struck me that it was much better to leave the camp via the Guard-room and use the roads to get there without the possibility of getting bogged down going cross-country. I left Pop Hemming to carry on landing the remaining aircraft and shot downstairs and into the Hillman parked outside, driving off as fast as I could with safety. My intuition proved correct for I arrived at the scene of the crash some minutes before the fire tender crew, who had run into difficulties opening the locked gates and then became bogged down before finding the road. By the light of the flickering flames from the burning wreckage I approached what was left of the main fuselage and cockpit; it was upside down straddling the grass verge and at the side of the road and a deep ditch that ran parallel to it, and was still on fire. There was little hope of the crew having survived such a horrendous crash, but to make certain I crawled along the ditch until I could almost touch the burning wreckage. I could see a black flying boot sticking out of the smashed cockpit and thinking that I might be able to drag the body clear I got hold of the boot and pulled; the boot and what remained in it came away easily and I left it where it fell and returned to the roadway to meet the now approaching crash tender whose crew would complete the gruesome salvage task. Afterwards I drove back to Graveley where debriefing of the crews had been completed and rang Group Ops to let them know the position. In three months of intensive operations against German targets this was only the third aircraft the Squadron had lost and the second crew killed, all apparently through accidents or pilot error.

On the two following nights the Squadron was sent to Hamburg and Cologne, all the aircraft returning safely in good order. On the morning of 14th October Operation "Hurricane" was started against Duisburg by the heavies of Bomber Command with the intention of demonstrating to Germans generally the now overwhelming superiority of the Allied Air Forces. More than 1,000 aircraft bombed in the first wave followed by a larger force of heavies from the American Eighth Air Force, escorted by fighters, which bombed targets in the Cologne area. The Bomber Command heavies then struck again at Duisburg in two waves two hours apart, including 39 Mosquitoes from the Light Night Striking Force.

Sandy and I went along as part of the force ahead of the Lancasters and Halifaxes and provided "Windowing", finally releasing our "cookie" on the Oboe marker in the centre of one of the huge fires started during the earlier raids. Our trip from start to finish took less than three hours. In less than 48 hours almost

9,000 tons of bombs had fallen on Duisburg in the heaviest raid of the war so far. And still it went on as on the following night I briefed the crews for Hamburg and on the next night another sortie to Cologne; all the crews returned safely from these operations. After eight consecutive nights the squadron deserved a break and early next morning word came from Group that we could stand down that night. I went to my office to deal with any paperwork that required my attention and to check the squadron operational record was being kept up to date.

The relative calm was disturbed when Paddy Menaul the Station Commander came in hot-foot with news for us. Apparently the Foreign Relations Department at the Air Ministry had decided to make a publicity film for showing in the South American countries where the Fellowship of the Bellows had been active. As a "Bellows" squadron 692 had been selected to play the major role in the film which was to be shot at Graveley on the 20th November. It was to take the form of a presentation parade at which a South American born Squadron Officer WAAF, (who was also the Chief Windlass of the organisation) would accompany the Argentina Ambassador and present a specially made and inscribed set of bellows to the Squadron. Present at the parade would be the AOC No 8 Group, Air Vice Marshal D.C.T. Bennett, the Director of Foreign Relations at the Air Ministry, Air Commodore Foster, and the AOC in C Bomber Command Air Chief Marshal Sir Arthur Harris. If a new Squadron crest could be designed and produced in time to be authorised by H.M. the King it would be presented to the Squadron at the same time, thereby adding a little more lustre to the proceedings. After some discussion of the problems likely to be encountered, it was agreed that the venue for the parade would have to be on the tarmac apron near the Squadron offices, and that I would mount a drill rehearsal for the squadron at the first convenient opportunity without interfering with operations. I would also initiate a competition for budding artists to put forward their ideas for a suitable crest having regard to the operational role of 692 squadron. I would then submit the

A photograph of the Squadron shield designed while Joe was CO, complete with King George's signature of approval.

Joe being presented with the new Shield by Donald Bewer, with 'Bomber' Harris looking on.

winning design to the office of the Chester Herald and liaise with him on the production of the finished article which would have to be signed in person by His Majesty before it was official. I phoned the Chester Herald's office and was given a lot of useful ideas and a dead-line was agreed to allow sufficient time for the crest to be produced, taken to Buckingham Palace for signature and then delivered to Graveley before the parade. Next morning, before the teleprinters began chattering their instructions from Group regarding "target for tonight", I gathered everything together in the briefing room and started things rolling on the Squadron crest competition.*

* (Editor's comment. Joe did not record that the crest was duly completed and presented as evidenced by the photograph of the shield, with King George's signature, and of the presentation ceremony).

★   ★   ★

Our target the night after the break was Hannover with thick frontal cloud covering much of the route. During the day No 3 Group had flow the first major operation in its new independent role using the new G-H blind bombing device on days when the ground was concealed by cloud with tops of the clouds no higher than 18,000 feet. Bonn had been the target and the attack had been a complete success with only one aircraft lost. Other Mosquitoes were being sent to Mannheim and Dusseldorf but all 692's aircraft were on the Hanover raid. The temptation was too much and leaving Wadsworth off the battle order to look after things I quickly included myself and Sandy, hoping that Pat Menaul would not notice the extra trip. The outward flight was quite uneventful and the fires started by the bombs in the target area were well concentrated, but on losing height on the way back the port engine iced up badly and I finished up landing on one engine with the port airscrew feathering. The total time for the trip even then was only three ours and twenty five minutes.

Next day it was back to normal, briefing the crews who formed part of a force of 48 Mosquitoes sent to Wiesbaden; all returned safely. At this stage I was beginning to find the restrictions placed on my operating with the squadron irksome and frustrating and I saw no reason why I shouldn't be allowed to do more. In this frame of mind it was just as well that the weather took a hand in the situation and operations were called off for the next 48 hours.

During that time I had an unexpected visit from St John Turner, the Intelligence Officer of my old 1473 Flight days and now at an airfield in East Anglia. During the long night stand-bys waiting to be sent off on investigational flights by 80 Signals Wing from Finmere, Turner had often talked about his pre-war days in the Diplomatic Service. Up to the time when the Nazis overran Europe he was serving on the Embassy staff at The Hague and had managed somehow to send all his household goods back to U.K. before being evacuated. Included in the packing cases were some excellent toys for his children, then three or four years old. However, the cases had been lost in transit and his children had grown out of the toys by then. He had often said that if the toys ever turned up he would see that I got a pedal car for Denise and now, true to his word, he had turned up out of the blue with it in time for Christmas. It was a lovely little machine, almost a miniature model of my old Austin Arrow "Amy" and a similar colour. Over the next few weeks I derived a lot of pleasure fitting it out with small gadgets and number plates and ensuring that it was in pristine condition ready for the big day.

My lucky star was in the ascendency it seemed for that night after dinner in the Mess I was chatting to some of my crews and enjoying a beer with them when the subject got around to my current baby Austin and I happened to mention that I would gladly let it go if I could find a more modern car, preferably a weatherproof saloon, for family use. At that, a Flight Lieutenant in the group, said that he had just the car for me, a 1937 Morris 8 saloon, and that he would be willing to take the Austin and some ready cash in exchange for it. We eventually agreed on the sum of £40 and I wrote out a cheque for him on the spot; we concluded the transaction after lunch the next day, both of us well satisfied with our bargains. My new acquisition, a dark blue two-door saloon seemed in good running order and was to prove invaluable over the next couple of years.

By 22nd October 1944 the weather had cleared sufficiently to the east to send a 45-strong force of Mosquitoes to Hamburg, and the following night 38 were sent to Berlin; guessing that the target might again be Berlin on the 24th I slipped Sandy and myself on the battle order hoping that Pat Menaul wouldn't notice that we had already exceeded our quota for the month, but the target turned out to be Hanover. The trip to the city proved uneventual on the way in but on the way back rocket-assisted night fighters lit up the sky ahead as they used the extra thrust to climb above the returning Mosquitoes, and then use the height to gain sufficient speed to make a single attack. I throttled back the engines and dropped the undercarriage as I carried out a 360 degree turn to search for them but saw nothing so I resumed course for home. Letting down over the North sea we received broadcast instructions to land at Coltishall, as further inland the whole of East Anglia was covered with a belt of fog and low stratus. All our aircraft returned and landed there safely and the crews, including myself, spent an uncomfortable night on the floor of a crew-room. By the time all the aircraft were refuelled by the overworked ground crew and the weather had cleared sufficiently for take-off it was mid-day, and we landed at Graveley for a late lunch feeling scruffy and tired to find that operations for that night were cancelled and we were stood down.

Next morning with little or no warning an Air Ministry Film unit making a film covering the many roles of the Mosquito aircraft appeared on the Station requiring some shots of briefing, bombing-up and take-offs, and most of the day was spent in providing the unit with suitable action. Fortunately operations for the coming night were once again cancelled, otherwise we would have been hard-pushed to get everything done in time.

1945 started in earnest with dawn attacks on 14 rail tunnel entrances in the wooded and hilly region of the Eifel between the Rhine and the Ardennes battle area. Each Mosquito was to dive down to low level following the rail track to where it entered the mouth of the tunnel and try to "skip" its 4,000 lb cookie fitted with a short delayed action fuse into the tunnel itself. I allowed the crews to draw lots for which end of the tunnel they would attack and an hour before first light watched them take off from the Control Tower before starting the long wait for their return. In the event all but one came back. The pilot had been considered lucky in drawing what had looked like the flattest and most open approach end of his tunnel but had not reckoned on a German train that had taken shelter inside and an alert gunner manning the 20 mm gun on the last wagon. The gunner put a burst in as the Mosquito approached head-on and it crashed into the hills above, the bomb exploding on impact.

All the other aircraft were down and the crews enjoying their late breakfasts before ten o'clock with a job well done when we were warned for operations again that evening, this time to Hanover. In a matter of 24 hours the Squadron carried out three major operations against Berlin, the rail tunnels and Hanover losing only one aircraft.

Things quietened down a little after the hectic start and a few days into January my six months extended semi-operational tour with 692 Squadron ran out. On the 28th Group posted me a few miles north to the Pathfinder Training Unit at Warboys where I was to sit out the remaining weeks of the war as Chief Flying Instructor. A few days after my arrival the A.O.C. Don Bennett phoned me up late one night to congratulate me on the award of the Distinguished Service Order which had just been notified by signal. I was over the moon and could hardly wait to pass the news on to Pamela at Easter Cottage. That weekend having raised enough petrol coupons to get the Morris 8 to Heacham and back, I set off in pouring rain on the Friday evening to see my family, using all the minor roads and short cuts that seemed feasible from the map to conserve petrol. As I turned into a darkened village street somewhere in the Fens the front off-side wheel suddenly parted company with the car and rolled off into the darkness, the studs on the hub flange having sheared for some reason. Getting out of the nearside door so as not to tilt the car on the hub I collected the wheel and walked along the street looking for some sign of life. There was no sign of a garage but a chink of light from a window with a badly fitting curtain attracted my attention, and the sign hanging above confirmed that it was the village pub. I opened the door and walked into the little bar parlour, still carrying the car wheel. The landlord proved to be very helpful and as I dried off in front of the fire with a glass of bitter ale he gave me the low down on the village facilities. The most important one as far as I was concerned was an agricultural machinery repair workshop just along the road that had a welding plant. The fitter came in for his pint at that moment so I paid for it and we got talking over what sort of a repair we could do. Once he realised that I was also a trained mechanic and could help he became quite enthusiastic, and in no time at all we had pushed the car on three wheels into the lighted workshop amongst rusted bits of farm machinery. I jacked up the front axle and stripped the hub passing it to my friend to drill out the remains of the broken studs. Meanwhile I searched around and found three suitably sized coach bolts with square nuts of the type used on farm machines. These were slotted into the newly drilled holes and my friend welded the round heads in position; I cleaned them up with a rusty file and re-assembled the hub bolting the wheel back in position by means of the square nuts and we were ready for the road again. I could hardly believe my luck, for the whole repair had only taken an hour. Also, other than accepting another pint before I set off, the welder absolutely refused any payment and to this day he has my heart-felt gratitude for being a friend in need. The wheel was still holding firm and true when I disposed of the car two years later.

Returning from Heacham I started to settle down in my job with the Pathfinder Training Unit alongside Hamish Mahaddie. He was in residence with his family in the small Station Commanders Quarters near the Mess, having replaced John Searby as C.O. some months before. By now the Mess bar was almost unrecognisable from earlier days being positively ecclesiastical, with beautiful stained glass windows and oaken carved pews fitted in situ. This was Hamish's doing, as apparently he had met a local Vicar whose church had been damaged by enemy action earlier in the war, although not enough to destroy the lovely stained glass. The vicar expressed his fears that local vandals might finish off what the Germans had started whereupon Hamish offered to have them brought to Warboys for safe custody. His offer was accepted and within days the windows and some oak pews were installed in the Mess bar where they stayed, a source of pleasure to the residents of the Mess and numerous visitors, until the war ended.

There was little pressure on me in my job as Chief Flying Instructor now that the end of the war was in sight and I began to make tentative enquiries locally about accommodation with the object of having Pamela and Denise nearby. At that moment I ran into more trouble with the car, expensive noises emanating from the clutch every time I changed gear. The experts in the M.T. Section were unanimous in their opinion, viz that the carbon faced clutch operating ring was worn out or disintegrating rapidly and needed replacing. I phoned around the few garages still open but none could offer me a quick repair. One did try to help by saying that if I could get someone to call in he would let me have the part required and I might be able to get it done at Warboys. It seemed the best solution so I arranged for the M.T. to call in on a duty run and I decided to do the job myself. The following Sunday I ran the Morris into an empty Nissen hut formerly used as a workshop, donned a borrowed set of overalls and got cracking. It took longer than I expected working without a handbook but I finished the job in time for tea and the car was now in good shape. That being so, when I was offered a furnished cottage in Needingsworth that had been used as overflow accommodation by the Ferryboat Inn nearby on the river, I was able to take it knowing that I had reliable transport. I then fetched Pamela and Denise from Heacham and installed them in a cottage near St. Ives. To all intents and purposes the strategic bomber offensive was over and at P.T.U. we were merely marking time and awaiting the inevitable end of the conflict in Europe, while hazarding guesses as to what yet lay in store for us in the Far Eastern theatre once it ended. Time alone would tell. Meanwhile we made ourselves as comfortable as possible in the cottage and with Spring on the way took Denise on little outings about the district and tried to forget all about it.

In April Hamish Mahaddie was posted, and his place taken by Laurie Deane now tour-expired from 83 Squadron and sporting a well earned DSO from his Master Bomber activities. In one of the boat houses along the river near St. Ives we kept an airborne life-boat of the type dropped by parachute to ditched airmen. To mark the occasion Laurie was made Captain and we spent the afternoon chugging up and down the River Ouse under the guise of a training session for the senior instructors. One sunny afternoon I took out a rowing boat and rowed Pamela and Denise; it was tiring work and after a while I headed for the bank intending to tie up to a tree. At the bank Denise tried to step ashore and only a lucky grab by Pamela saved her from a ducking.

As we dallied in the cottage and began to live as a family once more during those few weeks of April, events moved fast on the final breakthrough into Germany. Although the Ruhr was encircled early in the month it held out for nearly three weeks before the German troops finally surrendered the ruined cities to the Allies. A few days later, the Americans linked up with the Russians on the Elbe, Berlin fell to the Russians, and Montgomery moved northwards to capture Bremen, Hamburg and Lübeck and meet the Russians on the Baltic coast. In the sure knowledge that the war in Europe would be over within days and to be ready for whatever might be in store for me and the ensuing chaos, I took Denise and Pamela back to Heacham to join her mother for the time being. It was just as well, for on 8th May after nearly six years the last bomb was dropped, the fighting stopped and the war against Germany came to an end with the signing of the surrender on Luneberg Heath. Everyone went mad and VE Day celebrations broke out spontaneously everywhere. At Warboys all attempts at work were abandoned and many went A.W.O.L. to 'do their own thing'. I had a tank full of petrol in the car ready for the occasion and I too just quietly disappeared for the next 24 hours, turning up at Heacham where we all celebrated the red-letter day listening to BBC Radio programmes, playing card games and still hardly realising that it was really ended.

Returning to Warboys next day I found few of the staff around, and most of them were nursing prize hangovers and unfit for anything! I went to my office but there seemed to be nothing worth while doing. The sense of purpose that had sustained me throughout war operations was missing and I felt lost for some days. It was just as well that we were to keep busy in other directions, being called upon to repatriate some of the many thousands of prisoners of war now released from camps in East Germany. The Allied transportation organisation was unable to deal quickly with the problem due to the state of the pulverised road and rail networks throughout Germany. So Bomber Command laid on a massive air lift using aircraft and crews to fly to selected collecting points and return in a matter of hours with full loads of ex-prisoners. Many thousands of these mercy flights were made by our Lancasters and Halifaxes over the next few days.

Once the immediate crisis was over we turned to the ground crews who had worked so hard and under such appalling weather conditions to provide and service the aircraft for the bomber offensive. We owed them so much, we who had survived and returned safely, and our only way of saying thank you was to fly them around some of the major German cities on a form of "Cooks Tour" and let them see for themselves the punishment that had been meted out through their efforts. It was most illuminating to hear their comments on return from their five and a half hour marathon sight-seeing tour in the discomfort of a Lancaster fuselage. On my flights I took them over a route: Dungeness - Cap Gris Nez - StVith - Kaiser - Lauten-Karlsruhr - Mannheim - Worms - Darmstadt - Hanau - Mainz - Koblenz - Cologne - Aachen - Namur - Dunkirk returning via Ramsgate, a trip I'm sure they will all remember to the end of their days.

Preparing for Peace

In the Far East the war against Japan was still being fought with undiminished ferocity. Arrangements were under way in this country to form "Tiger Force" which was planned as a contribution to the American forces in that theatre. There was a massive pool of RAF aircrew, both officers and S.N.C.O.s, kicking their heels after being laid off from flying in the operational commands in Britain and it was decided to utilise these personnel wherever possible in much needed ground staff roles. To ensure that none of their previous skills and experience was overlooked the redundant aircrew were first sent in droves to Holding Units usually ex-O.T.U.s. At these they appeared before Re-assessment Boards hurriedly set up to interview each candidate, assess his capabilities and recommend him for the ground duties at which he appeared most useful. "P" Staff then took action to see that candidates were posted to such duties while still retaining their rank and pay as aircrew.

At the beginning of June, I received an immediate posting as the senior member of one such board being set up at the war-time O.T.U. at Bruntingthorpe some 15 miles from Leicester. Arriving at Bruntingthorp I was joined by other board members and we sorted out our terms of reference and modus operandi ready to start interviewing. From then on our board dealt with a seemingly endless procession of "bolshie" or resigned ex-aircrew, as we endeavoured to extract sufficient information from them to asses their capabilities and recommend their roles during the final phase of the war.

After several weeks of this soul-destroying routine all the board members were heartily sick of the job. Then out of the blue came a reprieve for me in the shape of a telephone call from my old friend Jackie Onions whom I had last seen at Bicester in 1943. Now

SPSO at 100 Group H.Q. Jackie had tracked me down to offer me a posting commanding a satellite station to Honiley just outside Stratford on Avon which would shortly become vacant. I jumped at the opportunity, whereupon Jackie arranged for me to be interviewed by Group Captain Messenger, the Station Commander at Honiley on 14th August. I duly reported there and after a satisfactory interview the Group Captain flew us over to Atherstone in the Station Proctor and showed me around. I also met the out-going Wing Commander who was being de-mobilised, and I was greatly impressed by seeing a G.C.A. Unit in action for the first time. When the Americans released the first atomic bombs on Hiroshima and Nagasaki resulting in the Japanese surrender on 19th August my board was disbanded, at the same time my posting to Atherstone was confirmed; once again I packed all my kit in the Morris and set off for my new station.

Atherstone was a wartime airfield made up from land requisitioned from local farms and estates; all the buildings were of a temporary nature, mostly Nissens, and for most of the war the airfield had formed part of No 22 O.T.U. It was conveniently situated near the main Stratford on Avon — Oxford road some three or four miles from the Bard's birthplace and surrounded by pleasant countryside. I arrived there to find that my predecessor had already left on demobilisation. He had lived in single quarters converted from a disused NAAFI store, one of the few single brick buildings on the camp, so I moved in there where I had the use of two bedrooms, bathroom and a small sitting room and kitchen. The building had definite possibilities for use as a temporary married quarter and only required a few extras to make it fairly comfortable, as it already had central heating radiators. Accordingly, I tackled the Station Commander to find out whether he would have any objections to me having my family join me on the airfield, and was much relieved to hear that he would turn a blind eye to anything of that nature. For the next week or two I had my hands full by day getting to know everything about the running of the airfield and the GCA School, and in the evenings putting into practice plans to make the quarter more acceptable for a family. The sitting room still had large double entrance doors used originally for delivering stores and was extremely cold and draughty. However, I found an airman who could lay bricks and between us we designed and built a chimney and fireplace in place of the doors; there was no shortage of logs from blown down trees around the airfield to make a cozy fire. A coffee table was next on the list so I enrolled in the evening wood-working class currently in vogue on the station and in a few hours made a passable round table, using waste 5 ply sheets that looked extremely good when finally smoothed down and painted. I ordered an electric cooker which was delivered and installed next day and arranged with the acting NCO to have single rations in kind delivered to the quarter once a week so that everything was above board, for officially I was still living as a single officer in the Mess. It only remained to collect Pamela and Denise from the cottage at Heacham. I made the trip there over the weekend, returning on the Sunday with the car loaded with all sorts of odds and ends designed to make the makeshift quarters a little less austere. With the daily help of the batwoman allocated to the building we were soon settled in and enjoying our new life as a family in the middle of the activities taking place on the camp, and I could now give my undivided attention to the running of the station.

All training of G.C.A. crews for the Royal Air Force was carried out at Atherstone on the three makes of American equipment, Bendix, Gilfillan and Westinghouse. Altogether some 32 sets of operational equipment and two complete ground simulators had been sent to us under Lease/Lend. Although initially designed as an approach and landing aid for United States carrier-borne aircraft operating in the Pacific theatre, the equipment was fast coming into use as a universal landing aid for all. It had been introduced into the RAF too late for it to be of service to Bomber Command. By the time sufficient RAF personnel had been trained in the States to operate and maintain the sets and then returned to this country to set up a School and train further operators to man more units, the war in Europe was practically over. Only a few units were operational at key airfields in N.W. Europe, Eindhoven, Hamburg and Gatow and one or two of the newly-designated Master airfields at Carnaby and Manston had started limited watches as a step towards being available for emergencies throughout the 24 hours.

But now that demobilisation was starting in earnest the RAF was experiencing extreme difficulties in keeping even those few GCA units it had fully manned, and the School was working flat out to provide enough trained replacements to keep them operational. The situation was so acute that the C.O. of the school, Squadron Leader Rex Brailsford, had been given authority to decide on the implement all postings of trained operators, using the School aircraft for moving them whenever time was of the essence in effecting a posting. The ex-Coastal Wellingtons formerly used on anti-U boat operations fitted with the Leigh light were particularly useful for ferrying personnel to and from N.W. Europe when not utilised on the daily training schedules alongside the basic Oxfords. The two Short Stirlings on the other hand were pretty useless for either task as they were seldom serviceable for flying, and in any event were a very expensive method of providing a blip for the training of ground operators as approach controllers.

As the autumn turned into winter I found life very satisfying, supervising all aspects of the smooth running of the station, taking part in the flying programmes and running into Stratford on Avon at weekends taking Pamela and Denise out to lunch and shopping. They too were happy in the quarters only a short distance from the airmens' dining hall. This became the station cinema in the evenings with several changes of programmes.

In October I flew the School Radar Officer, Flight Lieutenant A.C. Clarke* up to Carnaby to re-site the G.C.A. Unit there, and over lunch we had an interesting talk on his future plans when his demobilisation came through. "Nobby" had trained in the States where he had met the German rocket expert Von Braun. He had developed a consuming passion for space research and telemetry to the extent that he intended to leave his Civil Service job at the Treasury and enter University for a further Physics degree in these subjects. In the meantime he would keep himself by

---

* He was of course the famous Arthur C. Clarke who was to achieve world acclaim in space research and with his writings in science fiction.

writing space fiction books in his spare time. Nobby kept a large telescope in his quarters with which he scanned the heavens on clear nights. I joined him one evening moon-watching, and later on in November flew him to the R.A.E. Farnborough to see an exhibition of captured German "Vee" weapons, to his great delight.

There were two further events of note before Christmas that year, the first being when we took Denise to her first pantomine, a matinée performance at the Shakespearian theatre in Stratford. Then the Station laid on its own performance of "Babes in the Wood", a huge success by any standards. Afterwards most of the personnel went off on their first peace-time Christmas leave, and then it was the New Year.

★   ★   ★

1946 started quietly enough with as yet no indication of what it had in store for me. Whenever possible I flew Oxfords and Wellingtons on the GCA training programme and tried to keep myself in flying practice. Group Captain Messenger left Honiley and was replaced by Tim Vickers another signals specialist. We got on well together. At the beginning of March Turner-Hughes, the Armstrong Whitworth Chief Test pilot at nearby Baginton airfield contacted me in his role as Chairman of the Coventry branch of the Royal Aeronautical Society and asked me to give a talk on "Bomber Operations" at their next meeting in Coventry, to be held near to the damaged cathedral. Toc H, as he was almost universally known introduced me to the meeting and I then spoke for almost two hours before we all adjourned for refreshments; a few days later I had a very nice letter from him enclosing a press cutting from the Coventry evening paper reporting the event.

Also that month I ferried a number of newly trained operators to Gatow, staying on the following day to check the operational GCA unit based on the airfield and meet the crew. Afterwards the C.O. of the unit took me on a short trip into Berlin sight-seeing. We watched the black market operations taking place along the side of the Brandenburg Gate, the participants melting away with the approach of a military police unit, and the change-over of the guard at the Russian tank memorial nearby. We then visited Hitler's Chancellery in the Russian zone, picking our way gingerly around the huge entrance hall which had received a direct hit, (hopefully one of mine!) until we could reach the main corridor running between the ransacked offices. In the thirties, a favourite ploy of the Movietone news camera-men was to approach the intersecting double doors spaced at intervals along the highly-polished corridor, each guarded by two uniformed sentries. As the cameras reached the doors the sentries swung them wide open revealing a further stretch of wide corridor with two sentries in the distance who repeated the performance, and this could go on for some time giving an illusion of infinity in the corridors of power. Now, after some months in the hands of the Red Army it was a sorry sight. Every ministerial office leading off the corridor had been ransacked and the steel safes and cabinets blown open by explosives. The doors hung drunkenly, and everywhere the walls and floors were covered with graffiti and excrement. It was a relief to get out into the fresh air again only to be approached by a wounded German veteran of the Eastern Front trying to dispose of his Iron Cross for cigarettes or chocolate.

Returning to the mess at Gatow in time for dinner I was invited to make up a foursome at snooker afterwards. Underneath the building there were huge cellars and at some stage between the changes of ownership by Russian, American and British an excellent snooker table had found its way down there. My partner turned out to be the Station Catering Officer and we formed a good team, winning most of the frames. This led to a nice surprise for me the next morning. As I carried out the pre-flight checks on the aircraft, having been cleared along the corridor through the Eastern zone by the quadripartite Berlin Air Safety Centre, a van drew up and delivered two cases of French wine for me with the compliments of the Station Commander, Group Captain Somerville. He was living in a commandeered mansion on the lakes nearby with a millionaire life style, ably assisted by the Catering Officer. No doubt in the cellars would be a huge stock of looted wines from the occupation of France and in my opinion no better disposal of the stock was possible than the route my two cases were taking. Three hours later I touched down at Manston for Customs clearance given on the spot as the Customs Officer was busy dealing with an Anson that had landed earlier loaded to the gills with champagne intended for a mess party somewhere. Forty minutes later I landed back at Atherstone with my wine intact, and richer for the experience.

On the 26th of the month, just ten days later, further problems arose with the unit at Gatow; at the start of each month the four power's Commanders in Chief Germany flew into Berlin for their meeting, flying out again to report to their Governments immediately after the meeting. To ensure that adverse weather conditions would not prevent the meetings taking place the GCA unit at Gatow had to be fully manned and operationally "on its toes" on these occasions. A sudden emergency had me dashing along the Berlin corridor with replacement crew members once again and returning almost immediately via Manston — this time with nothing to declare.

During my absence notification had been received from the Air Ministry that we were to expect an unusual visitor during the next few days — a Red Army Signals Lieut. Colonel by the name of Stemasov from the Russian Embassy in Kensington Palace Gardens. Some weeks earlier there had been a major exhibition of current aircraft and Air Traffic Control aids to navigation and landing at RAF Bassingbourne. In addition to B.A.B.S. presently in use by Transport Command as the standard Blind Approach aid for their crews one of our G.C.A. Units had also been in the demonstration. Colonel Stemasov had seen the unit and been impressed so much that he had instigated a request through Embassy channels to be allowed to obtain further information through RAF sources. The visit, to last several days, was now approved and we were to provide him with single accommodation in the mess and give him as much technical information as he required. Stemasov duly turned up the following Monday, a youthful and highly intelligent officer with a charming manner who spoke perfect English. Although not a pilot, he wanted to try out the procedures himself and embarked on some hair raising trips in the Link Trainer prior to being taken into the air for actual demonstration flights. On his last night at Atherstone I arranged a small dinner party in his honour at the "Swans Nest" restaurant in

Stratford on Avon, attended by half a dozen of the School Staff, and although vodka was unavailable the Scotch flowed freely throughout the course of the evening. To finish off a pleasant evening we returned to the mess for a night-cap. I think we must have under-estimated the amount and the effect of the Scotch Stemasov had downed because for the first time during his visit he mounted his soap box in the bar and began a long discourse on the virtues of Soviet communism. He left next morning nursing a prize hangover and I received a note of thanks from him later and a Christmas card the following year.

★　　　★　　　★

Although life at Atherstone was very pleasant and summer was on the way with each week that passed I became more and more concerned about my future. My application for a permanent commission had gone in almost a year earlier, since when I had heard nothing, not even an acknowledgement that it had been received. The outbreak of war in 1939 had meant that my commission had been annotated "For the duration of hostilities only"; now in my thirties with nearly 17 years of service, thrice decorated, at the peak of my flying career and with the responsibility of a wife and daughter I was loath to pass it all up and have to start a new career. That left me in a Catch 22 situation. To apply for and be accepted for a Staff College course, a must at my age and seniority, I needed to first have a permanent commission. A short wartime Staff College course open to all would probably have led to my selection for a permanent commision early on, but I was fully employed on operational flying through the war years and missed that opportunity. What really irked me was having to interview applicants in my capacity as Commanding Officer, most of them with little experience or ability, and see them offered permanent commissions a few weeks later while I still waited. It all seemed very unjust to me at the time.

What really made me blow my top was when a junior Flight Lieutenant I had interviewed some weeks earlier had his name appear in Air Ministry Orders on one of the lists. I knew that throughout the whole of the war he had not flown operatiaonally, being on a limited medical category. The Commission Board now granted him a permanent commission subject only to him passing the full flying medical within a specified time limit. So he came to me with a request for three weeks special leave to attend a fitness course to prepare him for the Central Medical Board. I need hardly say that in due course he passed the medical and was confirmed in his appointment in the London Gazette; you can imagine what my feelings were at the news.

Towards the end of April I was called upon to take replacements to the Units then at Eindhoven and Hamburg-Fuhlsbuttel, and welcomed the opportunity to fly again on something more interesting than the local G.C.A. training circuits normally available to me when I wanted to get airborne and out of the office. On this occasion I was cleared by H.M. Customs to fly direct to Eindhoven thereby avoiding the usual delays associated with landing at Manston for clearance; that enabled me to deliver half my passenger load there and fly on to Hamburg with the rest that same day.

I returned to Eindhoven to pick up my return passengers for the U.K. in time to witness a most unusual event. The runways there had originally been made from blocks of stone giving a cobbled surface that provided a bumpy take off and landing for aircraft. In an attempt to give a smoother surface to the runway a layer of tarmac had been rolled on top of the cobbles and had proved a success at first. It so happened that the first De Havilland Vampire jets were on their way to Germany and had landed at Eindhoven to refuel before carrying on to their destination without experiencing any trouble. Take-off, however, was a different matter. At full throttle with the hot gases from the low mounted Goblin engines striking the surface of the tarmac proved too much and as the Vampires gathered speed sections of cobblestones lifted up behind them then fell back to the ground leaving the stretch of runway looking for all the world like the pack ice on a frozen river when the thaw begins. Repairs to the runway delayed my return until the next day, much to my disgust. A fortnight later when I made another trip through Eindhoven I had trouble. After taking off for

Celle, a fault developed with the constant speed unit on the port engine and I was forced to return to the airfield for repairs, the replacements being taken on to Celle by other means.

I arrived back at Atherstone on 14th May and two days later my name appeared in Air Ministry Orders alongside a number of other long serving pilots, most of whom I knew, as being selected for a medium service commission in the newly formed Air Traffic Control Branch. It was a bitter disappointment to me but the appeal I made through my Air Officer, Air Vice Marshal Addison, who had been my Group Captain at HQ80 Signals Wing in the early days of the war, fell on deaf ears. I was left with a simple choice of accept, or leave the service, and no matter how much I fumed when I thought about my shabby treatment, if I wanted to stay in the Royal Air Force I would have to accept. Having made the decision I let events take their course.

Lots of events were taking place that year; Atherstone had a close relationship with No 194 (B.S.A.) Squadron Air Training Corps and arrangements were being made for the squadron to spend its summer camp there with the C.O. who was the Chief Designer in the motor-cycle division of B.S.A.s. That year the football team reached the final of the A.T.C. Cup and I was invited to the Wolves ground where the final was taking place and met the B.S.A. Chairman Sir Bernard Docker for a drink in the boardroom before the match started; to our great delight the squadron carried off the cup after an exciting game.

About the middle of June I flew another load of replacements out to Gatow staying overnight in the mess. Round about midnight I was rudely awakened by a massive explosion somewhere in the city but nothing else followed so I went back to sleep again. Next morning I was informed that a Russian barracks block has been blown up by an underground organisation causing many casualties.

During my visits I heard many stories of the brutality of the occupying Russian troops in their sector of the city. Many of them were of Mongol extraction, unable to read or write, and who up to that time had never seen a watch, a camera or radio set. A fair proportion of them had been conscripted into the Red Army from regions thousands of miles away on the borders of the Soviet

Union. Now the war was over they were released from the Army and left to find their own way back. Rather than do that, quite a few of them formed into renegade bands living in cellars beneath the rubble and taking whatever they required in way of food, women and valuables at gun-point. One such band even went to far as to hold up a train on the Berlin underground and strip all the passengers of their possessions. An RAF bus full of personnel returning to Gatow one night pulled up at the traffic lights along the Unter Den Linden by the side of a rickety open Russian lorry with armed troops lolling in the back and the airmen started to make faces and signs at them in a friendly manner. The Russians were not amused, however, and one of them retaliated by emptying his tommy-gun along the side of the bus as it moved off wounding a number of passengers. Another evening an airman took his German girl-friend out for a drink in a bar near the Russian zone and when they tried to leave some drunken Red soldiers tried to grab the girl and molest her. The airman calmly pulled out a Luger and shot the soldier holding her and they left in a hurry, hotly pursued, to seek safety with a military patrol.

Later that morning I took off for the UK, landing at Manston for Customs clearance as I had done on past trips and expecting to get away within half an hour or so. The bearded Customs Officer was the same one who had dealt with me previously, but this time his manner and approach had changed completely and we were held up for over two hours while he went over the aircraft and our overnight bags with a fine tooth comb before giving us clearance to leave for Atherstone. I later heard what had caused him to change his attitude towards RAF personnel. Some days earlier an aircraft had landed with "nothing to declare" and had been cleared by him. A fault on one of the engines had necessitated the crew staying overnight and they had gone into Ramsgate for the evening. There they got slightly the worse for wear in one of the pubs and started shooting a line about how easily they had got into the country with a load of wine brought from France without paying duty. Unfortunately for them an off-duty Customs man was also having a drink in what was his local and he lost no time in passing on the information and seeing that the evaders were dealt with. As might be expected, our bearded friend's superiors came down heavily on him so he in turn gave any RAF personnel a hard time from then on — and who can blame him!

Early in July another flight to Gatow with G.C.A. replacements was scheduled and this was to be my last one from Atherstone. Squadron Leader Winter my Admin. Officer was almost due for his demobilisation and asked if he could come along for a sight-seeing tour, and Tim Vickers also came along. On the morning of July 3rd I made the five minute flight to Honiley with an already laden Wellington carrying ten passengers, collected the Group Captain, then took off again and set course for Gatow where we landed three hours later. I spent the following day looking into the problems of the G.C.A. Unit based at Gatow and saw little of the activities of my sight-seeing passengers until shortly before take off the next morning, when they arrived with a pile of luggage that was soon stowed away in the Wellington. As in the past I landed for customs clearance at Manston and reported to the office that I had nothing to declare in the aircraft, fully expecting a thorough search to be made. The senior man had gone to lunch and his deputy cleared me without going out to the aircraft so we started up and took off without further ado.

After landing at Atherstone I went to Air Traffic Control and looking out over the airfield noticed Winter supervising the unloading of the luggage most of which was taken off to his quarters. I found out later that he had spent most of his time in Berlin acquiring items on the black market and had taken with him a large stock of cigarettes and beverages in short supply to use as payment. I was extremely annoyed to find that I had been an unwitting assistant in his activities but by then it was too late to do anything about it as he was already demobilised.

On 23rd July I received bad news. My father had been admitted to hospital in Pontefract for a serious operation. The news came right out of the blue, as I had been unaware of any illness. Next morning I left in an Oxford aircraft for Snaith, the nearest airfield to home, where I was able to get a lift to Knottingley and from there by public transport to the hospital in Pontefract. By that time my father had come round from the operation and although he was suffering a good deal of pain he was able to talk with me. I stayed with him for as long as I was allowed then returned home to comfort my mother and stay overnight, intending to go to the hospital again next day. By the morning there was a slight improvement in his condition, so in the afternoon I flew back to Atherstone to collect my overnight bag and arranged to return by air next day for a longer stay. I saw my father again when I arrived in the late morning and he was still improving, so instead of staying on for an indefinite period my mother persuaded me to fly back to Atherstone that afternoon and keep in touch by telephone. I picked up the aircraft at Snaith and after chatting with Met about the weather conditons along the route took off in the Oxford on a hot, sultry afternoon and set course for Atherstone with Warrant Officer Andrews in the passenger seat. The weather on that day was unusual, with line squalls and associated thunderclouds towering above 20,000 feet in an unbroken line from the Pennines to the South Coast to the West and relatively clear in the East. We had started off in the clear, flying along this huge wall of cloud which had gradually forced us to the east of Atherstone, beneath the cloud; I was intending to keep on in the clear until I was due east of the airfield then call for a G.C.A. landing. I had not counted on what was to happen next.

Firstly the atmospherics in the thunderclouds with almost continuous lightning made it impossible to contact the G.C.A. unit on any channel, and secondly as I entered the dense and turbulent wall of black cloud at 2,000 feet the light wooden Oxford was caught in severe up-draughts and taken upwards at an alarming rate, the altimeter winding on the height as if it had gone mad. I pulled back the throttles and put the aircraft into a dive but it made no difference and we still kept on ascending. I started a turn on to the reciprocal and somehow we got round, a few minutes later emerging into clear air with a reading of 12,000 feet on the altimeter, the fastest lift I'd ever had in the air and in a nose down attitude! From that height I could see Bagington the Armstrong-Whitworth firm's aerodrome near Coventry so I dropped in to have a cup of tea with Turner-Hughes, their test pilot, and to ring through to Atherstone to check the conditions there. Atherstone was still "out" and I had to stay on at Bagington for another two hours before I was able to pick my way back in the murky aftermath of the storms. I reached there just in time to hear the

224

news that my father had died while I was on the way back. The funeral was held three days later at Farsley where we had a family vault in which both he and eventually my mother would be laid to rest. It was almost the end of July and mid-summer but it was a wet and miserable day and after the service the mourners appreciated the refreshments laid on by the café nearby before going their various ways.

And So He Bloody Well Should!

(Contributed by the editor)

With the death of his father, and his own narrow escape from disaster in bad weather as he flew from a visit to his sick bed, Joe's manuscript peters out. He left a series of chapter headings covering his continuing career in the RAF and in industry on his retirement but the chapters were never written. Compared with his achievements as a bomber pilot, however, Joe's post-war career pales into insignificance. He had trained from boyhood to be an instrument for implementing the Trenchard doctrine of waging war by bombing an enemy's homeland, and without the need to engage his armies or navy. It is in this rôle he should be remembered.

Now, 50 years on, the strategic bombing policy is still being questioned on both moral and materialistic grounds. Joe's manuscript does not show he was bothered by moral scruples as he released his bombs upon the enemy. Why should he have been? As a helpless spectator while flying to plot the German beams, he had seen bombs rain down indiscriminately on British cities. He knew as well as anyone that with the emergence of air power, war became total war. No longer would nations wage war by pitting their gladiators against each other while civilians remained immune from slaughter. And what is moral about that anyway?

The material aspects of the Trenchard doctrine are more debatable. Without doubt the war in Europe was not lost in the early years because of the shield of the Navy. And ultimately it was won by armies on the ground. The RAF had been built around the strategic bombing policy and Bomber Command had pursued this almost single mindedly. Who can know whether the war would have ended sooner, or later, if the RAF had been equipped to support the Navy or the Armies directly, as was the Luftwaffe, instead of as an independent strategic force? But that debate does not affect the judgement of Joe or his role in the war. He had played his part admirably and he can rest assured that:-

'Boom Trenchard loves me'

'And so he bloody well should!'

RECORD OF SERVICE

UNIT	DATES FROM	TO	UNIT	DATES FROM	TO
E. AND R. SCHOOL. READING.	4.2.36	36.3.36	A.T.C. NORTH COATES FITTIES	1.12.36	31.12.36.
No 6 F.T.S. NETHERAVON.	21.4.36	10.1.37	A.T.S. NETHERAVON.	21.9.36	11.1.37.
35 SQUADRON, WORTHY DOWN	11.1.37	20.4.38	A.T.C. ALDERGROVE.	12.4.37	4.5.37.
35 SQUADRON, COTTESMORE	30.4.38	3.5.39	FERRY FLIGHT, CARDINGTON.	29.9.37	11.10.37
35 SQUADRON, CRANFIELD.	- -	9.12.39	No 4 A.T.C. WEST. FREUGH.	3.1.38	30.1.38.
35 SQUADRON, BASSINGBOURN	9.12.39	10.2.40	MARTIN'S SCHOOL OF AIR NAVIGATION	4.11.38	4.2.39
35 SQUADRON, UPWOOD.	10.2.40	4.5.40	No 4 A.T.C. WEST FREUGH.	19.2.39	1.3.39
ASTRO. NAV. COURSE. ST. ATHANS	4.5.40	3.6.40	AIR GUNNERY, WESTON ZOYLAND.	7.9.39	15.9.39.
No 17 OTU. UPWOOD (B SQUDN)	3.6.40	21.6.40	B.A.T. AND D.U. BOSCOMBE DOWN	5.7.40	17.8.40
SQUIRES GATE, BLACKPOOL.	21.6.40	4.7.40	DETACHED FLIGHT. RAF WYTON.	17.8.40	1-1-41
109 SQUADRON, WYTON. [OBOE]	1.1.41	27.1.41	109 SQUADRON BOSC. DOWN	27.1.41	2.11.41
DETACHMENT, RAF HURN. 7 AND 15 OAKINGTON AND SQUADRONS WYTON.	2.11.41	11.11.41	AI 4A FLIGHT, BOSC. DOWN.	11.11.41	21.12.41
1473 UPPER R.C.M. FLIGHT, HEYFORD.	21.12.41	4.1.42	AI 4A FLIGHT, BOSC. DOWN.	4.1.42	8.3.42
1473 FLIGHT, RAF FELTWELL.	8.3.42	30.11.42	1473 FLIGHT, RAF FINMERE.	1-12-42	14.7.43
1473 FLIGHT, RAF FELTWELL.	14.7.43	30.1.43	N.T.U, RAF UPWOOD.	1-10-43	10.10.43
33 P.F.F. SQUADRON, WYTON	11.10.43.	17.4.44	33 P.FF. SQUADRON, CONINGSBY	17.4.44	19.7.44
692 SQUADRON, GRAVELEY	20-7-44	28-1-45.			

AIRCRAFT FLOWN

	AIRCRAFT	ENGINE	AIRCRAFT	ENGINE	AIRCRAFT	ENGINE	
1	M. HAWK T.	GYPSY VI	WELLINGTON 423	HERCULES XI	BRISTOL FIGHTER.	FALCON. ROLLS ROYCE	1
2	TUTOR	LYNX IV	LANCASTER III	MERLIN 23.	D.H.9A.	LIBERTY.	2
3	HART T.	KESTREL IB	OXFORD.	CHEETAH IX	AVRO 504N (D)	LYNX IV	3
4	AUDAX	KESTREL IB	MOSQUITO XVI	MERLIN 73	A.W. ATLAS (D)	JAGUAR	4
5	FAIREY III F	NAPIER XII	ANSON XIX	CHEETAH	A.W. SISKIN (D)	JAGUAR.	5
6	GORDON	PANTHER IL	LINCOLN	MERLIN	TOMTIT. (D)	GENET.	6
7	WELLESLEY	PEGASUS XX	PROCTOR	GYPSY IL	VALENCIA	PEGASUS .	7
8	BATTLE I.	MERLIN II	METEOR 7	DER JET	HORSLEY	CONDOR.	8
9	BATTLE I	MERLIN I	METEOR III	DER JENT.	BULLDOG (D)	JUPITER .	9
10	AVRO ANSON	CHEETAH IX	VAMPIRE TII	GOBLIN	D.H. RAPIDE	GYPSY M.	10
11	BLENHEIM MK I.	MERCURY VIII	PRENTICE	GYPSY	TIGER MOTH. (D)	GYPSY.	11
12	BLENHEIM MK IV	MERCURY XV			WESTLAND WALLACE	JUPITER.	12
13	MAGISTER	GYPSY VI			MILES MARTINET.		
14	. WHITLEY V.	MERLIN IVAM			PROCTOR.	GYPSY M.	
15	VIRGINIA.	JUPITER IVA			EXPEDITOR C.45.		
16	.MENTOR	GYPSY QUEEN.			YORK.	MERLINS .	
17	WELLINGTON	PEGASUS 18			D.H. DOVE, REV-V	GYPSY.	
18	WELLINGTON	P. AND W. TWIN WASPS.			DAKOTA.	P.4 W.	
19	HESTON PHOENIX	GYPSY SIX.			VIRGINIA		
20	TIGER MOTH.	GYPSY.					
21	SHORT STIRLING	HERCULES .					
22	LEOPARD MOTH.	GYPSY.					
23	MOSQUITO IV	MERLIN 21.					
24	HALIFAX II	MERLIN XX					

LINK TRAINER.

| YEAR | | AIRCRAFT | | PILOT, OR | 2ND PILOT, PUPIL | DUTY |
MONTH	DATE	Type	No.	1ST PILOT	OR PASSENGER	(INCLUDING RESULTS AND REMARKS)

DATE.	PRACTICE	TIME	DATE.	TOTALS BROUGHT FORWARD PRACTICE	TIME
13.10.38	1.	.30	16.6.39	CROSS COUNTRY TEST.	1.00
17.10.38	2.	.30	3.7.39	LORENZ	30
21.10.38	3.	.30	20.7.39	LORENZ	30
24.10.38	5.	.30	20.7.39	LORENZ	30
28.10.38	5.	.30	20.7.39	LORENZ	30
27.3.39	2.3.4.	.30	3.8.39	ZZ APPROACHES	30
27.3.39	3.4.5	.30	3.8.39	ZZ APPROACHES	30
27.3.39	5.	.30	9.8.39	LORENZ	30
27.3.39	"T" TEST.	.15	9.8.39	LORENZ.	30
28.3.39	REVISION. "U" TEST.	.30	6-10-43	BEAM APPROACH.	.40
27.3.39	10.11.12. ROUGH AIR.	.30	13-10-43	FIGS.8 AND BEAM.	.20
31.3.39	"T" TEST. FULL BUMPS.	15.		FIGURES OF 8.	.20
8.5.39	10.11.12.	.30			
8.5.39	10.11.12.	.30			
16.5.39	LORENZ	.15			
16.5.39	LORENZ	15			
17.5.39	1. LORENZ	30			
17.5.39	LORENZ.	15.			
12.6.39	REVISION	15			
12.6.39	LORENZ.	20			
13.6.39	LORENZ	30			
13.6.39	LORENZ	30			
13.6.39	LORENZ.	15			

GRAND TOTAL [Cols. (1) to (10)]

.................Hrs...................Mins.

TOTALS CARRIED FORWARD